The Southwestern Journals of Zebulon Pike,
1806–1807

FRONTISPIECE: Zebulon Pike and his men in Santa Fe, after a painting by Frederick Remington. Remington painted this work in 1906 as part of a series on "The Great Explorers" for *Collier's Weekly*. He destroyed the original oil in 1908.

The Southwestern Journals of Zebulon Pike, 1806–1807

EDITED BY STEPHEN HARDING HART
AND ARCHER BUTLER HULBERT

NEW INTRODUCTION BY
MARK L. GARDNER

UNIVERSITY OF NEW MEXICO PRESS   ❧   ALBUQUERQUE

Introduction © 2006 by Mark L. Gardner
Two previously published volumes comprise *The Southwestern Journals of Zebulon Pike, 1806–1807.* Permission to reprint *Zebulon Pike's Arkansaw Journal,* edited by Stephen Harding Hart and Archer Butler Hulbert (© 1932), and *Southwest on the Turquoise Trail,* edited by Archer Butler Hulbert (© 1933), granted by Joanne Hulbert Yeager and Nancy Hulbert Olsen, executrices for Dorothy Printup Wing. Text as comprised for *The Southwestern Journals of Zebulon Pike, 1806–1807* © 1960 by Dorothy Printup Wing
Printed in the United States of America

11   10   09   08   07   1   2   3   4   5   6   7

PAPERBOUND ISBN 978-0-8263-3390-2

LIBRARY OF CONGRESS CATALOGING-IN-PUBLICATION DATA

Pike, Zebulon Montgomery, 1779–1813.
  [Account of expeditions to the sources of the Mississippi. Selections]
  The southwestern journals of Zebulon Pike, 1806–1807 / edited by Stephen
Harding Hart and Archer Butler Hulbert ; new introduction by Mark L. Gardner.
    v. cm.
  The journal is part of the author's An account of expeditions to the sources of the Mississippi.
  Includes bibliographical references and index.
  Contents: Introduction / Mark Gardner — Zebulon M. Pike : his life and papers / Stephen Harding Hart — The purpose of Pike's expedition / Archer B. Hulbert — Journal of voyage to the sources of the Arkansaw : instructions to Lieutenant Pike — Journal of a voyage / Zebulon Montgomery Pike — Diary of a tour, made through the interior provinces of New Spain, in the year 1807, by Z.M. Pike, of the Army of the United States, when under an escort of Spanish dragoons.
    ISBN-13: 978-0-8263-3389-6 (cloth : alk. paper)
    ISBN-10: 0-8263-3389-3 (cloth : alk. paper)
    1. Pike, Zebulon Montgomery, 1779–1813—Diaries. 2. Explorers—Southwest, New—Diaries. 3. Soldiers—Southwest, New—Diaries. 4. Southwest, New—Discovery and exploration. 5. Southwest, New—Description and travel. I. Hart, Stephen Harding. II. Hulbert, Archer Butler, 1873–1933. III. Gardner, Mark L. IV. Title.
F592.P638 2006
917.9—dc22

                                      2005032952

Frontispiece and figures 1–4 courtesy Mark L. Gardner. Figure 5 and maps 2–4 were part of the original 1932 Hart/Hulbert edition of Pike's journals. Map 1, cartography by Robert Houdek, 2005.

Design and composition: Melissa Tandysh

Contents

Fig. 4: Zebulon Montgomery Pike.
A nineteenth-century engraving based on the noted
Charles Wilson Peale portrait of Pike.

Introduction

The other nation that demands our vigilant caution, and forces us to contain, in part, its expansion, is the new power known as the Republic of the United Anglo-American Provinces. These states, which have risen so suddenly to such a colossal height, have extended to points so dangerously near and surround us so closely that we must fear the expansion of their borders over Louisiana and Florida and their proximity to the province of Texas, where they can enter undetected.

—Lieutenant José Cortés, 1799

Should an army of Americans ever march into the country [Mexico] . . . they will only have to march from province to province in triumph, and be hailed by the united voices of grateful millions as their deliverers and saviours [*sic*], whilst our national character would be resounded to the most distant nations of the earth.

—Captain Z. M. Pike, April 12, 1808

IT SEEMS THAT ZEBULON MONTGOMERY PIKE HAS ALWAYS PLAYED SECOND fiddle to fellow explorers Meriwether Lewis and William Clark. As I write this, the United States is nearing the end of a years-long bicentennial celebration of the famed 1804–6 expedition that commenced even before the start of the official anniversary. The number of Lewis and Clark books and articles would fill a library. There have been nationally televised documentaries, an IMAX film, commemorative postage stamps, and a major traveling exhibition (not to mention all the requisite Lewis and Clark exhibits and educational programs at numerous regional institutions). The general hoopla has truly been overwhelming, to put it nicely.

Zebulon Montgomery Pike, whose small Southwestern expedition set out the same year that Lewis and Clark returned to St. Louis, has paled in comparison. Granted, America's most famous mountain bears his name (a mountain he never climbed), yet very few Americans today could say anything about who Pike was or what he did. Such was not the case, however, in the early nineteenth century. Pike's report on his previous exploration to the headwaters of the Mississippi River in 1805–6 was published as a pamphlet and in a handful of Eastern newspapers,[1] undoubtedly the first public notice of the lieutenant who had not yet celebrated his thirtieth birthday. Then came the 1810 publication of Pike's one and only book, which included his journals, scientific observations, and maps from both the Mississippi expedition and the 1806–7 expedition to "the south-western boundary of Louisiana [Territory]."[2]

At nearly five hundred pages (embracing appendices), Pike's tome was a daunting read, and it was not without its critics, who, interestingly, included the book's own publisher. In a footnote to Pike's preface to the volume, John Conrad, a junior member of the publishing firm of C. & A. Conrad & Co. of Philadelphia, admitted that "he very much doubts whether any book ever went to press under so many disadvantages as the one now presented to the public. Some of those disadvantages must be obvious to every man who reads the work."[3] A reviewer for *Analectic Magazine*, published in Philadelphia, acknowledged that while Pike's book was "highly useful" as a topographical survey, "it can scarcely be accounted an amusing production, or interesting to those readers who are perpetually on the search for the pathetic and the marvellous [*sic*]."[4] Another reviewer, however, found much about the work to recommend. Although "a mere journal of occurences [*sic*],"

> they present a variety of interesting situations, and engage deeply the attention of the reader. The narration, though simple, bears the original impression of the spot; and carries with it that most desirable of all qualities in a traveller, an innate air of truth. While they

interest our feelings in the toils and dangers of Mr. Pike and his companions, they lead us through a variety of country, of people, and of manners; and the narrative thus produces a romantick [*sic*] and interesting effect.[5]

Despite the mixed reviews, Pike's book reached a relatively large audience, which included European readers as well. A London edition appeared in 1811, followed by translations into French (1812), Dutch (1813), and German (1813).[6] Although Pike and his men would not receive double pay and grants of land as had members of the Lewis and Clark Expedition (an expedition, Pike pointed out, that received a much larger appropriation of funds than his own), Pike would see several promotions in rank, the first, that of captain, coming shortly after he had embarked upon his Southwestern adventure in 1806.[7] He received the rank of major in 1808, lieutenant colonel the following year, full colonel in 1812, and finally brigadier general in 1813. His

FIG. 2: Death of Pike: Zebulon Pike receives a fatal wound when the abandoned British powder magazine explodes at the Battle of York, Ontario, April 27, 1813. An engraving from Charles J. Peterson's *The Military Heroes of the War of 1812 and the War with Mexico*, 1848.

hero's death at the age of thirty-four during the War of 1812 guaranteed him a chapter in many a book devoted to American biography or military deeds published in the first half of the nineteenth century.[8]

Pike quickly slipped out of the American consciousness, though, with the outbreak of the Civil War, which conflict produced a plethora of dashing military heroes, both North and South. A centennial celebration of Pike's Southwestern expedition in Colorado Springs in 1906 generated fleeting national attention. There have been reprints of Pike's journals over the years, but these have been aimed at antiquarians and scholars. And despite this current anniversary in 2006—obviously, Americans love to celebrate anniversaries—Pike will never see the huge resurgence in popularity that Lewis and Clark have experienced, even though Pike and the cast of characters associated with him are equally as interesting. All of this is strangely ironic, of course, when one considers the fact that Pike's Southwestern expedition actually had more profound consequences than Lewis and Clark's.

First of all, even with his organizational flaws, Pike got his journals and observations into print in a reasonably timely manner. His book was available to the public three years after his return to the States. Lewis and Clark's official account appeared in 1814 (two volumes priced at $6.00 a set), practically *eight years* after the conclusion of their expedition and four years after the publication of Pike's volume. On the rapidly advancing Missouri River frontier, eight years was an eternity. In fact, a large commercial trading venture to the Rocky Mountains started up the Missouri from St. Louis in 1807, some of the members former participants in the Lewis and Clark Expedition.[9] By 1814, there were many American trappers and traders who knew the Upper Missouri, Yellowstone River, and numerous lesser drainages like the backs of their hands. French, Spanish, and British traders had all preceded Lewis and Clark to the Upper Missouri country, and sailing ships of various nationalities had long been trading with the Pacific Coast Indians. They had no need of Lewis and Clark's belated publication.

Of course, had Pike stayed well within U.S.-claimed territory, then I likely would not be writing about him now. But the fact is, he didn't. Pike and his men strayed into Spanish territory, were summarily gathered up by Spanish soldiers and escorted to Santa Fe and then Chihuahua, receiving a lavish eyeful of Spain's northern frontier in the process. For a country extremely paranoid about its neighbors in North America, as Spain was,

Spanish officials would have done well to have escorted Pike back across the border in the direction from whence he came.[10] Instead, they revealed a world to Pike about which there was *much* interest in the United States, especially on the Missouri frontier. Pike made careful notes—written and mental—and put them all in his book. Consequently, readers learned in 1810 that the province of Nueva Vizcaya (the present-day Mexican states of Durango and Chihuahua) "abounds in silver and gold mines." Even more tantalizing, though, were Pike's observations on the value of textiles in the goods-starved province of New Mexico: fine cloths sold for an astounding $20 a yard, superfine cloths, $25 a yard.[11] The effects of this new information were aptly described by Santa Fe Trail chronicler Josiah Gregg in 1844: "The Santa Fe trade attracted very little notice . . . until the return of Captain Pike, whose exciting descriptions of the new El Dorado spread like wildfire throughout the western country."[12]

Pike's revelations resulted in more than one attempt at opening trade between Missouri and the "new El Dorado" of New Mexico. But because protective Spanish officials did not look kindly on foreign trespassers (as Pike could well attest), these expeditions ended largely in disaster, with goods confiscated and owners imprisoned—yet the traders kept coming. When Mexico finally threw off the Spanish yoke in 1821—and with it, Spain's former trade barriers—Americans were bartering goods in Santa Fe that very same year, literally before the revolutionary dust had settled. The Santa Fe trade quickly developed into a major frontier enterprise. In 1833, merchandise hauled down the Santa Fe Trail was valued at $180,000. Ten years later, it amounted to $450,000, with much of the goods actually intended for markets in Chihuahua.[13] Then, in 1846, thirty-six years after the publication of Pike's journals, an American army under Stephen Watts Kearny seized New Mexico for the United States during the U.S.-Mexican War (turns out the Republic of Mexico should have been as paranoid as Spain).

In the end, Pike's second expedition may be viewed not only as the impetus for the famed Santa Fe trade, but also as a reconnaissance for Manifest Destiny. The Corps of Discovery, on the other hand, although an extraordinary human achievement, was, at its most basic level, an on-the-spot inspection of a recent acquisition.[14] When it comes to significance, Zebulon Montgomery Pike plays second fiddle to no one.

The following edition of Pike's journals was first published in Colorado in 1932 and 1933. It does not reproduce Pike's complete report of 1810, but only his account of the 1806–7 journey to the upper Arkansas and northern Mexico or "New Spain," commonly referred to today as Pike's "second" or "Southwestern" expedition. Edited and annotated by Stephen Harding Hart (1908–93) and Archer Butler Hulbert (1873–1933), it appeared in two parts in the first two volumes of an eight-volume series published by the Stewart Commission of Colorado College and the Denver Public Library under the title *Overland to the Pacific*. The parts have been united into one for this reprint.[15] Another change from the original Harding/Hart edition regards the editors' footnotes. These have been converted to endnotes to begin at the conclusion of the Pike journal. However, documents and letters pertinent to the expedition, as well as the editors' commentary on Pike's route, remain at the foot of the pages as originally placed by the editors.

A few words are due regarding editors Hart and Hulbert. A native of Colorado, Stephen Harding Hart attended Yale University, Harvard Law School, the University of Denver Law School, and New College, Oxford, England. It was while at Yale that Hart conducted most of his research on Pike's Southwestern expedition. He appears to have been the first scholar to make a serious study of the maps that had been confiscated from Pike by Spanish officials in 1807, and an essay Hart prepared from his Pike research won Yale's George Washington Eggleston Prize in 1929. This same scholarship formed the basis of Hart's contribution to the 1933 reprint of Pike's journals.

Interestingly enough, Hart did not pursue a career in history but instead turned to the law and politics. From 1937 to 1943, he did stints in both houses of the Colorado legislature, and in 1947 he cofounded the very successful Denver law firm of Holland & Hart, which today ranks as Colorado's largest legal firm. Hart always retained a passionate interest in Colorado history, however, helming the Colorado Historical Society as its president for over a decade (plus a number of years as a member of its board of directors). He also received the appointment as the state's first historic preservation officer in 1967, serving eleven years in that position. Today, the Colorado Historical Society's research library is named for Stephen H. Hart.[16]

Archer Butler Hulbert is largely unknown today, but in the early twentieth century, he was one of America's most prolific scholars. A graduate of Marietta College, Ohio, Hulbert went on to become a student of the influential historian of the American frontier Frederick Jackson Turner at

Harvard University. Hulbert's specialty was western transportation and migration, and he published numerous volumes on rivers, canals, early roads, and western trails, as well as a popular U.S. history textbook for high schools. A bibliography of his writings, including articles, numbers 115 items.[17] By far Hulbert's most famous and popular work was *Forty-Niners; the Chronicle of the California Trail* (Boston: Little, Brown & Co., 1931). In what was really part fiction, part history, Hulbert wove together a plethora of primary accounts to create the trail "diary" of a young gold-seeker in 1849. His manuscript won the *Atlantic Monthly's* nonfiction prize—$5,000 and a publishing contract—in 1931.[18]

At the time of the publication of *Forty-Niners*, Hulbert was professor of history at Colorado College (he had come there in 1920), as well as director of the College's Stewart Commission on Western History. The Commission had been established in 1925 through Hulbert's friendship with Colorado College trustee Philip B. Stewart, a Colorado Springs businessman and friend and hunting partner of Theodore Roosevelt. The role of the Commission was to provide financial support for Hulbert's book projects, and its principal benefactors were Stewart and his wife, Frances, an avid collector of Southwest Indian textiles, jewelry, and other crafts.[19] In 1926, Hulbert began the research for the *Overland to the Pacific* series, "a documentary history of the Overland surge of the American people to the Pacific Ocean."[20] The first volume in the series, *Zebulon Pike's Arkansaw Journal*, appeared in 1932 to generally positive reviews (historian Herbert E. Bolton called it "a triumph").[21]

Volume two, *Southwest on the Turquoise Trail: The First Diaries on the Road to Santa Fe*, was available in August 1933, and volume three, *Where Rolls the Oregon*, was released on December 22 of that same year. Two days later, on Christmas Eve, Hulbert died at his home in Colorado Springs of influenza. According to his obituary, he was in a weakened condition due to excessive work while in New York City revising his high school history textbook and thus "unable to throw off the illness of the last week."[22] He was sixty years old. The final five volumes of the *Overland to the Pacific Series* were completed under the direction of Hulbert's wife Dorothy.[23]

The purpose of this current reprint, which is now perhaps obvious, is to provide a convenient one-volume edition of Pike's Southwestern journals in commemoration of the expedition's bicentennial. There is an added bonus, however, in that included here, as in the original volume, are Hart's essay on

Pike and his papers and Hulbert's essay on the purpose of Pike's expedition. I have not commented on the long controversy surrounding whether or not Pike was a "spy" in connection with the conspiratorial intrigues of his commander, General James Wilkinson, and Aaron Burr, because the reader will find this fully examined in Hulbert's vigorous defense of the young lieutenant. In fact, Hulbert was so emphatic in defending Pike that he drew forth comments from more than one reviewer. "[T]he ardor with which they flay Pike's detractors carries at times more the tone of the advocate than the historian," wrote one.[24] Another commented that Hulbert was "rather bellicose in tone, and handy with his epithets," yet "not without justification."[25] Subsequent Pike scholars, however, have joined Hulbert in discounting the notion that Pike was anything more than a disoriented explorer and patriotic intelligence gatherer.[26]

It is important to point out again that the edition reprinted here first appeared over seventy years ago. As well as a work of scholarship focusing on Pike and his Southwestern expedition, it is also an artifact of its time, a notable entry in the limited Pike historiography. There are a few items, then, that bear updating here. First, Stephen Hart notes that at the time of

Fig. 3. This vintage postcard was sold in Colorado during the centennial celebration of Pike's Southwestern expedition in 1906.

the writing of his essay, the Pike papers recovered from Mexico were in the archives of the U.S. War Department. They now reside in the collections of the National Archives. Second, Hart and Hulbert incorrectly identified the location of the Republican Pawnee village Pike visited in 1806 as being in Republic County, Kansas (where the State of Kansas had erected a historical monument in 1901 and held a centennial celebration in 1906), when the actual location was by the late 1920s known to be in Nebraska. This resulted in an irate review and response from the Nebraska State Historical Society.[27] Hulbert made note of the controversy in his volume two of the *Overland to the Pacific* series. Third, there is still serious debate locally as to exactly what prominence or high point Pike reached on his failed attempt to climb the mountain that would bear his name—Pikes Peak. Hart and Hulbert zeroed in on a prominence dubbed "Mount Miller" (named for one of Pike's party), while in recent years scholarship has focused on Mount Rosa.[28]

Those wanting to pursue a deeper investigation of Pike and both of his expeditions should consult Donald Jackson's two-volume *The Journals of Zebulon Montgomery Pike, with Letters and Related Documents* (Norman: University of Oklahoma Press, 1966), the definitive work on the subject. For those interested in acquiring a first edition of Pike's book, which cost a considerable $3.50 in 1810, copies (with all the maps intact), when available, range in price from $28,500 to $45,000. A bargain for one man's legacy.

Mark L. Gardner

Notes

1. Henry R. Wagner and Charles L. Camp, *The Plains & The Rockies: A Critical Bibliography of Exploration, Adventure and Travel in the American West, 1800–1865,* fourth edition, revised, enlarged and edited by Robert H. Becker (San Francisco: John Howell-Books, 1982), 31–32.

2. Z. M. Pike, *An Account of Expeditions to the Sources of the Mississippi, and Through the Western Parts of Louisiana, to the Sources of the Arkansaw, Kans, La Platte, and Pierre Juan, Rivers . . .* (Philadelphia: C. & A. Conrad & Co., 1810), [4].

3. Ibid., [5]. Donald Jackson identifies the author of the publisher's note in *The Journals of Zebulon Montgomery Pike, with Letters and Related Documents,* edited by Donald Jackson, 2 vols. (Norman: University of Oklahoma Press, 1966), 1: xxvi n. 5.

4. *Analectic Magazine* 3 (February 1814): 104. This was a review of the 1811 London edition of Pike's journals.

5. *Select Reviews of Literature, and Spirit of Foreign Magazines* 6 (July 1811): 45.

6. Wagner & Camp, 52–55.

7. More than thirty years after Pike's death, his widow, Clara, petitioned Congress for compensation for Pike's services on his two exploring expeditions. She received $3,000. See U.S. Congress, Senate, *Mr. Benton made the following Report* [on petition of Mrs. General Pike], S. Rep. 66, 26th Cong., 1st sess., 1846, serial 473, 1–4.

8. See, for example, Charles J. Peterson's *The Military Heroes of the War of 1812 and of the War with Mexico* (Philadelphia: W. A. Leary, 1848), in which we learn that Pike's "loss was deeply regretted by the nation, which had formed a high estimate of his ability" (91–92).

9. Richard Edward Oglesby, *Manuel Lisa and the Opening of the Missouri Fur Trade* (Norman: University of Oklahoma Press, 1963), 40–41.

10. Note the 1799 warning of Lieutenant José Cortés, quoted above, in José Cortés, *Views from the Apache Frontier: Report on the Northern Provinces of New Spain,* edited by Elizabeth A. H. John (Norman: University of Oklahoma Press, 1989), 42.

11. Pike, Appendix to Part III, 18 and 8.

12. Josiah Gregg, *Commerce of the Prairies,* ed. Max L. Moorhead (Norman: University of Oklahoma Press, 1954), 10–11.

13. Ibid., 332.

14. A vehement revisionist view of the significance of the Lewis and Clark Expedition (or, rather, lack thereof) is David Plotz, "Lewis and Clark: Stop Celebrating. They Don't Matter," *Slate Magazine,* August 16, 2002 (*Slate* is an online magazine. Plotz's article is available for viewing at http://www.slate.com/id/2069382)

15. The full citations for the two volumes are Stephen Harding Hart and Archer Butler Hulbert, eds., *Zebulon Pike's Arkansaw Journal: In Search of the Southern Louisiana Purchase Boundary Line,* Overland to the Pacific,

vol. 1 (Colorado Springs and Denver: The Stewart Commission of Colorado College and the Denver Public Library, 1932), and Archer Butler Hulbert, ed., *Southwest on the Turquoise Trail: The First Diaries on the Road to Santa Fe*, Overland to the Pacific, vol. 2 (Colorado Springs and Denver: The Stewart Commission of Colorado College and the Denver Public Library, 1933).

16. Joseph W. Halpern, "Six of the Greatest: Stephen H. Hart," *The Colorado Lawyer* 32 (July 2003): 19 (this article is available online at http://www.cobar.org/tcl/tcl_articles.cfm?ArticleID=2794); and Jim Kirksey, "Prominent attorney, lawmaker Hart dies," *Denver Post*, November 9, 1993.

17. The bibliography is part of the extensive Archer Butler Hulbert Papers manuscript collection held by Special Collections, Tutt Library, Colorado College, Colorado Springs, Colorado.

18. Steven Carter Kottsy, "The Westward Movements of Archer Butler Hulbert: American History as Lived and Written, 1873–1933," Ph.D. diss., University of Cincinnati, 1992, 693–98.

19. Ibid., 641–42; and Joanne Hulbert Yeager, "Archer Butler Hulbert, 1873–1933," *Wagon Tracks: Santa Fe Trail Association Quarterly* 18 (November 2003): 22. In the 1930s, the Stewarts donated 320 items, Southwest Indian textiles and silver jewelry, to the New Mexico Laboratory of Anthropology, Santa Fe. They remain part of the Museum of New Mexico's permanent collections today.

20. Prospectus for *Overland to the Pacific*, author's collection.

21. "Volume 1 of *Overland, Pike's Arkansaw Journal*, is a triumph. If it is a sample of the whole, the success of the Series is assured. The plan thus to publish the original narratives of the Anglo-American West is splendid." Herbert E. Bolton, as quoted on the dust jacket to *Southwest on the Turquoise Trail*.

22. "Dr. Hulbert of Colorado College, Dies," *Colorado Springs Gazette-Telegraph*, December 25, 1933.

23. Yeager, "Archer Butler Hulbert," 23.

24. LeRoy R. Hafen, Review of *Zebulon Pike's Arkansaw Journal . . . , The Mississippi Valley Historical Review* 20 (June 1933): 118.

25. Marian Dargan, Review of *Zebulon Pike's Arkansaw Journal . . . , The New Mexico Historical Review* 8 (January 1933): 63.

26. Stephen G. Hyslop, "Zebulon Montgomery Pike's Southwestern Expedition: Bibliography for a Neglected Chapter of Our History," *Wagon Tracks: Santa Fe Trail Association Quarterly* 17 (May 2003): 6–7.

27. Review of *Zebulon Pike's Arkansaw Journal . . . , Nebraska History Magazine* 13 (Oct.-Dec. 1932): 298–300.

28. See Dave Philipps, "What Peak Did Pike Climb? Lawyer Tracks Final Destination of Wayward Trek to Mount Rosa," *Colorado Springs Gazette*, April 25, 2004.

FIG. 4: Zebulon Montgomery Pike,
after the Charles Wilson Peale portrait.

PART ONE

Zebulon M. Pike: His Life and Papers

1.

THE LIFE OF GENERAL ZEBULON MONTGOMERY PIKE IS REMARKABLE
for his two expeditions of exploration into the West and his death while
commanding the American forces which captured York, now Toronto,
during the War of 1812. The most convenient material for the study of
Pike's explorations is presented in the introduction and text of Captain
Elliott Coues' *The Expeditions of Zebulon M. Pike*, and that for the study
of his military exploits is found in General Henry Whiting's *Life of Zebulon
Montgomery Pike* in Sparks' *Library of American Biography*.[1] Coues shows
Pike the explorer, Whiting emphasizes Pike the soldier, but together they
give an excellent, balanced biography.[2]

Pike was born on January 5, 1779, near Trenton, New Jersey. His
father, Zebulon Pike, a Major in the United States Army, fought in the
Revolutionary War and retired with the rank of Lieutenant Colonel. After
very little schooling, Pike, then fifteen years old, entered the army with
nothing but his ambition and resolute spirit. He married, in 1801, Clarissa
Brown, daughter of the Revolutionary Captain John Brown and had several children, of whom one, a son, survived him, and only one, a daughter,
reached maturity. This daughter, Clarissa Harlowe Pike, named probably
by a happy combination of his wife's name and that of Samuel Richardson's
great heroine, married John Cleves Symmes Harrison, son of General

William Henry Harrison, and uncle of President Benjamin Harrison. In 1802, one year after his marriage, when Pike became First Lieutenant in the First Regiment of the United States Infantry, he was described as an efficient and zealous officer, strict in discipline, and gentlemanly and reserved in manner. He was studious, devoting his time to extending his military education, to reading, and to studying French.

When the United States acquired Louisiana from France, Lieutenant Pike was chosen, then twenty-six years old, to lead one of the parties to explore it, for its extent and boundaries were unknown. President Jefferson sent Lewis and Clark to march to the Pacific; and General Wilkinson, who was Governor of Louisiana and Pike's superior officer, sent Pike, in 1805, with three non-commissioned officers and fourteen enlisted men, to explore the Mississippi to its head. His objects were to select sites for military posts, to treat with the Indians, and to discover what he could about the British traders operating in American territory. According to his historian, Coues, Pike "literally performed the duties of astronomer, surveyor, commanding officer, clerk, spy, guide, and hunter." It was a responsible position for a young man, especially since his party was out all winter, but he acquitted himself well and, in the words of General A. W. Greely, "more than carried out his orders."

Pike's success on the Mississippi expedition led almost immediately to his being chosen by General Wilkinson, in 1806, to direct an undertaking of even greater importance and difficulty. Only the same ambition and spirit of enterprise enabled him to accomplish it.

The ostensible purposes of the journey were to restore freed captives to the Osage Nation and to affect a permanent peace between that nation and the Kansas, to establish friendly relations with the Comanches, and to acquire a knowledge of the Southwestern boundary. "The late dangers and hardships I had undergone," Pike confessed, "together with the idea of again leaving my family—made me hesitate, but the ambition of a soldier, and the spirit of enterprise which was inherent in my breast, induced me to agree to his [Wilkinson's] proposition."

Pike's route took him first up the Missouri and Osage Rivers to the villages of the Osage Indians, then overland out of the present state of Missouri into Kansas and through Kansas to visit the Pawnees on the Republican River. Marching south to the Arkansas River and then up it, he traversed Kansas again and Colorado, ending his expedition across the territorial boundary of Louisiana, just south of Alamosa, Colo., on the Conejos River.

The Spaniards had recently made a raid through Kansas with a force of some three hundred sixty regular dragoons and mounted militia, holding two hundred forty in reserve on the Arkansas River, the whole command under Lieutenant Don Facundo Malgares. The purposes of this move seem to have been to hold the Indians to their allegiance to Spain and to intimidate, if not attack, Pike. When the latter arrived at the Pawnee villages, therefore, just after the magnificent flourish by the Spanish, the Indians were far from being impressed by his meagre band of twenty men. They were most hostile toward him and contemptuous of his claims. By mere force of character, however, and calm disregard of danger, Pike not only saved his party from destruction, but bullied the Indians into substituting the American for the Spanish flag during his stay.

On November 24, 1806, he left his party, then building a hut on the present site of Pueblo, Colorado, and with three of his men tried to gain the peak now named for him. His men wore light overalls and no stockings. When he embarked upon this mountain climbing adventure he expected to reach the summit in about twenty-four hours. Instead he marched two and a half days when, topping a ridge at the head of Turkey Creek waist deep in snow, he beheld the summit of his "Grand Peak" sixteen miles in the distance. "It was as high again as what we had ascended," he wrote, "and it would have taken a whole day's march to arrive at its base, when I believe no human being could have ascended to its pinnacle." The explorers had slept without blankets and had been without food for thirty-six hours. Under such circumstances Pike gave up his attempt. Rejoining the main body, he pushed into the mountains and discovered South Park and the head of the Arkansas River. In search of the Red River, he returned by way of the Royal Gorge, and, leaving the disabled remnant of his pack train, and part of his baggage, in a small fort garrisoned with two men at the mouth of the Gorge, he started southwest towards the Sangre de Cristo Range.

Winter had already settled down. The men, who were not supplied with equipment for cold weather, cut up their only blankets for socks. They made foot-coverings out of raw buffalo hide. Since the pack train had been left behind at the Gorge, the soldiers were compelled to carry everything— sometimes as much as seventy pounds for a man. Yet they marched twenty or twenty-five miles a day. Game was their only food—"without salt or any other thing whatever"—and that soon became scarce. On one occasion Pike went hunting with only one companion because the rest of the men were broken down by hunger and cold. After walking all day in vain, the two spent the night unsheltered in a blizzard rather than dishearten their comrades by returning to camp empty-handed. On the morrow they killed a buffalo and reached camp at midnight with the first food the party had had in four days.

Through all these sufferings Pike perseveringly and rashly pushed on, over the Sangre de Cristo Range, and into the San Luis Valley, where he crossed the Rio Grande River and built a stockade in Spanish territory on the south bank of the Conejos River. This stockade on the Conejos was situate not far from Santa Fe. There he remained until the Spaniards, learning of his breach of neutrality, sent a force and took him, a willing and observant prisoner into Mexico. Before he marched from his fort on the Conejos, he ordered a sergeant and one man to go back and bring in the two frozen men and also the two men left with the baggage and disabled horses. Pike left a party in the stockade to await the return of all men in the rear and ordered the sergeant (Meek) to "come in" to Santa Fé "as he never would come without a fight, if not ordered." Traveling through Mexico a prisoner, Zebulon Pike made notes of the country and inhabitants, which his men concealed in the barrels of their guns. He was taken to Chihuahua before General Salcedo. This polite officer, after confiscating his papers, which were returned to our War Department in 1910, treated him kindly and sent him overland, at the expense of the United States, to the American army post at Natchitoches, on the Red River in Louisiana, where he arrived July 1, 1807.

Having completed his expeditions, he published, in 1810, his book. Pike, although serious and studious, wrote inaccurately and ungrammatically. His punctuation and spelling were poor, and his book badly arranged. His book, however, contained much valuable information and remained long an authority on western matters. Indeed, it was rearranged and published, with normal spelling and grammar, in England (1811) and translated into French (1812), Dutch (1812–13), and German (1813). There are, moreover, three modern American editions (1889, 1895, 1925). He appears to have written the work more for fame than for money.

Fame was the reward, also, of his explorations, for although he made an attempt to obtain an appropriation from Congress for himself and his men, he failed. He obtained, however, a rapid advance in rank, which gave him the colonelcy of the Fifteenth Infantry before the War of 1812 began. At that time probably no other officer (and no other regiment) in the army was held in higher estimation. He enjoyed among his superiors a well-earned reputation for boldness, enterprise, and fitness to command. He inspired all men under him with confidence in his ability.

In the spring of 1813 he commanded the American forces attacking York. Landing his men, he captured the fort. In the engagement, however, he was mortally wounded by the explosion of the British magazine. He died April 27, 1813, on board the flagship *Madison*, just as the captured British flag was placed beneath his head. His victory was one of the few successful battles of the war, and his death was mourned by the whole nation.

Although only thirty-four, the attack on York was ordered by "Brigadier-general Z. M. Pike." Yet his appointment as Brigadier-general in the United States Army was not confirmed until after his death. The last letter he wrote, to his father, contained the following sentence: "If success attends my steps, honor and glory await my name—if defeat, still shall it be said that we died like brave men and conferred honor, even in death, on the American name." Pike gave two maxims to his son: "First, preserve your honor free from blemish; second, be always ready to die for your country,"

2.

Pike's southwestern expedition was a military reconnaissance. One of its primary purposes was to procure and bring back to the government information about the tremendous Louisiana territory which the United States had recently acquired.[3] Little was known of the region which Jefferson had purchased and practically nothing of the country near the head waters of the Arkansas and Platte Rivers. Americans had scarcely entered this area. It had never been mapped. Wilkinson in his letter of instruction to Pike[4] had required him "to remark particularly upon the geographical structure, the natural history, and the population of the country" through which he passed. Pike, as usual, carried out his orders, with thoroughness.

He observed the features of the terrain, noted them in his *Journal*, and completely charted his route. He constructed traverse tables in which he entered from day to day his courses and distances. From these and from daily observations by eye and instruments he drew plots showing in detail the courses of rivers and tributaries, islands, the disposition and relative height of hills, bluffs, or mountains, the location of Indian villages, sand dunes, and timbered sections—anything that appeared to him important. He indicated his route overland by a dotted line, numbered his camps, and marked them by crosses or circles. He showed, too, the route taken by Malgares' Spanish expedition and marked its camps when he could find them. All this he did very neatly and clearly, labeling the features in his nice hand. The situation under which the charts were constructed is indicated by Pike, in his preface to the original edition. There he described himself as "returning in the evening, hungry and fatigued, to sit down in the open air, by firelight, to copy the notes and plot the courses of the day."

The maps thus constructed he projected in a manuscript book, the same one he had carried with him on his voyage to the source of the Mississippi and which contained the similar charts he had drawn of the Mississippi expedition together with traverse and meteorological tables of both his expeditions. Professor Herbert E. Bolton has described its final form:

"One of its titles—it has one at each end—is 'Book, containing Meteorological Observations, courses and chart of part of the Mississippi, Missouri and Osage rivers, with the route by land from the Osage Nation, taken by Lt. Z. M. Pike in the years 1805 and '06, being part of a complete survey which he made of the Mississippi river from St. Louis, Louisiana, to its Source.' The other title is 'Book, containing Traverse Table and Chart of part of the Mississippi, Missouri and Osage rivers, with the route by land from the Osage rivers, taken by Lieut. Z. M. Pike in the year 1805 and 06, being part of a complete Survey which he made of the Mississippi River from St. Louis to its Source.' The contents of the book may be summarized as follows:

1. Eleven quarto pages of meteorological observations covering the period from August, 1805, to March 2, 1807, the date of Pike's arrival at Santa Fé. . . .

2. Twenty-eight pages of traverse tables, covering the period stated above. In these tables there are separate columns for date, course, distance, shores, rivers, islands, rapids, and for remarks on mines, quarries, timbers, bars, creeks, shoals, etc.

3. Twenty-five section maps, covering fifteen pages, of the Mississippi River above St. Louis, and about an equal number, covering thirty-two pages, of Pike's route from St. Louis to Santa Fé. The first set is in

ink, with the addition of colors, the second in black ink only. They are executed with considerable care, and are well preserved. They contain, besides information concerning Pike's route, valuable data in regard to geographical names and to settlements of both whites and Indians. Whoever undertakes a new edition of Pike's narrative will probably wish to incorporate reproductions of all the maps in this book."[5]

Pike began the maps of the Arkansas Journey with very elaborate charts of the Missouri and Osage rivers. As travelling became more difficult, however, from the Osage towns, north to the Pawnee villages, and south to the Arkansas River, he made simpler but still accurate sketches. Through all the terrible experiences on the upper Arkansas and in the Wet Mountain Valley he continued to plot his route still clearly and carefully. One map he duplicated, considering his first attempt incorrect. The final ones, of the valley of the Rio Grande, are on a large scale and show much of the surrounding country and mountain ranges. With them, as a final flourish, Pike ended the series.

The adventures of the book containing Pike's maps and tables are almost as interesting as its contents. These began Feb. 26, 1807, with the capture of Pike by the Spaniards. In Spanish territory, in his little fort on the Conejos River, he had been waiting for more than a month recuperating from his hardships and expecting the Spanish capture. After being taken, he was conducted south toward the seats of Spanish government, at first having the undisturbed possession of his papers. Here was enacted the amusing incident related in his letter of July 5, 1807 (p. 179) of his secreting his papers in the clothing of his men. The ruse was endangered by "the ladies of Santa Fe" who treated the men so liberally to wine that, intoxication threatening, Pike quickly retrieved his papers from all the soldiers who could be found and put them in his trunk. The trunk, however, was "benevolently assimilated" by his suspicious hosts the next morning. One brave soldier had not been found the night before. He had in his possession Pike's precious *Journal!* Thus when Pike's papers were finally confiscated at Chihuahua, his *Journal* was saved.

Of this examination and final confiscation of his papers, Pike gave two published accounts, one in a letter to General Wilkinson dated Natchitoches, July 5, 1807, and the other in his *Journal.* These accounts, like most of Pike's writings, are vague in detail, but they agree in all important statements.[6]

A translation of the Inventory given to Pike upon confiscation of his papers, was included in his book. It reads as follows:

"INVENTORY of papers which the lieutenant of infantry of the United States of America, Montgomery Pike, in the superior government, and commandant general of the internal provinces of New Spain as belonging to a voyage which he executed from St. Louis up the Illinois to the population of New Mexico, to visit the Indian nations, and reconnoitre the country and intermediate rivers, as it appears his expedition was undertaken by provision of the government of the said United States and the orders of General Wilkinson.

No. 1. Letter from general Wilkinson to Pike, dated 24th June, 1806.

No. 2. Another from the same to Pike, 18th July, 1806.

No. 3. Another from the same to the same officer, 19th July, 1806.

No. 4. Another from the same to Pike, dated 6th August, 1806.

No. 5. Letter from lieutenant Wilkinson to his father, 27th October, 1806.

No. 6. Another from the same to the same, 28th October, 1806.

No. 7. Letter from Pike to general Wilkinson, 22d July, 1806.

No. 8. Letter from lieutenant Wilkinson to lieutenant Pike, 26th October, 1806.

No. 9. Proclamation of general Wilkinson, prohibiting any citizen of the United States trading with the Indian nations without his permission, or that of the government, dated 10th July, 1805.

No. 10. A letter from Charles Junot, agent for the Indians, to general Wilkinson, dated 10th July, 1806.

No. 11. Notes of lieutenant Pike on the voyage from New Mexico, to Chihuahua, of four pages.

No. 12. A rough manuscript of the Missouri and Osage rivers.

No. 13. Letter from sergeant Ballenger to general Wilkinson, without date.

No. 14. Letter from lieutenant Wilkinson to Pike, without date.

No. 15. A certificate in the French language of a certain Baptist Lamie [Jean Baptiste Duchouquette] found among those nations, and specifying his motives for being there.

No. 16. A bundle of papers in the French language, which contained notes on the harangues and manifestoes which lieutenant Pike had delivered to the Indian nations.

No. 17. A passport of lieutenant Pike to the Indian Winapicane, a captain of the little Osage.

No. 18. A small draught or map of the country which is situated between the Mississippi and Santa Fe, with a description of that town, and of having met with three thousand Camanches.

No. 19. A book 8vo, manuscript, which contains the diary of lieutenant Pike, from January 1807, to the 2d March of the same year, when he arrived at Santa Fe, in 75 pages.

No. 20. A book 4to. manuscript, in paste board, with copies of letters to the secretary of war and general Wilkinson, and various observations relative to the commission of the lieutenant, in 67 pages.

No. 21. A manuscript book in folio, containing different plans of countries &c. with a diary with Rhumbs distances, and worked observations and meteorological tables which arose from a revisal of the voyages, by the said lieutenant Pike, in 40 pages.

Don Francisco Valasco, first officer of the secretaries of the commandant generalship of the internal provinces of New Spain, and Juan Pedro Walker Alferez, of the company of horse of the royal presidio of Janos.

We certify that the lieutenant of American infantry, Montgomery Pike, when presented to the commandant general of the before mentioned provinces, Don Nimesio Salcedo, likewise produced a small trunk which he brought with him, and that in the presence of the undersigned, opened himself, and took out different books and papers, when having separated with his own hands, under our cognizance, all that appeared to be, or that he said was private, or had no connection with the voyage; delivered the remainder to the demand of the commandant general which were solely those comprehended in the foregoing inventory which we have formed, and for the verification of which we have signed these presents at Chihuahua, the 8th of April, 1807.

(Signed)   Francisco Valasco.[7]
Juan Pedro Walker."

Thereafter Pike continued his journey under guard, through Mexico and back into the United States, leaving at Chihuahua a great part of his papers, among them the important book of tables and charts.

In Mexico the papers remained, lost as far as Americans were concerned, for 100 years, until all of them, except items 19 and 20 which are still lost, were discovered by Dr. Herbert E. Bolton of the University of California, now President of the American Historical Association. He reported the find in an article which appeared in the *American Historical Review*, July 1908. Their location he described as follows:

> The originals are preserved at the City of Mexico in the archive of the Secretariat of Foreign Relations. They are filed in *Caxa* 1817–1824 of "Asientas Internationales" in a bundle marked "Boundaries, concerning the search for, and delivery to the boundary commission of the documents which were taken from the traveller Pike." This bundle, in turn, is enclosed within the *carpeta* of an *expedienta* marked "1824. The United States. Treaties concerning the fixing of the boundaries between Mexico and the United States in conformity with the third article of the treaties of Washington dated February 22, 1819."[8]

From the correspondence filed with these papers Dr. Bolton learned their adventures between their seizure at Chihuahua and their discovery at the City of Mexico. He related their complicated handling as follows:

> "On September 21, 1827, Don Miguel Ramos Arispe, Minister of the Department of Justice of the federal government, and president of the commission appointed to determine the United States and Mexico, wrote to the Minister of Relations that be thought it probable that the papers taken from 'the traveller Paike' might be at Chihuahua in the Archives of the old commandancy-general and asked that they be searched for, and if found, put at

the disposal of the boundary commission. The request was at once referred to Simon Elias, governor of Chihuahua, and by him, in turn, to Jose de Zuloaga, *comisario* of that state, and custodian of the archive of the commandancy-general. After some delay the papers were found in the archive designated, and, on October 20, they were transmitted by Zuloaga to the governor, who, three days later, despatched them to Mexico, together with the original list made when the papers had been confiscated. On November 21 a receipt for all of the papers was signed by the Minister of Relations. A copy of the list was at once made, and the original list returned to Chihuahua. On the same day, November 21, the papers were sent to Arispe, who returned them, in their entirety, clearly, on January 24, 1828."[9]

In his article Dr. Bolton published reproductions of the most convenient papers. He did not print Item 4, a letter from General Wilkinson to Pike dated August 6, 1806, and Item 7, a letter from Pike to Wilkin son, July 22, 1806, for they had been published in Pike's original report. Item 12, also omitted, was a rough pencil sketch of the Missouri and Osage rivers, and considered as "quite superceeded by the finished chart which Pike inserted in his book." Item 18, a drawing of the country between the Missouri River and Santa Fe, was on so small a scale that Dr. Bolton rightly concluded it could furnish no useful conclusions.[10] Item 21, however, the book of tables and charts, Bolton described "a valuable document" and regretted that its form rendered it unsuitable for printing in the *American Historical Review.* All three of these documents are, in a way, as important as those actually printed, particularly No. 21.

Besides writing his article in the *American Historical Review* and printing the suitable papers, Dr. Bolton informed the government of his very fortunate discovery. His information led to the writing of the following letter from Henry Lane Wilson, Ambassador of the United States to Enrique C. Creel, the Mexican Minister of Foreign Affairs:

AMERICAN EMBASSY
Mexico

Personal
File 329.

May 17, 1910.

My dear Mr. Creel:

Your Excellency is doubtless aware of the geographical explorations of Lieut. Zebulon Pike, U. S. A., and of his having been made a prisoner by a force at Santa Fe in 1806, when he unwittingly crossed over into Spanish territory.

On that occasion, certain papers were taken from Lieut. Pike: and as my Government considered them of great historic value, the Embassy, under date of May 24, 1906, requested to be advised if these documents could be found in the Archives of Mexico; but though a search was instituted therefor, they could not be located.

The Embassy has been informed by Dr. Herbert E. Bolton, of the Carnegie Institution of Washington, that during the course of his researches in 1907 and 1908 through the various Archives of Your Excellency's Government, he was so fortunate as to discover the missing documents. Should Dr. Bolton's statement be corroborated, I beg to be advised whether it would be possible to return the papers to my Government, by which they are much desired.

As the United States has already indicated its policy by restoring the Palenque Cross to Mexico on its own initiative, I feel it unnecessary to state that my Government would be pleased to reciprocate the above courtesy, should the occasion offer; and in the hope that it may be consistently possible to return the documents in question.

I am, my dear Mr. Creel,

Very sincerely yours,
Henry Lane Wilson.

This letter was graciously answered by the transmittal of papers and the following note:

"Secretariat
    of
Foreign Relations
Department of Boundaries
Number 2114
Abstract
    Secretariat of Foreign Relations
        Mexico: 15 of July, 1910

Mr. Ambassador:

With reference to the communication of your Excellency, Number 329, under date of the 17 of May last, and in conformity with the desires which in that communication you are pleased to express, I have the honor to transmit to your Excellency, as a token of respect and esteem to the Government of the United States of America, the documents which were taken from the Lieutenant of the American Army, Zebulon Pike, in the year 1806, and which have been found in the archives of this Secretariat.

In this respect I am pleased to repeat to your Excellency the assurance of my high consideration.

Signature: Enrique C. Creel

Dispached by Pina.

To His Excellency Henry Lane Wilson,
Ambassador Extraordinary and
Plenipotentiary of the United States
of America.

Present."

Secretary Wilson acknowledged the receipt and expressed his appreciation for the return of papers in the following:

"AMERICAN EMBASSY
Mexico

File 329.

July 17, 1910.

His Excellency Enrique C, Creel,
Minister for Foreign Affairs.

Mr. Minister:

In behalf of my Government, I have the honor to offer to Your Excellency not only sincere thanks for the return of the Zebulon Pike documents, but also profound appreciation of the sentiments of cordial friendship expressed in Your Excellency's note of the 15th instant (No. 2114), wherewith the papers in question were transmitted to the Embassy.

Assuring Your Excellency that these sentiments are fully reciprocated, and thanking you again for returning these documents to my Government, by which they are much valued, I take pleasure in renewing to Your Excellency the assurance of my high consideration.

Henry Lane Wilson.

(Secretaria de
    Recidida
    19 Jul. 1910.
Reg. No. 1926
    Mexico."

This correspondence and the transmission of the papers somehow passed unnoticed. When, therefore, in 1925, Mr. R. H. Hart, a member of the Colorado State Historical Society, attempted to have the maps copied for study and publication, Dr. Bolton's article remained the latest authority on their location. Following the elaborate directions given in it, Mr. Hart, through Mr. Lawrence C. Phipps, Jr. and Mr. A. B. West, instituted a search in the archives of the Secretariat of Foreign Relations at the City of Mexico. The result of this search was, at first, the disappointing news that Mexican officials were having difficulty in locating the maps. It seemed that some of the records in the archives of the Secretariat of Foreign Relations had been moved to the National Palace. Finally search was abandoned.

In the meantime Mr. Hart, suspecting what had actually happened, that the papers had been transmitted to Washington, wrote to the War Department asking if their records showed whether the Pike papers were ever recovered, through the Army, or through the State Department.[11] This request revealed only that nothing could be found "to show whether they were recovered or not."[12] Thus all threads failed, and it seemed as if the maps would be lost for another hundred years or perhaps forever.

In 1927, however, the cover[13] which had enclosed Pike's records was discovered in the Secretariat of Foreign Relations in Mexico City by Mr. C. W. Lathrop acting on advice from Mr. Hart and Mr. Phipps. In it was the correspondence between Ambassador Wilson and Secretary Creel relating to the transfer of the Pike papers to Washington. Photographic copies of the cover and correspondence were procured to insure against further loss, and the search was renewed.

The Wilson-Creel correspondence indicated that the papers should be in the archives of the Department of State. Inquiry there, however, revealed that they had been transmitted to the War Department, August 5, 1910.[14] Confronted with this evidence, the War Department prosecuted a search. For some time, however, it was without results, for the shifting of records at the time of the World War had caused some confusion.[15] Finally after a month of search all the items exactly as described by Dr. Bolton were discovered. They were in the Archives Division, Adjutant General's office. There they rest, after travels fully as long as Pike's and through territory as terrifying.

3.

Until the discovery of the maps here used to check Pike's travels there were only three important original sources of information available for study of Pike's Southwestern Expedition: the correspondence and documents of President Jefferson, General Dearborn, and General Wilkinson, relative to the purpose of the expedition; the papers discovered and published by Dr. Herbert E. Bolton; and Pike's own published book.[16]

The first of these sources deals with the background of the expedition, its purposes, and the suspicious role of Wilkinson. It has been thoroughly exploited by previous commentators. Dr. Elliott Coues in his *Expeditions of Zebulon Montgomery Pike*, Dr. Isaac J. Cox, in *The Early Explorations of Louisiana*, and the editor of the *American Historical Review* in his remarks following Dr. Bolton's article, have extracted all possible information from these documents.

The second is the papers discovered by Dr. Bolton, noted above.

The third, Pike's book, by far the most important of the sources, is worthy of more detailed consideration.

When Pike had concluded his travels, he seems to have written about them for glory more than profit—for reputation was always uppermost in his mind. But he had an eye for sales and royalties, as the following fragment from a letter to General Dearborn suggests:[17]

"I have entered into an agreement with the firm of Conrad, Lucas & Co of this place to print and publish my Tours, for which I allow them 20 pr. Cent on all the sales, and pay besides the expences of printing &c.—This, with bad debts and other Casualities will leave to myself but an extreame small profit but as a soldiers views are more Generally directed to fame than interest I hope that one object will at least be accomplished.—The Work will not exceed four dollars pr. Copy but the exact price we cannot yet ascertain but hope Genl. Dearborne will give it all the patronage which he may deem it entitled to; and Signify to Messrs. Conrad and Lucas the number of Copies you will take on % of your Department."

Publication was attended with difficulties. Pike's training as a soldier and his experiences among Indians had not prepared him for editorial duties. "Like many another gallant soldier, versed in the arts of war," Pike "was quite innocent of literary strategy, though capable of heading an impetuous assault on the parts of speech."[18] Pike, too, was hurried and ill. His papers, moreover, were, as he says, "In a mutilated state, from the absolute necessity I was under to write on small pieces in the Spanish country; also from being injured in the gunbarrels," [where he had hidden them] "some of which I filed three times off to take out the papers."[19] The following note to the original edition was certainly justified:

"The publisher owes it to truth, and to Colonel Pike, to state that he very much doubts whether any book ever went to press under so many disadvantages as the one now presented to the public."[20]

This original edition, published in 1810 at Philadelphia, was poorly arranged. It was indexed badly and was padded with numerous appendices containing haphazard letters, memoranda, meteorological tables, and formal notes on geography, ethnology, and military and commercial topics. It included, on the other hand, a set of six interesting maps covering the entire country traversed on Pike's two journeys. Two of these maps, those referring to the Southwestern Expedition, are of particular interest, for they are the ones superseded by those cited here. These two maps, together with the other four Pike published, were prepared by the draughtsman, Anthony Nau, and will hereafter be referred to as the Nau maps, to differentiate between them and Pike's own charts.

In constructing these southwestern Nau maps Pike was severely handicapped by the loss of the papers which had been confiscated by the Spaniards. Among the lost papers were the charts which he had carefully prepared of his whole route day by day from St. Louis to the Rio Conejos. On these he had hoped to base his finished maps of the interior provinces of Louisiana. He was deprived, too, of the best substitute for these charts, his original table of courses and distances, which had been confiscated with the rest of his papers.

The loss of his papers he bewailed frequently in letters to General Wilkinson and the Secretary of War:

> "It must be recollected that the Spanish General seized on all my Documents in his power; Amongst which [were] the book of Charts protracted, daily, from my notes and the eye; and although I retained a copy of Courses, Distances, &c—by which I have been enabled to retrace my plans, and routes, yet they necessarily are not so perfect as the Original and daily protractions would have made them."

It was not to Pike's interest, however, publicly to emphasize his losses, but rather to show what he had accomplished in spite of them. He glossed over them in the published work and emphasized the resources and materials still in his hands.

With these materials he could have made commendable maps of the Southwestern Expedition, although naturally not as accurate or detailed as his daily charts, for these materials were fairly complete and authoritative. They were as follows: the *Journal* which he saved, containing each day's march and occasional descriptions of the country; a transcript which Dr. Robinson, one of the company, had made of all the courses and distances, except the excursion to South Park and the headwaters of the Platte; a "few notes . . . of the Latt . . . from letters" to General Wilkinson; and "a very elegant protracted sketch of the route" as far as the Arkansas, which Lieutenant Wilkinson copied and carried with him down that river after he had parted from Pike.[21] Poor use was made of these materials, however, for the Nau maps are careless and inaccurate. Camps, rivers, directions and distances were omitted, twisted, or out of proportion. Even that part of the itinerary, as far as the Arkansas, for which Pike had the use of Wilkinson's "elegant protracted sketch," is confused and incorrect. Although the Nau maps are attractive in appearance, they are of slight value when compared to the original charts.

The Nau maps, in one form or another, were included in all later editions of Pike's work. The first of these was published, in London in 1811. Its editor, Dr. Thomas Rees, somewhat improved the awkward arrangement, spelling, and grammar of the first edition. On the London, therefore, instead of the Philadelphia version, were based all the editions which followed—a French edition at Paris, 1812; a Dutch edition at Amsterdam, 1812–13; and finally a German edition. In 1889 the London version was reprinted in Denver, Colo., with a valuable introduction by William M. Maguire. There are two forms of the Denver work, differing, however, only in binding, margin, and such external features.[22] The most modern reprint, an attractive, unpretentious little volume contains only the Southwestern Expedition. It was edited by Dr. Milo Milton Quaife, based on the original American edition, and published in 1925 by the Lakeside Press, Chicago. No writer on Pike has shown the poise and balance exhibited by Dr. Quaife.

The standard edition of Pike, however, a monument of editorial skill and labor, is that of the late Dr. Elliott Coues. It was published by Harper in New York in 1895. Coues' *Memoir of Zebulon Montgomery Pike* is an excellent, thoroughly documented, work. His notes to the *Journal* while verbose, are voluminous, scholarly, and, considering the material at his disposal were accurate. They are even interesting, an unusual quality in footnotes. They explain the text, but in terms of geography and nomenclature of four decades ago and they locate Pike's route and camp sites. In this last task, Coues was unavoidably handicapped. He had only the mileages and spasmodic geographic descriptions of the *Journal,* and the inaccurate and small-scale tracings and camp marks of the Nau maps. Using these as a basis for his identifications, he located Pike's route and camps by means of a series of remarkable guesses and deductions. The inaccuracies and scarcity of his material, however, led him into many errors, usually small, though sometimes as great as thirty or thirty-five miles. These errors of Coues are corrected and his accurate judgments are confirmed by the original charts on which the ensuing annotations are based—with a reproduction of some of Pike's actual maps.

STEPHEN HARDING HART

New College,
Oxford

PART TWO

The Purpose of Pike's Expedition

With the exception of Fremont's journals perhaps no document on western travel has given rise to so much discussion as that which has centered about Zebulon Pike's expedition of 1806.

On a review of this literature, in the light of Pike's *Journal* as interpreted by Mr. Hart's exposition of Pike's maps, one is struck, first, by the fact that, in answering such accusations as that Pike was "highly unethical and untruthful at the very least and with a fair chance of being distinctly traitorous,"[23] almost every witness has been given a full chance to be heard except the accused himself. What Pike wrote has been read with Twentieth Century eyes and an understanding of the Great Plains and Rockies a century and a quarter behind the times. Full attention has been paid to all prejudicial evidence that can be adduced or inferred from Wilkinson, Burr, Jefferson, Dearborn, Salcedo, Robinson, Foronda, Rowan, Hunt, Adair and Kibby. Pike himself has been quite utterly neglected with one exception, to be as noted elsewhere.

This is due to the fact that—as usual—our journals and documents on western travel have been edited by Atlantic Americans—or at least by those so ignorant of western lore and plainsmanship that judgment gives way to an inaccuracy that mitigates against a clear understanding and smacks of everything but scholarship. In the case of Pike, for instance, no one of his critics has studied his diary with a consciousness of his lack of

plainsmanship, or a realization of his misconceptions on a score of topics; no such critic has once pointed out the unbelievable lack of judgment
which sent him into the Great Plains without a competent frontiersman
and mountaineer as a guide—when a score of such men were available;
no one, even while ardently espousing the whim that Pike's real mission
was that of spying out New Mexico for Wilkinson and Burr, has suggested
that few men could have been selected so poorly equipped in every way
for such a mission; or that Pike, at every turn throughout the journey, did
something that he must have known would seriously handicap him in the
role of "spy"—like boldly risking the alienation of the Osages, or actually
seeking the Comanches when they were possibly at war with the Spaniards,
or ignoring every known route from the Arkansas River toward Santa Fe
until starvation drove him south.

The lack here complained of not only leads to editorial sins of omis-
sion such as obliviousness to Pike's shortcomings and errors in estimating,
guessing and forecasting. It leads to serious errors of commission, as illustrated by the ridicule poured upon Pike for his references to reaching a
divide (Tennessee Pass) beyond which lay the "Pierre Juan," the Yellowstone
River. Any reasonable amount of knowledge of the Rockies of 1806 would
have saved any editor the embarrassment of attributing to Pike (despite
the zestful rodomontades of an ambitious twenty-six-year-old) an foolish
boast that amounted to a lie; when, as a matter of fact, Pike's information
was correct although he did not rightly interpret it any more than have his
equally-ignorant editors.

Now the testimony of Pike comes to us solely from his *Journal*. True,
it is not wholly a contemporaneous, day-by-day record. While formed from
day-to-day entries of distances travelled and comments on events and geographical observations, it was supplemented by memories of his experiences,
the whole, being fashioned into a running narrative when Pike returned
home—with comments and corrections thrown in "after the event." Of
this, more later; our point, here, is not the contents and character of the
Journal but its treatment hitherto. It has not been approached with the purpose of learning from it. The common attitude to the document is represented by such comments as: "the details of Pike's journey need not detain
us long"; and "Pike's journey over the plains of Kansas was of no particular
interest." If Pike is quoted on any point by such an editor, his testimony
is usually cited as "Pike claims," "Pike seemed to think" or "Pike would

have us believe"—such references being made with irrelevant abstraction, as though the person writing was conscious of having momentarily sunk to a low level of authority.

Passing the point (to be noted later) that through Pike's *Journal* the American people were to get their very first picture of the Great Plains and Rockies, editors and analysts have essayed the task of giving Pike his place in history while ignorant of both the meaning of his words and the limitations of his fitness, but armed with an intimate knowledge of the international complications of his day so far as they related to active diplomats in Foreign Offices. They have then proceeded to find in Pike's records only what they sought. His simple story was, in their hands, oriented beyond recognition. Into it they read explanations, interpretations and correlations which implied a knowledge of international affairs on the part of Pike equal to their own, than which nothing could be more false. Surfeited with this European background, and reflecting the hollowness and hypocracy of international diplomacy of 1806, they begin their study of Pike's simple tale mentally averse to taking his plain words at their own meaning, unwilling to find anything on the surface. To do their duty they must try to detect a trick in each word, a hidden meaning in every sentence, the code of a spy in Pike's very astronomical observations! I mean that literally. This novel idea originated with a Spanish official who, on reading General Wilkinson's directions to Pike for using certain instruments which were sent to him, observed that if Pike knew anything about the business such directions were superfluous; otherwise they were not sufficient to teach Pike anything. They were, therefore, a secret code! No one could blame any writer for citing this delicious piece of mediævalism. But have Pike's historians done so for the merriment of the thing? Has one of them ever raised a finger to check Wilkinson's directions or Pike's observations to test whether they were authentic—and thus prove the insinuation to be false? No. Not one. As a matter of fact, every direction given Pike by Wilkinson as to the use of instruments was correct, commonplace and is thoroughly understood as "standard" by those acquainted with the science who read them today. Yet no critic of Pike has cared, hitherto, to establish this simple fact,

Thus, by raising a suspicion, here, and not nailing it for a lie; by trying to find in a superficial observation there, an insidious, hidden meaning; by taking some of the ebullitions of an ambitious, high-spirited young officer at face value, these biographers of Pike's tip-toe after him across the Great Plains filled with goose-flesh at the thought that every crimson *opuntia rhodantha* (cactus) may be a red Comanche in disguise and every "Spanish Bayonet" may be a sharpshooter of Malgares', the Spanish cavalry leader. To them any innocent *castilleja integra* (Indian Paint Brush) may be frescoing a new international complication and any sage brush reek of espionage, filibustering and sabotage. Whereas the plain truth lies on the surface, whether scholasticism and antiquarianism cares to look for it there or not. The sole validity acquired by these suspicions and aspersions cast on Pike is secured by the mere physical act of raising them. The sign "Is this man a crook?" nailed on any man's home would lead to curious questionings and compel uncomfortable denials. Even high grade commentators on Pike show an inconsistency in attempting to impute to him disloyal ambitions. Others so severely qualify their premises as to neutralize the argument or succeed, somewhere, in so actually disallowing their own accusations as to make them untenable. One of the best of these scholars frankly states that an examination of all the sources fail to show that Pike was guilty of more than a warm friendship for Wilkinson, and admits that, while Pike acted unwittingly as Wilkinson's agent in a filibustering scheme (i.e. "a spy upon Spanish territory"), he was, from a national point of view, "justified in assuming this role" in view of the equivocal dealings of Spanish colonial authorities.[24]

Low grade literary fortune hunters, who have exploited sensationally Pike's "treachery" and "disloyalty" for gain, have made a record for producing some delightful historical nonsense out of Pike's "hostile advance" on Santa Fé, or his "military demonstration" against New Mexico.

If the stark horror of the thing was not mitigated by the fact that no one of Pike's men actually froze to death, how piquant a picture—this "reconnoissance in force" (as Mr. Coues called it) on Santa Fé of twelve famished men, nine of them with frozen feet and not guns enough among them to go around! How terrible the "belligerent aspect" of five men, most of whom had had their fingers frozen; a fact mentioned by a Spanish officer but not by Pike! And, forgetting for the instant, that some of these men went through life on stumps of legs only, how picturesque, this "military demonstration" against New Mexico of eleven men mushing through the giant Sangre de Cristo Range of Colorado in zero weather, clothed only in cotton overalls and cotton shirts, their blankets having been cut up for socks, hoping soon to be "captured" and saved from death—leaving behind in the Wet Mountain Valley five comrades, some of whom picked the bones from their frozen feet and sent them forward to Pike by the first who were able to travel in mute appeal that his promise of succor should not be forgotten!

Is it not time that such rubbish should be denied the right to pass for "history"—even if published by "our best people"? Is it not time that Zebulon Pike be divested of both the trappings of mediæval diplomatic mummery and the gooseflesh of sensational "historians" and that his story should be examined for its own sake, its own testimony, its own tell-tale evidences of common truth and common errors—even if his maps had not been found to throw their significant light on this real, human tale that Pike told? Is it not time that we read Pike's *Journal* with some sense of relative values? Is it not important that he, first of Americans, describes the lush and beautiful Kansas lowlands—or at least as important as any hocus-pocus about General Wilkinson's relations with the British minister? Is it not a national literary, as well as historical, heritage, this glowing account of the verdure of the matchless Great Plains—and much more important to us now than the 1806 machinations of Manuel de Lisa? Did not the weight of Pike's testimony as to the fertility of the West, which could support the numberless millions of buffaloes which he saw, affect the imagination and the thinking of men—far beyond his academic platitudes about the Great Desert line being a natural boundary of empire? Is it not impressive that Pike first pictures for us the old Santa Fe trail, almost a generation before Brown and Sibley surveyed it—but who mentions this when Wilkinson's alleged "secret instructions" to Pike can be made the subject of spinal-column-tickling gossip? Was he not the first explorer to advocate a transcontinental highway from Atlantic to Pacific and to assure the world that the Rockies could be as successfully crossed as the Alleghenies? Did not Pike first report the Peak which was generously named for him two decades later; make an attempt to reach it in zero weather clad only in cotton overalls; measure its height fairly accurately, considering its Great Plains pedestal was overestimated in altitude; study it from every side except the north? But carping "historians" still state both that Pike then "modestly" named the Peak for himself, which is a lie, and that it was "wrongly" named for him at a later date, which is an injustice—never seeing the human angle of the episode which reveals the real modesty of the young man for never thinking of naming it for himself? Is not beautiful South Park; the black grandeur of the Royal Gorge; the ineffable glory of the Sangre de Cristo Range and the majesty of the San Luis Valley, first described for Americans in Pike's pages? Is this to be ignored because prejudiced critics are so partisan that, if a word of Pike's is found to agree with their biased views, it is quoted eagerly as thoroughly reliable, whereas no entry containing an implication contrary to their views can be mentioned except with a slurring "Pike claimed" or "Pike alleged"?

Such is "scholarship" when a document like Pike's *Journal* is studied to prove a pet theory instead of looking at it, even-eyed, for the truth!

Again, it is unfortunate to edit a *Journal* like Pike's without giving the reader a peek into letters that were written contemporaneously by the diarist himself. Such letters are exceedingly informing. Journal entries must, necessarily, be short, cryptic; a letter tells the thing out in plain story form; and it may illumine a whole episode by intimate flashes which, because of their informality, would be excluded from an official journal. In the case of Pike, the contemporaneous letters do not in the least further the "spy" theory—save as the freedom of a confidential letter allows some of Pike's youthful exuberance to effervesce. And Oh! what advantage his critics have taken of such effervescence! And yet in the self same correspondence is to be found the very key to the whole Pike-New Mexico episode—never once, even by accident, noted by a single critic!

So let us read Pike's *Journal* for what it contains—not for what men have read into it. It is a genuine document. Both the political hocus-pocus read into the tale, as well as any pretense to "pathfinder" heroism (beyond boyish rodomontade), are belied by those principles of unconscious testimony and internal consistency which must mark any bona fide document. Every such piece of writing affords plenty of rogue's-yarn proofs of authority and authenticity by the inimitable and unpremeditated evidence afforded by the consistency of both its truths *and its errors*. Every such document comes into the court of critical cross-questioning to justify or to condemn its author, nor can the essence of its vital testimony be augmented or suppressed without either so altering its literary flavor (by tampering with modes of expression or by coarsely realigning the writer's original principles, purposes or prospectives) as to give the lie to every such innovation. For a document which was recast after the experiences which gave it birth, Pike's *Journal* is a singular literary relic. The corrections of mistakes and misunderstandings are not woven into its fabric but are inter-jected like footnotes or in parentheses. The integrity of the document is interestingly checked by Pike's recovered maps—which Pike of course did not possess at the time of rewriting. In four instances his entry of "Red River" on the line of the Arkansas is crossed out and the word "Arkansas" is written beneath. But his entry "Red River" on the line of the Rio Grande stands unchanged!

The story that Pike unfolds in his steady going *Journal* creates in the openminded person its effective impression by a consistency that could not have been artificially maintained by a course of rewriting; a consistency in purpose; a consistency in outlook; a consistency in its reference to back-ground or past occurrences; in its orderly sequence of acquisition of new information whether true or false; *in adhering logically to errors and misun-derstandings and misjudgments.* Pike knew, when editing his *Journal* for the printer, of the "spy" accusation. Yet, though wounded to the heart by this attack on his reputation, he disdained to make his *Journal* a defense. In fact he leaned the other way, by telling his plain tale just about as his original notes must have told it, with patent evidences of short-comings, misgivings, bad guesses, poorly based surmises, foolhardy experiments, geographical blunders, childish mistakes—and yet, withal, a sprinkling of youthful bom-bast, martinet pertness and cocky military braggadocio. The simple qual-ity of Pike's ingenuousness is signally illustrated by his writing to General Wilkinson from Mexico July 5, 1807 (p. 182) that his enforced detainment there had given him a chance to secure as much information about the country as if he had been expressly sent for that purpose. And is it a sign of fairness, to say nothing of sportsmanship, that his issuing a *Journal* full of such loop-holes for an attack on his ability as a leader is never named to his credit, while, on the other hand, every boyish boast of his amusing military prowess is cited in capital letters and italics (so to speak) to substantiate the figment of a diabolical intrigue which he was plotting by his "filibustering attack" on the unsuspecting Dons—with only three men able to walk and with only forty pounds of lead at the start, of which at least 500 rounds had already been fired!

But the raw absurdity of the thing has led us ourselves into error! The Dons were not "unsuspecting." They knew of Pike's advance toward the frontier even before he started! And here we face some interesting consider-ations which no critic has deigned to consider: namely, the long list of facts which make it foolish to believe that Pike's "spying" activities could have had any place in his contemplation when the journey to the West was being considered—although, incidentally, of course, it was reasonable to suppose that Pike should record what he saw and obtain information of use to the authorities whatever the future might bring. And why not? Had he not done just that very thing, as Dr. M. M. Quaife has brought out in his well-balanced Introduction to *Zebulon M. Pike's Southwestern Expedition.* Why this furor over the character of Pike's "guilty inroad" toward the Southwest when he had just made a similar, and perhaps less justifiable, one to the North—bringing back all kinds of information regarding the political and strategic character of Anglo-British border rivalries? Any one word of Pike's many belligerent paragraphs addressed to British fur companies on the shadowy borderland in the North had had more sting in it than anything that ever passed between Pike and the Spaniards during all his acquaintance with them!

If Pike's adventure in the Southwest was intended to be what his critics claim (providing you credit General Wilkinson with any brains at all, and no one ever denied that) Pike certainly would not have been chosen for the mission, in the first place. Too many men at least somewhat versed in the essentials of the delicate business—a knowledge of New Mexico and its men of real consequence and, above all, of the Spanish language—could have been had if spying out the land for Aaron Burr was really desired. Moreover, such an one, going in the guise of a trader, let us say, would have attracted nothing like the attention and suspicion of a troop of armed horsemen; nor would the former arouse the hostility of Spain's Indian allies as would the latter. More than that, if Wilkinson and Burr had seriously wanted a reconnoissance of New Mexico they would have wanted it in 1805—not 1806 or 1807. A serious reconnoissance of New Mexico required an accurate military strategist; Pike with his imperfect instruments could not get the correct altitude of Pike's Peak within 4000 feet, and misjudged the latitude of both present Great Bend, Kan., and Pueblo, Colo., from thirty-five to forty miles. Only an expert, supplied with the best instruments and the best methods of transporting them, could have fixed altitude, latitude and longitude correctly.

No publicity whatever would have been permitted a bona fide effort to acquire the information Pike's critics claim he sought; as it was, the Spanish government heard of Pike's advance before he started, and sent out the Malgares column of 600 horse to challenge any American alienation of Spanish Indian allies—if not to baulk, or actually to punish, Pike if possible!

Overlooking the publicity and ostentation of Pike's preparations and departure, no expedition for the primary purpose attributed to Pike would have taken the route dictated to him—nor would it have been burdened with the delivery of the Indian wards entrusted to his charge. Nor would such a party have been sent out on a slow-moving mission without being equipped for winter—if any serious reconnaissance of New Mexico was contemplated; nor have been started so late in the season or have been expected to arrive at Pike's fixed destination (Natchitoches) so soon.

If so romantic a destination or purpose for Pike was in General Wilkinson's mind, is it sensible to think that he would have suggested the return of his own (Wilkinson's) son—who accompanied Pike—when the Arkansas River had been reached? And let Pike (of whom the son was jealous) go ahead alone and win laurels and glory? And miss the whole romance of the thing? Moreover, two letters discovered by Dr. Bolton in Mexico show that Pike expected to ascend the Arkansas and descend the Red and reach Natchitoches as soon as Lieutenant Wilkinson did—or sooner.[25] So rapid a tour left no time for any such reconnoitering program as called for by the argument of his critics.

As suggested elsewhere, incidentally, the conduct of the expedition gives the lie to the supposition that anything except the ordinary, routine investigation of Spanish-American boundary was Pike's purpose; otherwise it is unthinkable that Pike would have treated the Osages as brusquely as he did; that he would have gone hunting endlessly for Comanches who were reported both as Spanish allies and as at war with Spain; that he would have ventured beyond the Osage allies without competent guides; that he would have ignored every route which turned south from the Arkansas to New Mexico just as winter was coming down from the North; or that, under such circumstances, he would have ventured one step into the Rockies when he arrived at the frowning portals of the Royal Gorge. To cap the climax, Pike is ordered to secure from the Comanches several chiefs who will accompany him homeward down Red River and proceed to Washington to hear the "Great White Father" himself speak on the subject of future peace. Whether the Comanches were at peace or at war with Spain, it is equally bewildering to conceive of Pike's being handicapped by such impedimenta while making a "reconnoissance in force" upon New Mexico. The idea is too eccentric to be entertained. If they were allies of Spain they would be useless; if at war with Spain they would get Pike shot on sight.

The basis of the allegations supporting the theory that Pike was an active, conscious "spy" for the separatist advocates supposed to be headed by Burr depend, in the first place, upon sly boasts of filibustering made by Wilkinson; in the second place, upon the airy, youthful exultations of Pike's which seem to some to be so dripping with intrigue; and, in the third place, upon certain common-place, everyday comments and forecasts and opinions reported by Pike which no soldier, with an ounce of sense, could have ventured into the Great Plains in 1806 without making—at a moment when no one knew whether the United States and Spain would at all be able to keep from coming to blows over the question of Mississippi River commerce and hazy boundary line disputes. However, the fact remains, that at no time in Pike's march was he on more debatable ground than were Lewis and Clark the moment they crossed the Rockies.

The first basis—Wilkinson's later sly boasts of abetting intrigue through Pike—can be thrown out of court at sight. And is it not a dry comment on the simple honesty of Pike's detractors that they leave no stone unturned, no vituperative language unemployed, no scathing denunciation overlooked to impress their readers with a full knowledge of Wilkinson's loathsome dishonesty and innocence of every human attribute indicative of truthfulness—until it comes to quoting him on the purpose of Pike's wily journey of intrigue! On all other topics Wilkinson is, to them, beneath contempt; but, with reference to Pike's mission, he is cited as a paragon of truthfulness! Dr. Quaife has expressed this same idea by complaining that Pike's critics never seem to recall that so perfect a crook as Wilkinson was just as likely to be double crossing his Spanish employees by means of Pike as his fellowcountrymen. In other words, the man's unreliability was potentially all-comprehending.

The second basis is Pike's verbal, sophomoric flourishings *a la militaire*. They are, however, no less, and no more, excusable than what might have been found in almost any western army officer's journal in these days of troublesome joint ownership of the Mississippi River. Countless officers' accounts just as sophomorically incriminating as anything recorded by Pike are to be found in diaries, journals, newspapers and magazines of the day.

Of course Pike, venturing out upon a doubtful border, must have had in mind every such problem of topography, distances and routes—his orders practically called for data on every such topic. How criminally negligent would not our War Department have been if it failed to gather every bit of intelligence that was possible concerning every topographical feature of the Spanish-American borderland! The fact that Pike discusses the Santa Fé Trail route to Santa Fé from the standpoint of a practical army route, and describes pugnaciously what he could do were he given an army to lead over it, is offered as full proof that he was an intriguing spy; whereas if he had not reported on all such major topics he ought to have been stripped of his commission!

Under this head, Pike's statement to Wilkinson in his letter of July 22nd that he would advance the subterfuge, if captured by the Spaniards, that he did not know his whereabouts has been cited as proof of the insidious character of his expedition. If Baron von Humboldt was able to draw neither the Red River, Cimarron or Canadian correctly even on a map at this time, and Major Long could not do it two decades later, was it surprising that Pike actually did get confused when out in the wilds and call the Rio Grande the "Red"? If capture threatened, Pike stated that, "unless they give us ample assurances of just and honorable treatment, according to the custom of nations in like cases, I would resist, even if the inequality was as great as at the affair of Bender [Russia], or the streights of Thermopylae." To attempt to make capital out of this bit of Don Quixotism shows to what length Pike's romancers enjoy going! Equally difficult is their task with reference to the alleged strong fort Pike erected on the Conejos where he proceeded to "dig in" behind a thirty-six foot, three-sided, wood-and-earthen fortress surrounded by a moat. Effort has been made to show what a menace to Spain was this slight protection against the Indians constructed by Pike's crippled force. He is quoted as saying, with a burst of courage, that in it he could defy Malgares 100 strong. But no one so quoting him—and how typical of all these carping innuendoes it is!—completes the quotation. Malgares had 600 troopers, not 100, in the first place; and in the second place, Pike states (February 6th, 1807) that his work was powerful enough to afford him defense for one or two days—but that on the *first or second* night he would have to run! Referring to the same matter at another time (April 20) he stated that he could have held out until his provisions were exhausted. Meanwhile he, the commander of the party, had to provide with his own gun *every mouthful that his men had to eat!*

In the light of these crimes committed against the name of Pike, is it not possible, now, to reconstruct his story briefly and thus, not only to formulate a reasonable working basis for an explanation of its various episodes, but to introduce the rightful perspective and to correlate the testimony of the newly-found Pike maps to this historic journey? Only thus can the countless insinuations and suspicions of Pike's actions be answered. The *Journal* which follows can be studied to corroborate or refute every statement which we advance.

At the moment of the opening of the story we find Osage Indians who had been on a visit to the "Great White Father" at Washington, and others of the same tribe who have been recovered from captivity, are at St. Louis ready to be convoyed to their western Missouri homes. This duty always fell, of course, to the War Department. Lieutenant Pike, just returned from a successful and interesting reconnoissance of the Upper Mississippi River and some exciting treaty-making experiences with Indians in that section, was assigned by General Wilkinson, head of the army, to escort the Osages westward. Critics who have attempted to entangle Pike in Wilkinson's intrigues with Aaron Burr and Spanish officials have stated that secret instructions now issued to Pike called for the spying out of routes to, and conditions in, New Mexico under the guise of his also being ordered to explore the upper Arkansas River and the portages between it and the Red River. They point out that the plan was General Wilkinson's—and not that of President Jefferson's—as in the case of Lewis and Clark (now on their way home from the Pacific) or the Freeman-Dunbar survey of the lower Red River.

The point is not honestly made. Those who advanced it knew that to the War Department, only, was assigned such duties as convoying Indians across the frontiers; no other branch of the government had done, or could do, this. Despite its singular and complexing outcome (resulting in Pike's capture) the government did recognize and support the expedition and Secretary of War Dearborn stated that it received President Jefferson's approbation and that Pike's services were held in "high estimation" by him.[26] If only the President of the United States had authorized military reconnoissances in the West nine-tenths of all that were made would never have occured, as Mr. Coues himself knew perfectly well.

This consideration, however, opens up the neglected key view-point (mentioned by no critic) which forms a working basis for a clear understanding of the mysteries of the entire episode. Pike, young, ardent, typically bellicose (for a twenty-six-year-old-officer) and never more an ardent admirer of his Chief than when anticipating glory to be won under him on the field of battle, was more practical than his biographers. War with Spain was unlikely, but fame was right now being won on the Great West frontier—in fathoming its character, its wealth and its intriguing boundary lines. Of Lewis and Clark, in particular, and of Freeman, Dunbar and Sibley incidentally, Pike was a jealous admirer. His Mississippi River exploration of the season previous had given him a niche by which to climb to fame. He had performed creditably. This new assignment, with its chance to match his wits in the tepees of half-hearted American Kansas Indian allies, and with the Comanches on the upper reaches of the Arkansas, the warlike Spanish allies, together with the added reputation of mapping the upper Red River, as Freeman and Dunbar had as yet been unable to do, was immensely to his liking. In the end he cherished the hope of being made the head of a Commission to survey the Louisiana Purchase boundary line. Pike, in the first chance to write to General Wilkinson while in Mexico, takes the opportunity to ask (p. 178) the General's help to secure such an appointment. When you know that fact, you have the secret, the open sesame, of all the real riddles of Pike's eccentric experience with Indian duplicity, suspicious Spanish complacency and the rigors of a Rocky Mountain winter in 1806. Nine-tenths of the blather-dash of his critics is answered by it; the other tenth must be accounted for only on the ground that Pike's ardent spirit did not wish his commander to think him lukewarm or pusillanimous in the "bright face of danger." He was just exactly the kind of an officer in whose pocket, as he lay dead on a battlefield, you might expect to find (as was found in Pike's) a message to his son to keep honor unsullied and always to be ready to die for country.

Reading the accompanying *Journal* with that theory in mind, and with the corroborating evidence of Pike's actual maps before one's eyes, practically every anomaly in his progress into the Plains, and his otherwise inexplicable advance into the Rockies in midwinter, becomes as reasonable as would be possible in the case of an ambitious, over-zealous youth, itching for fame.

Pike's first business was the delivery of his Osage wards to their relatives.

No army officer ever found such a mission anything but difficult. Few men knew the contemporaneous relations of any bickering tribes—least of all those existing between Osages, Kansas, Pawnees and Comanches in 1806. Pike's case was made doubly hard because the Spanish trapper-baron, Manuel de Lisa of St Louis, was intent upon neutralizing American interest in the Osage-Pawnee-Comanche country and linking up Spanish alliance with these tribes to his plan to establish a three-cornered trade between St. Louis, the Indians and Santa Fé. In passing, it is an item of note that detractors of Pike, while perfectly cognizant of the influence of these St. Louis rivals, have done him the injustice of confusing the evidence and feign doubt as to whether Pike was not a party to, or responsible for, some of Lisa's intriguing interference; this is another instance of playing fast and loose with facts in order to create a diversion in favor of a pet theory.

Leaving Belle Fontaine near St. Louis July 15th, Pike reached his first destination, the Osage towns in present-day Kansas, August 18th. Proceeding forward with three Osage guides (who took the party by a long, roundabout route to avoid the dreaded "Kans") the chief town of the Grand Pawnees, near Republic City, Kansas, was reached on September 25th. After twelve days of hectic parleying with these Spanish-inclined Pawnees (who had been visited within a few weeks by Malgares' Spanish column) Pike's little force struck out, on Malgares' "Spanish trace," for the Arkansas River with two Osage guides, on October 7th.

We have no data on which to base a judgment of Pike's quality as a leader during this Indian phase, so to speak, of his expedition. The best one can say is that he got out of his numerous dilemmas without the loss of a man and proceeded forward instead of backward—as the Pawnees heartily advised. His record shows that he was guided by some excellent principles, like preventing a wanton destruction of game "as the laws of morality forbid it," and in demanding justice from the redskins; "if you have justice on your side," he remarked, "and do not enforce it, they universally despise you." It is doubtful whether an officer ever had much better proof of the respect of his men for him than Pike had before the end of his long, strange tour. In Santa Fé he was compelled to punish them severely for intoxication—when they bore secreted in their clothing Pike's *Journal*, Charts and meteorological observations. But their respect for him prevented them from divulging his secret.

Pike did not however, keep on good terms with his colleague, Lieutenant

Wilkinson, the son of his admired Chief. How early this disaffection arose, and how serious it may have been, is left to the reader's imagination. The facts known are that in the son's report to his father, the General, he discounts the value of Pike's proposed exploration of the upper Arkansas; and, in a letter addressed to the General from the banks of the Arkansas before beginning his descent of that river, he complains bitterly of the limited outfit which Pike furnished him. In its proper place young Wilkinson's complaint will be found, together with Pike's terse reply.[27] While the writer thinks that the young man should have been turned up and spanked, each reader can decide that for himself. He complained of the small ration of powder and lead issued to him. Pike allowed Wilkinson's party of five, (who were making a homeward journey) nineteen pounds of powder and thirty-nine of lead; while Pike's party of sixteen, heading toward the mountains, with every mouthful of food for untold weeks to be supplied by their guns, had thirty-five pounds of powder and forty of lead!

The matter of real import is, however, whether this Wilkinson dispute throws any light on Pike's mission to the interior. It is plain that the young man has a very definite idea of Pike's purpose in ascending the Arkansas, for his querelous letter states that a map of the lower river and a sketch of the adjacent country which he is to make is of as much importance to General Wilkinson "as one of Red River, its confluent streams and country." In fact he says it is of more importance, because he did not know that the Freeman-Sparks Red River expedition had already been stopped by the Spaniards in what is now Little River County, Ark.

Even if one admits that General Wilkinson might not have wished that his son (though practically of Pike's own age) should accompany Pike on an alleged "filibustering" reconnoitre of New Mexico, is it reasonable to suppose the young man would have been kept in ignorance of the secret? This seems to the present writer illogical and absurd. Otherwise if young Wilkinson knew of the "real" reason of Pike's advance up the Arkansas—he would never have uttered in writing expressions so roundly discounting the value of Pike's advance inland. It is impossible to believe that General Wilkinson would have subjected his son to the embarrassment of having been fooled, by both his own father and by Pike, as to the alleged major purpose of the latter's Arkansas reconnoissance.

At this camp near Great Bend, Kansas, Pike bids Wilkinson and his party farewell, and turns westward toward the mountains. The records of his feelings and purposes at the moment are limited but they afford some information, although no one hitherto has taken pains to catalogue and correlate them.

1. It is unknown what maps Pike may have had which purported to delineate the heads of the Red and Arkansas rivers save such as Humboldt's and others mentioned. Of them he merely remarks, later, that they represented the Red as lying south of the Arkansas and interlocking to some degree with its head waters.[28]

2. As to information acquired from the Indians, it is sure Pike had learned something, and equally clear that some of it was misunderstood. It can be believed that he had left no opportunity neglected to acquire information—probably even getting something from the Indians (who soon turned hostile) whom he met in eastern Colorado a few days later. We know that while in the Pawnee land he "spared no pains in reconnoitring or obtaining information from the savages in our route."[29] That he secured some facts as to the main road to Santa Fé is known from his comment on the *indirect route* followed by the Malgares column which, he states, "was by no means the direct one from Santa Fe."[30] However much or little Pike knew of the direct route to Santa Fé, it is conservative to say that he must in any case have known that it turned south from the Arkansas River to avoid the Rockies. That was surely the one thing of prime importance that anyone would have learned. He had with him what, evidently, was a traders' map of the later "Cimarron desert" route of the Santa Fé trail[31] and which left the Arkansas in western Kansas. Pike did not follow it.

3. As to his proposed westward advance Pike wrote to General Wilkinson from the Arkansas: "From this point, we shall ascend the river until we strike the mountains, or find the Tetaus [Comanches]; and from thence bear more to the S. [outh] until we find the head of the *Red River*, where we shall be detained some time, after which nothing shall cause a halt until my arrival at Natchitoches."

4. Pike's letter to the General from the Arkansas (Oct. 24th) refers to the unexpected expenses of the expedition and compares the cost and relative value of his Mississippi trip of 1805 and this one to the Arkansas with that of Lewis and Clark to the Pacific. Pike's purpose was not to minimize the work of that overland expedition but, rather,

to emphasize the large field he himself was covering and the value of his work in the light of the trifling appropriation ($600.00), made for the present tour. Proponents of the "spy theory" have kept quite silent about this inconsiderable appropriation for an expedition so important to General Wilkinson's future as they wish to think Pike's was! If his "secret instructions" intimated larger financial support, Pike certainly would never have written as he now did about exceeding the quota fixed. But the chief point here is the first intimation of Pike's friendly jealousy of Lewis and Clark's fame as explorers. True, it is only intimated; but it becomes a major point of interest for us since, as suggested, practically every so called "mystery" of Pike's expedition is explained by Pike's eagerness to rival Lewis, Clark, Freeman, Sibley, Hunter and Dunbar as an explorer.

We now see Pike with fifteen companions beginning the ascent of the Arkansas on Tuesday, October 28th, with a reasonable number of excess guns, to remedy any deficiency from breakage, and thirty-five pounds of powder, forty pounds of lead and 120 cartridges. The Spanish "road" or "trace," followed by Malgares column and marked by horses dung, abandoned Spanish tent pins and other camp litter, was pursued by Pike. Within fifteen days Pike, too, realized that he never could accomplish the proposed round trip back to "Natchitoches" before winter set in, and "determined to spare no pains to accomplish every object even should it oblige me to spend another winter, in the desert." This conclusion seems to have been prompted by the sight of his rapidly failing horses, four of which gave out Nov. 10th-12th. On the 15th the Rockies came in sight. These were the first critical days of the advance; their momentous character has not been indicated previously. Choices now made settled the fate of the expedition.

1. The horses were giving out.
2. The Arkansas was breaking up into many brooklets (see entries of Nov. 22nd and 23rd) which seemed to mean that its "head" was not far away.
3. Colder nights indicated the rapid approach of winter at that altitude.
4. The party was not in the least equipped for winter weather.
5. Inroads on its thirty-five pounds of powder and forty pounds of lead spelled trouble.

6. Game was drifting into the mountains, the invariable refuge from the blizzards on the plains which neither man or beast could weather.

7. A returning war party of Grand Pawnees was met on the 22nd. They had been in search of Comanches, evidently in the direction of present South Park. None had been found. There was no chance in the world that Pike's slow-moving outfit could do what a raiding band of Pawnees on the war path had failed to do—find Comanches.

In such a case what did Pike's and Robinson's choices indicate was their chief purpose, their "mission?" Make contact with Santa Fé? "Spy" out New Mexico? Map the road thither for an army of conquest? Collect the debts of an absconder living in Santa Fé?

On the contrary, Pike devotes himself to a program of Arkansas River exploration and determines to put his men in a defensible position "and ascend the north fork [Fountain Creek from Pueblo, Colo.] to the high point of the blue mountain [Pike's Peak]—in order to be enabled from its pinical to lay down the various branches and positions of the country."

The reason that all the mystery has been woven into Pike's journey is because critics have been satisfied only with mystery. No one has faced Pike's case in these days of mid-November frankly and realized that he did not have the horse power now to return by any route to the frontiers; or analyzed his choices. This is explained by the fact that nothing that Pike and Robinson chose to do now conforms to the "spy" and "filibuster intrigue" theory. In fact, the plain truth is more discouraging to such an interpretation even than that. If Pike and Robinson had had no commercial or political reasons to turn south now it would have seemed sane and wise to do so; if there had been none of the alleged lure of intrigue in that direction (inspired by "secret instruction") it would have seemed the only reasonable thing to have done. These men surely knew that the nearest settlements lay in that direction; they knew the Santa Fé "direct" route left the Arkansas hereabouts; they knew winter was in the offing and their horses weakening. If they had had no other reasons for going into New Mexico except to save the party it would now have seemed the one and only sensible thing to have done. But not even those considerations (let alone the alleged "secret instructions") turned them toward Santa Fé. In fact for fifty-one days the party floundered in the Arkansas Valley and South Park, with starvation never more than a step behind them, and never struck south for the land legend says that they were so intent to reconnoiter until, their horses all being killed or critically maimed, they did so on foot (January 14th), each man carrying seventy pounds of freight!

If we study Pike's record and maps candidly no mystery interposes itself—not even in connection with his bizarre references either to the Spanish "trace," or to the "Yellowstone River" or to being able, in one day, to walk between the heads of the Colorado, Yellowstone, Platte and Arkansas rivers. Undoubtedly encouraged in his ambitions to win laurels as an explorer by the loyal Robinson, Pike turns (Nov. 25th) toward present Pike's Peak with the Doctor and two companions. Bitter weather and poor luck with game found the four back in camp on the 29th having only reached the top of the ridge at the head of Turkey Creek, sixteen miles south of the Peak. Snow on this ridge was found to be waist deep. A particularly ignorant critic of the Lieutenant's slurringly states that he now "modestly" named the Peak for himself on his map.[32] His own map (p. 145) shows that he gave it no name. His *Journal* shows that he called it the "Blue Mountain" (p. 141) and "North Mountain" (p. 147). The Nau Map shows it as "Highest Peak." The appropriateness of naming the Peak for Lieutenant Pike has been touched upon heretofore.

Arriving again at his temporary camp on the present site of Pueblo, Colo., on the evening of the 29th, further vital decisions faced Robinson and Pike. The purpose of the attempted scaling of the Peak had miscarried, although mortal men, outfitted as illy as were Pike's, could have done no more. The earnestness of the leader's ambition (undoubtedly fostered as we have suggested, by Dr. Robinson) to master and map the topography of the Arkansas River from some more accessible point of vantage than the Pike's Peak comes out boldly with Pike's *Journal* entry of the 30th: "Marched at eleven o'clock, it snowing very fast, but my impatience to be moving would not permit my lying still at that camp." Thus Robinson and Pike forego another chance to turn south (up the well-travelled route to Raton Pass and New Mexico) and to follow that alleged mission of reconnoitering the Spanish domain—even in the face of weather which made the nearby mountains seem death traps from every angle except that of securing game.

On Dec. 7th and 8th, at the mouth of present-day Royal Gorge (Canon City, Colo.), the "Spanish Trace" is lost in the snow at the mouth of the gorge—where that route turned south up Grape Creek.

The problem here—unnoticed by previous editors—is: Why was the Grape Creek route to Wet Mountain Valley taken so nonchalantly and without remark on January 14th but was not now perceived? Or did Pike and Robinson know, as they now struck north again (up Four Mile Creek) to South Park that they were leaving Malgares "Spanish Trace"? I think the answer to this question explains several curiosities, namely both Pike's continued vague use of the expression "Spanish Trace," and his mystifying reference to the Yellowstone River. It must be that Pike and Robinson had heard from Osage, Kans or Pawnee of the famous Spanish Trace which led from Santa Fé to California and crossed the Colorado River above the Grand Canon. But the same Trace sent a branch up the Colorado River, through Middle Park and down the North Platte to Casper, Wyo., north of which lay the buffalo hunting grounds *par excellence*, those of the Bighorn, Powder and Tongue tributaries of the Yellowstone.[33]

What has heretofore seemed Pike's nonsensical mention of the Yellowstone, and his constant hazy reference to a "Spanish Trace," may be attributed entirely to misunderstood Indian reports of a Spanish Trace from the Colorado River northwest to the buffalo grounds of the Yellowstone basin. There is no other explanation for a sane man's speaking of the Yellowstone River in Central Colorado; although its southernly tributary was stated by some to rise as far down as the latitude of Long's Peak.[34] And, as we have seen (Note 28), the Kiowas called the Canadian (then supposed to be the Red) the Colorado River. Thus, all three of the mysteries of Pike's looking for (1) "Yellowstone," (2) a "Spanish Trace" and (3) a "Red River" in the South Park of Colorado in 1806 are cleared at one stroke. No other explanation accounts for them. Malgares' Spanish Trace was lost at Canon City. The misty rumor of a Spanish Trace was picked up to the north (South Park) and with it both a rumor of a "Yellowstone" and a "Red River." This was the Spanish Trace known to Purseley and, later, to Pattie, running from Colorado ("Red") River to the Yellowstone hunting grounds by way of the North Platte. A branch no doubt reached the same destination by way of the South Platte, coursing north from present-day Greeley, Colo., northward.

Thus, from being meaningless babble, the account Pike gives of his twenty-six days (Dec. 10th—January 5th 1807) of floundering up into South Park from the mouth of the Royal Gorge (Canon City) and finally down to the Arkansas River again by way of Trout Creek Pass, becomes a genuine account of being mislead toward a Spanish Trace to the Yellowstone

Country through a confounding of Indian reports received from Osage or Pawnee. The reason why the Arkansas River (which was struck just below Buena Vista, Colo.) was thought to be the Red River was due to the belief that the Arkansas River became little brooks at the Royal Gorge. In its icebound condition it was not believed that the whole river poured down through that narrow chasm. One is amazed at the fact, even looking at the Gorge today.

In view of the sarcasm wasted on Pike for believing that the Arkansas which he found at the mouth of Trout Creek on December 21st was Red River—implying that he knew better—is set in its true colors by the recovery of his maps which were made at the time. They are not unlike one rising from the dead, after a century and a quarter of sleep, to point a recriminating finger at Pike's belittlers. Across the South Park map (p. 150), a beautiful one for proportions considering the almost ghoulish conditions of near-famine under which it was made, is written the evidence of Pike's misunderstanding. All the divides to west, south and southeast are marked as divides between the Platte and "Red River." In each case the words "Red River" are crossed out and "Arkansaw" is written in their place—a correction made after his learning the truth and before the maps were taken from him. What a body blow to the "spy" theory of his mission! For how useful to his supposed alibi given to the Spaniards it would have been to let them find his map of the Arkansas River everywhere marked "Red River!"

The terrible march down the Arkansas (Dec. 21st—Jan. 5th), and the discovery, from the height above the Gorge's mouth, that the party had merely returned to the camp, left Dec. 10th at present-day Canon City, will remain one of the tragic episodes of western history.

No one interested in Pike's wild journey down the icy Arkansas in 1806 could fail to be interested in his camp on Christmas eve at the mouth of Squaw Creek just above Salida, Colo. His reference to the coming day, and the memories it provoked, is made more memorable by his brave attempt to record satisfaction in being able to delineate "the geography of the sources of the then supposed Red River, as I well know the indefatigable researches of doctor Hunter, Dunbar and Freeman, had left nothing unnoticed in the extent of their voyage up said river, I determined that its upper branches should be equally well explored; as in this voyage I had already ascertained the sources of the Osage, and White [Neosho]

Rivers, (been around the head of Kans River) and on the headwaters of the Platte." Those who doubt Pike's determination to perform real service as an explorer, and who hold his main mission to have been merely flighty freelancing in the role of spy, may well study this diary-entry on the frozen Arkansas on Christmas Day, 1806. Only these real services saved him from bitterest mortification when, on January 5th, he learned that he was still on the Arkansas and not the Red.

Pike and Robinson at the mouth of the Gorge are now confronted with their final crisis. Such of their horses as survive are useless. In the severe weather conditions which prevailed game sufficient for the entire party evidently could not be obtained at that camp-site since the noise of their guns tended to drive game far out on a continually widening radius, compelling marches of ten to twenty miles to obtain a single kill. This spelled starvation. Many possibilities were considered.

At last, as a *denier resort*, it was determined to do what would have been done seven or eight weeks before if the "spy" or "military reconnoissance" purpose had been the party's object. Two men are left with the horses and some baggage in an improvised hut while the rest of the party strike south in search of Red River—hunting game for food. The typical suspicion of critics like Coues, who could find no reason for the march south except "the mysterious *crux* of the orders" Pike had from Wilkinson, and attributed to Pike the purpose of reconnoitering New Mexico, is amusingly refuted by the fact that Pike's interpreter is one of the men now left behind! Of the fourteen who start south on the Malgares trace (the finding of which is not even mentioned!), carrying seventy pounds of impedimenta each through the snows (Jan. 14th—Jan. 30th) of Wet Mountain Valley to the base of the icy Sangre de Cristo Range, nine have their feet frozen. Two are left in one trail-side camp, and one in another. Half famished, the remaining nine do what few well-fed, properly equipped, hardy men would care to attempt today, namely, scale Madenos Pass of the Sangre de Cristo Range in zero weather and descend into the San Luis Valley. Critics of Pike have gruesomely misunderstood the case, ignoring the fact that the party had to keep moving, and with one thought in mind—game and fire-wood. The more grossly ignorant of these critics now set a high record by implying that when Pike reached the "Red River" (Rio Grande, as it proved to be) his claim of not being on Spanish soil was stopped and rendered untenable by the fact that he crossed it—*to the only trees in sight!*

1. Pike's map (p. 169) shows that he marked the Rio Grande as "Red River," *and had never had an opportunity to correct the mistake before his maps were taken from him.* If it was the Rio Grande, our claim extended to it, including the right of navigation."[35] And surely the fiercest Spanish partisan would not have gainsaid the party's right, under international law, to save their lives by going where firewood could be secured.
2. If it was the Red River, as Pike's recovered map still proves he thought it was, the American claim was as good on one side as the other. Would any spirited lieutenant on the frontier claim less than his President at Washington?

Pike now had to "dig in," get game (which seemed to be comparatively abundant) and hope for a peaceful capture before those thirty-five pounds of powder and forty pounds of lead were exhausted. Finding a wooded spot five miles up the Conejos tributary of "Red River," at famous Ojo Caliente, Pike began the construction of a little three-sided barricade, facing the river, February 1st. One week proved that any hope of securing sufficient game to keep the party in health, and to succor the five marooned comrades scattered along the snow-drifted Sangre de Cristo trail, was a sanguine, if not a criminally, hopeless one. Three deer were killed between Jan. 31st and Feb. 5th. On that day Pike and Robinson chased "some deer for several hours without success." All of Pike's detractors have overlooked the one really significant argument which could have been used to discredit his claim that he believed he was on the Red River and intended to descend it—the fact that in four weeks not an ax was lifted to shape a board or plank for transport or canoe! Such was not Pike's plan or hope. Rather, on the morrow, the final act of the episode was launched. Dr. Robinson prepared to "march alone for Santa Fé." No hope of relief for the party existed except by this manœuvre. A plausible excuse, to cover the real purpose of the journey (namely the discovering of Pike's party to the Spaniards in hope of succor), existed in the claim of the St. Louis merchant, Morrison, brought by Pike on Baptiste Lalande, supposed to live in Santa Fé.

Pike's hostile commentators, leaping at straws, have seized upon the Lieutenant's statement that this claim (carried to Santa Fé by Robinson) was "spurious *in his hands*" implied that his trip to Santa Fe was merely for spying purposes and that the business matter was a pure bluff. They ignore the pre-Victorian use of the word "spurious." Pike, not Robinson, had been entrusted with the Morrison claim. In that sense a non-commissioned person was chosen to present the claim—a "spurious," not the real, appointed agent. The paper was given "the proper appearance" (i. e. as though Dr. Robinson *had* been commissioned to serve it) and he departed with it February 7th, Critics have revelled in Pike's footnote (written in Washington, D. C.) describing the "real" purpose of the Doctor's visit, namely, "to gain a knowledge of the country, the prospect of trade, [Spanish] force etc." The formal brusqueness of this after-the-event braggadocio is written plain on the surface. It was a gallant effort to cover with a bold spirit the absolute wrecking of the expedition; the awful condition of at least three of Pike's force left behind the Sangre de Cristo Range; the two with frozen feet with him then in camp and the hopelessness of doing any Red River exploring with cripples!

On the evening of the day of Robinson's departure Pike sent off a detail of five men "to recross the mountains, in order to bring in the baggage left with the frozen lads, and to see if they were yet able to come." With half his force gone, Pike was left with four men, two of them cripples. The two able-bodied ones were set to work on the fortification, with Pike, the commander, "to support them by the chase." The timing here is noteworthy. Robinson, and the escort for the beleagured "frozen lads," left the Ojo Caliente the same day. This meant that those left behind would be able to come up in time for the expected "capture."

On Feb. 16th the looked for scouts from Santa Fé arrived; they departed on the 17th. The timing was fairly accurate. Three men who had been left on the trail came in during the same night, with two more, including Menaugh, being expected on the morrow. With their arrival, Pike ordered Meek and Miller to prepare to go back for the two men, horses and baggage which had been left at the mouth of the Gorge. On the 22nd, when Pike figured it "was time" for the capture, he established a lookout for the purpose of hailing the expected Spanish force. He was four days too soon. The Spanish party under Saltelo and Fernandez arrived the 26th—and the Arkansas phase of Pike's exploration was at an end.

The record Pike formulated from his notes, published in 1810, opened the eyes of Americans to the West as nothing had done before. His report was given to the world four years before Paul Allen prepared and published his history of the Lewis and Clark expedition. While both publications held out no inviting picture of western adventure and indeed, a very discouraging one so far as immigration was concerned, Pike's account of the enforced continuation of his tour through New Mexico, under the title "through the Interior Provinces of New Spain," gave Americans alluring pages to read on a topic only slightly known to them, and awakened, in Moses Austin for instance, interest and speculation that had a genuine part in later American history.

All this, of course, was an accident of the expedition. The actual hoped-for result, so far as Pike was concerned, was never realized. On April 20th, 1807, from Chihuahua, Pike, still sanguine of high honors to be won as an explorer, wrote his patron "should the line of demarcation be amicably adjusted between the United States and Spain, I hope to obtain the appointment of one of the commissioners, as I make bold to assert that, with respect to the arrangements equipment etc. necessary, and a knowledge of the country through which the boundary line must pass, I am better instructed than any other officer of my age in our service; and, if joined to a colleague of profound astronomical knowledge, we could surmount every difficulty—I conceive the information I hold of considerable consequence in the determination of the line of limits and that (if not already determined) I can throw considerable light on the subject."

Pike was not fated to be the surveyor of the Louisiana Purchase boundary line as he hoped. The Spanish rebuff to the Red River Expedition of 1806 lessened the government's eagerness to continue work which might precipitate war; nor did Pike's own "capture," and the succeeding international correspondence, serve to allay such considerations. On the other hand Pike's friend, General Wilkinson, had so lost caste that no further work of promotion suggested by him would have received approbation. More than all else, the gathering storm cloud preceeding the War of 1812 now drew attention away from the western theatre. Crossing Lake Erie to the attack on Toronto in that war, Pike, as effervescent and undaunted as ever, cited Wolfe's last words at Quebec and, like Wolfe, was killed in the moment of victory.

Yet Zebulon Pike has his hoped-for reward. He is known for as distinct a service as any of his competitors; and the accident of his capture and journey through New Spain resulted in giving the world his half-original and half-paraphrased account of the great southwest that voiced "The Lure of the Rockies and Rio Grande" beyond any account left by any contemporary. The best-known landmark in America hands his name down to all generations to come. And that name is one we can remember with pride and satisfaction—as did Thomas Jefferson when he described the explorer's perplexities to James Madison in his letter of May 24, 1808: "I think that the truth as to Pike's mission might be so simply stated as to need no argument to show that his getting on the Rio Grande was mere error, which ought to have called for the setting him right, instead of forcing him through the interior country."

Archer B. Hulbert

Colorado College
Colorado Springs,
Colorado

PART THREE

Journal of a Voyage to the Sources of the Arkansaw Etc.[36]

INSTRUCTIONS TO LIEUTENANT PIKE

St. Louis, 24 June, 1806.

Sir,

You are to proceed without delay to the Cantonment on the Missouri, where you are to embark the late Osage Captives, and the Deputation, recently returned from Washington, with their presents and Baggage; and are to transport the whole up the Missouri and Osage Rivers to the Town of the Grand Osage.

The safe delivery of this charge at the point of Destination, constitutes the primary object of your expedition; and therefore you are to move with such caution, as may prevent surprize from any hostile Bands and are to repel with your utmost force, any outrage which may be attempted.

Having safely deposited your passengers and their property, you are to turn your attention to the accomplishment of a permanent Peace between the Canzes and Osage Nations; for which purpose you must effect a meeting between the Head Chiefs of these Nations: and are to employ such arguments deduced from their own obvious Interests as well as the inclinations, desires, and commands of the President of the United States as may facilitate your purpose and accomplish the end.

A third object of considerable magnitude will then claim your consideration; It is to effect an Interview, and establish a good understanding with the Ya,i,tans; I,etans; or Camanchees.

For this purpose you must Interest White Hair, of the Grand Osage, with whom and a suitable Deputation you will visit the Panis [Pawnee] republic, where you may find Interpreters; and to inform yourself of the most feasible plan, by which to bring the Cammanchees to a Conference.

Should you succeed in this attempt (and no pains must be spaired to effect it) you will endeavour to make peace between that distant powerfull nation, and the nations which inhabit the country between us and them, particularly the Osage; and finally you will endeavour to induce eight or ten of their distinguished Chiefs, to make a visit to the seat of Government next September, and you may attach to this deputation four or five Panis and the same number of Canzes chiefs.

As your Interview with the Cammanchees will probably lead you to the Head Branches of the Arkansaw and Red Rivers you may find yourself approximated to the settlements of New Mexico, and therefore it will be necessary you should move with great circumspection, to keep clear of any Hunting or reconnoitring Parties from that Province, and to prevent alarm or offence, because the affairs of Spain and the United States appear to be on the point of amicable adjustment, and moreover it is the desire of the President to cultivate the Friendship and Harmonious Intercourse of all the Nations of the Earth, and particularly our near Neighbours the Spaniards. In the course of your tour, you are to remark particularly upon the Geographical structure, the Natural History, and population, of the country through which you may pass, taking particular care to collect and preserve specimens of every thing curious in the mineral or botanical Worlds, which can be preserved and are portable: Let your courses be regulated by your compass, and your distances by your Watch, to be noted in a field Book, and I would advise you when circumstances permit, to protract and lay down in a seperate Book the march of the Day at every evenings halt.

The Instruments which I have furnished you will enable you to ascertain the Variation of the magnetic needle and the Lattitude with exactitude, and at every remarkable point I wish you to employ your Telescope in observing the eclipses of Jupiters Satillites, having previously regulated and adjusted your Watch by your Sextant, taking care to note with great niceity the periods of immersion and emersion of the eclipsed Satellite. These observations may enable us after your return, by application to the appropriate Tables, to asscertain the Longitude.—It is an object of much Interests with the Executive, to asscertain the Direction, extent, and navagation of the Arkansaw and Red River's; as far therefore as may be compatible with these Instructions and practicable to the means you may command, I wish you to carry your Views to those Subjects, and should circumstances conspire to favour the enterprize, that you may detach a party with a few Osage to descend the Arkansaw, under the orders of Lt Wilkinson[37] or Serg[t], Ballenger, properly Instructed, and equipt, to take the Courses and distances, to remark on the soil, Timber, etc., and to Note the tributary streams.[38] This Party will, after reaching our Post on the Arkensaw, descend to Fort Adams and there wait further orders; and you, yourself, may descend the Red River accompanied by a party of the most respectable Commanches to the Post of Natchitoches and there receive further orders from me.

To Disburse you necessary expences and to aid your negotiations, you are here with furnished Six hundred Dollars worth of Goods, for the appropriation of which, you are to render a strict account, vouched by Documents to be attested by one of your Party.

Wishing you a safe and successful expedition,

I am Sir,

With much Respect and Esteem,

Sir

Your ob[t] Ser[t].

Ja: Wilkinson (rubric).

Lt. Z. M. Pike.

ADDITIONAL INSTRUCTIONS TO LIEUTENANT PIKE.[39]

Cantonment, Missouri,
July 12th, 1806.

SIR:

THE health of the Osages being now generally restored, and all hopes of the speedy recovery of their prisoners, from the hands of the Potowatomies, being at an end, they have become desirous to commence their journey for their villages, you are therefore to proceed tomorrow.

In addition to the instructions given you on the 24th ultimo, I must request you to have the talks under cover delivered to White Hair and the Grand Peste, the chief of the Osage band, which is settled on the waters of the Arkansaw together with the belts which accompany them. You will also receive herewith a small belt for the Panis and a large one for the Tetaus or Camanches.

Should you find it necessary, you are to give orders to Maugraine the resident interpreter at the Grand Osage to attend you.

I beg you to take measures for the security and safe return of your boats from the Grand Osage to this place.

Dr. Robinson will accompany you as a volunteer.[40] He will be furnished medicines, and for the accommodations which you give him, he is bound to attend your sick.

Should you discover any unlicensed traders in your route, or any person from this territory, or from the United States, without a proper licence or passport, you are to arrest such person or persons and dispose of their property as the law directs.

My confidence in your caution and discretion, has prevented my urging you to be vigilant in guarding against the strategems and treachery of the Indians, holding yourself above alarm or surprise, the composition of your party, though it be small, will secure to you the respect of an host of untutored savages.

You are to communicate from the Grand Osage and from every other practicable point, directly to the secretary of war, transmitting your letters to this place under cover, to the commanding officer, or by any more convenient route.

I wish you health and a successful and honorable enterprise, and am,

Yours with friendship,
(Signed) JAMES WILKINSON.

Lieutenant Z. M. Pike.

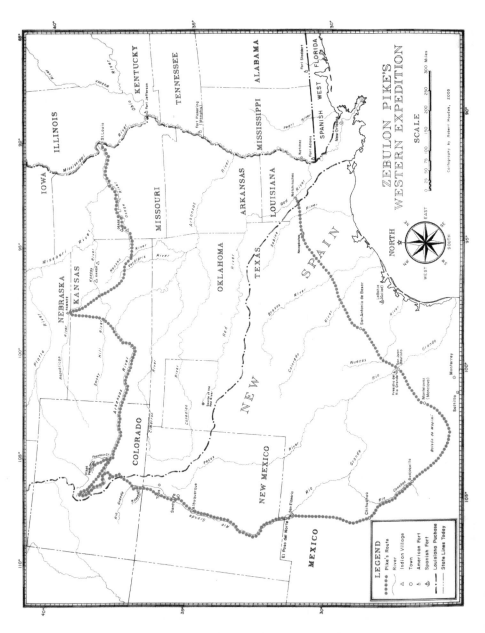

MAP 4: Zebulon Pike's Southwestern Expedition.
Cartography by Robert Houdek.

PART FOUR

Journal of a Voyage[44]

15th July, 1806.—WE SAILED FROM THE LANDING AT BELLE FONTAINE, about 3 o'clock P. M. in two boats. Our party consisted of two lieutenants, one surgeon, one sergeant, two corporals, sixteen privates, and one interpreter. We had also under our charge, chiefs of the Osage and Pawnees, who, with a number of women and children, had been to Washington. These Indians had been redeemed from captivity among the Potowatomies, and were now to be returned to their friends, at the Osage towns. The whole number of Indians amounted to fifty one.

We ascended the river about six miles, and encamped on the south wide behind an island. This day my boat swung round twice; once when we had a towrope on shore, which it snaped off in an instant. The Indians did not encamp with us at night. Distance 6 miles.

_____

On July 15, 1806, Lieutenant Zebulon Montgomery Pike embarked on his second expedition, this time to the southwest. His party consisted of seventy-four persons, red and white. Under his charge were fifty-one Indians, chiefs of the Osages and Pawnees, with a number of women and children. The chiefs had just returned from a sight-seeing tour of Washington. The women and children, however, had had more serious experiences. They were members of a Little Osage hunting

16th July, Wednesday.—We rejoined our red brethren at breakfast, after which we again separated, and with very severe labor arrived late in the evening opposite to the village of St. Charles, where the Indians joined us. Distance 15 miles.

---

party which had been surprised in 1803 by Indian enemies. One autumn morning about ten o'clock, when the Osage warriors were off hunting, a Potawatomi band attacked the camp of the Osage women and children, killed a third of them and made captive about sixty more. Some forty-six of these had been redeemed by the government of the United States and were now being returned to their people. The actions of that country were not wholly humanitarian, however, for the return of the captives secured the friendship of the Osages, a step necessary to the success of Pike's expedition.

Pike sailed from Belle Fontaine, located in the south center of Pike's Chart No. 33 on the Missouri fourteen miles north of St. Louis in what is now St. Ferdinand township, St. Louis county, Mo. The place soon became notable as the site of the first military post established in the newly acquired territory of St. Louis.[42]

Ascending the Missouri, Pike and his troops followed its course in two boats, a barge and a batteau or pirogue; the Indians, on the other hand, marched along banks under guard of a few soldiers.

Travelling thus, they made six miles the first day and encamped, in the words of the *Journal,* "on the south side behind an island." This camp, like all of Pike's camps, he located on his chart and numbered. Camp was on the south bank of the Missouri, west of Belle Fontaine, at present Carbunker's Point. The island, mentioned in the *Journal* and shown in the chart is Pelican Island, which now separates Car of Commerce bend from Pelican bend.

July 16. July 16 was a hard day and the expedition made only fifteen miles. It was not until late in the evening that the party arrived opposite St. Charles, seat of St. Charles Co. Pike's men were soft, but they soon became accustomed to rowing and poling their heavy boats as much as forty miles a day with no more strain than this day's fifteen miles. Pike's village of St. Charles has expanded into modern St. Charles, the seat of the county of the same name. Founded in 1769, only five years later than St. Louis, it was the first settlement in Northern Missouri. The name given to it was Les Petites Cotes. The town site was located by Blanchette, a Frenchman, surnamed Le Chasseur, who built the first post in the town and established there a military post.[43]

17th July, Thursday.—We crossed the river to learn if any communications had arrived from St. Louis, and if there was any news of other Indian enemies of the Osages. Called at Mr. James Morrison's and was introduced to a Mr. Henry (of New Jersey), about eight and twenty years of age: he spoke a little Spanish, and French tolerably well: he wished to go with me as a volunteer. From this place I wrote letters back to Belle Fontaine, whilst the Indians were

---

July 17th. Pike made little progress this day. He spent the hours visiting in St. Charles, writing letters, and quieting the Indians who had become alarmed by rumors of "Sacs, Ioways, and Reynards." He was amazed, too, by the arrest of his interpreter, Vasquez, who was obliged to return to St. Louis to account for a debt. He encamped "about three-fourths of a mile above the village," on the north bank. Pike's letter to General Wilkinson, written here read as follows:

St. Charles, July 17th, 1806.

DEAR SIR,

WE arrived here last evening all well, except some of the soldiers from fatigue, as in the present state of the water we are obliged to row altogether.

We were disappointed in obtaining any information from St. Louis, or baggage for our Panis [Pawnees]. I do not know how it will be digested by them.

We likewise were disappointed in receiving a line from you, as we had here expected, and in the hopes of which I shall yet detain until twelve o'clock, and then take my departure. Our Osage conduct themselves pretty well, and are very obedient to orders; at first they had an idea a little too free relative to other people's property, but at present stand corrected.

I understood from you that they were equipped by Mr. Tillier, with every thing necessary for their voyage to their towns, consequently, although they have been applying to me for a variety of articles, none of which have they been gratified with, but powder and ball, which is necessary for their own defense.

The general will pardon this scrawl; and should he send an express after us, please to let Mrs. Pike know of the opportunity.[44]

I am, dear Sir.

With high respect,

Your obedient servant,

(Signed)   Z. M. Pike, LT.

General Wilkinson.

crossing the river. A man by the name of Ramsay reported to the Indians that 500 Sacs, Ioways and Reynards, were at the mouth of Big Maniton. This gave them considerable uneasiness and it took me some time to do away the impression it made upon them; for I by no means believed it. We were about sailing when my interpreter was arrested by the sheriff, at the suit of Manuel de Liza,[46] for a debt between three and four hundred dollars, and was obliged to return to St. Louis. This made it necessary for me to write another letter to the general. We encamped about three-fourths of a mile above the village.

General Wilkinson's answer was unequivocal; it read:[45]

Cantonment

Missouri

July 18, 06.

Dear Sir

I have rec d. your letters of yesterday and concerning yr Interpreter without date. I had taken arrangements to secure Bennette, when he appeared here and I have now become his security. Manual is a Black Spaniard. He dined here yesterday and left here this morning before the arrival of your letters—this was well for Him.

I have seen too much of the World to fall in love with Strangers, particularly men of fine European and Asiatic languages, found in the wilds of the Missouri— the natural question is, how came so many accomplishments and useful qualities buried alive? Yet no Rule without an exception. But still Henry can gain much of you without being to contribute anything—the association is therefore unequal. If I am Cynical I have cause for it, in the very source of this letter. You must not credit [believe] your Red companions, for lying and stealing is their occupation, when unemployed in the chase. They recd. powder, Ball and every thing else from Mr. Tillier—he gave them 28 lbs of Powder. I shall dress [straighten] Manual [de Lisa] and Cadet aussi. I will teach them how to interrupt national movements, by their despicable Intrigues. I wrote you this morning by Hall of the artillery.

My son has the foundation of a good Constitution but it must be *tempered* by degrees—do not push Him beyond his capacities in hardships to suddenly. He will I hope attempt any thing but let the stuff be hardened by degrees. I have nothing further to add but my blessings and best wishes to you all

Ja. Wilkinson (rubric).

Lt Pike

18th July, Friday.—Lieutenant Wilkinson and Dr. Robinson went with the Indians across the country to the village La Charette. Mr. George Henry engaged, under oath, to accompany me on my tour. We wrote to the general, and enclosed him one of Henry's engagements. After we had made our little arrangements we marched by land joined the boats (which had sailed early) at twelve o'clock. Two of the men being sick, I steered one boat and Mr. Henry the other, by which means we were enabled to keep employed our full complement of oars, although we put the sick men on shore. Encamped on the north side. About eleven o'clock at night a tremendous thunderstorm arose, and it continued to blow and rain, with thunder and lightning, until day. Distance 15 miles.

July 18. On July 18 with George Henry and Pike steering the boats, the expedition progressed favorably and made its fourth encampment at what is now called Green's Chute, about two miles south of the present town of Cottleville, St. Charles Co.

Comparison at this point of Pike's original charts with the Nau maps affords a striking contrast. The original chart shows everything not only clearly but accurately. Bends, islands, bluffs, and tributaries can all be easily recognized on a modern map. The islands opposite camp 4 are Bonhomme and Johnson; that between camp 4 and St. Charles is Catfish island; the sharp twist here is Howard's Bend; and the slight bluff on the north, between camps 4 and 5, is near Weldon Springs. The Nau map shows, on the contrary, only an unrecognizable nest of islands in a straight channel. It makes the river flow south, too, instead of southeast. On the Nau map continuous bluffs, by which nothing can be recognized, line the river for miles, and the bends are haphazard. A mark placed on the west bank shows only that Pike camped somewhere above St. Charles.

Mr. Coues, naturally, could make nothing of this map, so he had to locate camp solely by means of the mileage as recorded in the *Journal,* a method which was never trustworthy. Since the *Journal* gave this day's march as 15 miles, Coues placed camp above Bonhomme and Posts islands about Cottleville landing. But this seemed to Coues excessive, so he remained in doubt (page 362, n. 9). His suspicion now proves to have been well founded, for camp was lower down, and Pike's computation of mileage was excessive.

19th July, Saturday.—In consequence of the rain, we did not put off until past nine o'clock; my sick men marched. I had some reason to suspect, that one of them intended never joining us again. At dinner time the sick man of my own boat came on board; I then went on board the other,

---

Pike's letter of this day to General Wilkinson read:

St. Charles, 19th July, 1806—In the morning.

DEAR GENERAL,

ENCLOSED you have one of the articles, subscribed by Mr. Henry, mentioned in my note of yesterday. I hope the general may approve of the contents.

Lieut. Wilkinson and Dr. Robinson marched (with one soldier) this morning, and the boats have proceeded under the conduct of Ballenger; I shall overtake them in an hour or two.

Numerous reports have been made to the [our] Indians, calculated to impress them with an idea that there is a small army of their enemies waiting to receive us at the entrance of the Grand Osage. But I have partly succeeded in scouting the idea from their minds.[47]

No news of Chouteau nor Panis Trunks.

I am, dear general,
Your obedient servant,
(Signed)   Z. M. PIKE Lt.

General Wilkinson.

On this same date General Wilkinson wrote again:

Cantonment
July 19th 1806.

Dear Sir,

I send after you the Circumferenter [horizontal compass] and Bark left by Dr. Robinson. I expect the Bearer may find you at Charette. We have philadel[a]. Papers to the 24th ult.[mo]—not a word of news from Europe. It is reported on vague grounds that Miranda has failed, and it is suggested that France and Spain will demand some retribution for our

and we continued to run races all day, and although this boat had hitherto kept behind; yet I arrived at the encamping ground with her, nearly half an hour before the other. The current not generally so strong as below. Distance 14 miles.

Countenance of this attempt, but this is a mere party ebullition. I think He will succeed because the British will aid Him.

You will *see* and *feel* the I,e,tans [Comanches], before you committ yourselves to them, and you must indeed be extremely guarded with respect to the Spaniards—neither alarm nor offend them unnecessarily. write me as long as you can by this Route, under cover to the Commanding officer here and address me at Fort Adams. I wish you would send a Runner to the osage from the Panis, after you have taken your measures with the I,e,tans, and transmit me a Sketch of your route, and of the Country before you agreably to your information. This may be important in providing against a total loss by misfortune—indeed you may send in your Interpreter Mongrain Express, with a letter of general Information to the Secy. of War, to accompany that which I have required above for myself. You may perhaps be able to guess, when I may look for you at Natchitoche. Write this by the return of the express and tell me how you *all* come on. be attentive in forming your Statistical Table of the Population, to give the names of Chiefs as well as Nations and Tribes, exactly after the manner you have adopted with the Secant and Sautieurs. Farewell, my friend, omit nothing to give utility and Importance to your tour, and the sooner you can reach Natchitoches the better, consistently with the necessary investigations.[48]

Your friend and sevt
Ja. Wilkinson (rubric).

Lt Pike.

July 19. A day of boat racing. In the morning Pike's boat won. After dinner he changed boats and proved himself a good coxswain by bringing the second one to campground half an hour before the other. This camp, the fifth, was on the north bank of the Missouri, in the vicinity of the railroad station called Defiance and opposite a group of houses, called Port Royal, Chart No. 33.

20th July, Sunday.—Embarked about sun-rise. Wishing to ascertain the temperature of the water, I discovered my large thermometer to be missing, which probably had fallen into the river. Passed one settlement on the north side, and, after turning the point to the south, saw two more houses on the south side. We encamped in a long reach, which bore north and west. The absentees had not yet joined us. Distance 15 miles.

Along this stretch, the Missouri flows between high bluffs separated far enough to admit large areas of alluvial flood plains first on one side then on the other between the bluffs and the water. The river gradually swings back and forth between the bluffs, continually changing its course and the position and conformation of the islands. In the one hundred and twenty-five years since Pike charted it, the course has changed decidedly, a fact which makes difficult the comparison of present maps with those of Pike and the identification of the features of one with those of the other.

In spite of this confusion, however, several points are clear. The islands below camp five ought to be Howell Island and those little ones clustered about it. Pike's Riviere Bonhomme is certainly not present Bonhomme Creek, but rather one much higher, perhaps Big Tavern Creek, which slips into the Missouri at St. Albans. The position of Big Tavern Creek corresponds perfectly in respect to bluffs, bends in the river, and the little promontory which juts into the river just southwest of St. Albans. The settlement on the north bank is near the site of the present town of Augusta. Perhaps it is the ancestor of that place. The settlement on the south was in the vicinity of Boles, on Dunn Spring Creek, which may in those days have flowed directly into the Missouri. Both of these settlements are mentioned in the *Journal*, July 20, when Pike passed them.

The run on which the northern settlement is located and which Pike calls Femme Osage River is not the present Femme Osage Creek. The modern stream of that name falls in fifteen miles lower down. What Pike intended was the stream formed by the union of present Bigelow and Sehrt Creeks.

Mr. Coues expressed uncertainty concerning the location of this fifth encampment of July 19; the Nau map and the text disagreed. The map puts this camp considerably below Femme Osage, below even the Bonhomme River. The *Journal*, however, by the mileages of the 19th and 20th brought him far past those rivers. Relying entirely on the *Journal*, Coues set Pike in the vicinity of St. Albans—a trifle too far—for, as noted above, Pike's computation of mileage for July 19 was excessive. Coues' difficulty would have been cleared if he had known what the original map makes clear, that Pike was mistaken in his designation of Femme Osage and

21st July, Monday.—It commenced raining near day, and continued until 4 o'clock in the afternoon: the rain was immensely heavy, with thunder and lightning remarkably severe. This obliged me to lay by; for, if we proceeded with our boats, it necessarily exposed our baggage much more than when at rest; for the tarpauling could then cover all. We set sail at a quarter past four o'clock, and arrived at the village La Cherette a little after

---

Bonhomme Creeks. Pike made the same error both on the original charts and on Nau's draught.

The "cave remarkable" referred to on the chart "is the cave formerly, and perhaps still, known as the Tavern." From it probably Tavern Rock and Big and Little Tavern creeks were named. If so, it seems to be placed a little too far west.

July 20. Pike made about fifteen uneventful miles. Some of his men were sick, so he had excused them the day before from rowing and had let them march along the bank. He suspected that one of them, Kennerman, intended to desert—a suspicion which was confirmed, for he never rejoined the party.

Mr. Coues located this day's encampment, number 6, correctly "at the mouth of Dubois or Wood cr., where there is now a place called South Point. This is directly opposite the line between St. Charles and Warren cos. on the N.; it is about 2 m. below Washington, Franklin Co., and at the 67th mile-point from the mouth of the Missouri. Pike maps the stream in the right place but by the name of "Ash R." (pages 363 n. 12). Coues' reference to Ash River, however, may be amended. On Nau's map this trace seems to refer to Dubois Creek. On the original chart, however, "Ash Creek" is placed in the position of St. John's or Bourbouse Creek, two miles or so above the present town of Washington, Franklin Co., and opposite St. John's island and the graceful bay on the north bank where was the Village de Charette.

July 21–22. Pike arrived at the Village de Charette, a frontier settlement of seven houses. The town of that name has disappeared. In its place is Marthasville, Warren Co., "3 miles north of which stands still the house," said Coues, "in which Daniel Boone died."

It appears from comparison of Pike's Chart with the United States Geological Survey quadrangle that the course of the Missouri changed interestingly during the years between 1806 and 1907. The flats west of Marthasville have increased much in area, allowing Charette Creek a mile longer independent course before it merges with the Missouri. In Pike's time islands and flowing waters occupied much of this plain. Sheltans or Boeuf Island at the mouth of Boeuf Creek (called by Pike rivere au Boeuf) has also grown considerably.

dusk of the evening, here we found lieutenant Wilkinson and Dr. Robinson with the Indians—also, Baroney (our interpreter) with letters from the general and our friends. The weather still continued cloudy, with rain. We were received into the house of a Mr. Chartron, and every accommodation in his power offered us. Distance 6 miles.

22d July, Tuesday.—We arranged our boats, dried our loading, and wrote letters for Belle Fontaine.

23d. July, Wednesday.—I dispatched an express to the general, with advertisements relative to Kennerman, the soldier who had deserted. We embarked after breakfast, and made good progress: lieutenant Wilkinson steered one boat and I the other, in order to detach all the men on shore, with the Indians, that we could spare. We crossed to the south side, a little

---

Pike's letter of the 22nd to General Wilkinson read:

Village de Charette, 22d July, 1806.

DEAR GENERAL:

I HAVE the honor to acknowledge the receipt of your two obliging favors of the 18th and 19th inst. the particular contents of each, shall be punctually attended to.

I assure *you* sir, that I am extremely pleased with the idea that Messrs. ——and——will meet with their merited reward, and I on my part, am determined to shew them that it is not their sinister movements that can derange the objects of our voyage; the greatest embarrassment they have yet occasioned me, has been by the detention of the Panis's baggage, who have been much mortified on the occasion. But I question much if under similar impressions and circumstances, many white men would have borne their loss with more philosophy, than our young savages.

I conceive that I cannot dispose of one of my guns better, than to give it to *Frank,* whose *fusee* was left at Chouteau's; also, each of them a soldier's coat; this is all the remuneration I will pretend to make them, and I hope [it] may bring them to a good humor.

You will probably be surprised at the slow progress we have made, but, are already informed of the cause of our detention at St. Charles; and since have been detained two days, on account of the rain; and although we were able to prevent the water from entering immediately on the top

below Shepherd River, Dr. Robinson killed a deer, which was the first killed by the party. Distance 13 miles.[49]

24th July, Thursday.—We embarked at half past 6 o'clock. Very foggy. The Indians accompanied by only three of my people. Lieutenant Wilkinson being a little indisposed, I was obliged to let Baroney steer his boat. We made an excellent day's journey, and encamped five miles from the Gasconade river. Killed three deer, one bear and three turkies. But three or four of the Indians arrived; the others encamped a small distance below. Distance 18 miles.[50]

25th July, Friday.—We embarked at half past 6 o'clock, and arrived at the entrance of the Gasconade river half past eight o'clock, at which place I determined to remain the day, as my Indians and foot people were yet in

---

of the boat where covered, yet the quantity which she made at both ends, occasioned so much dampness under the loading, as to injure both my own corn, and that of the Indians, with other small articles, which they had at various times taken from under the loading, and not returned to their proper places; but they appear satisfied, that we have paid all possible attention to prevent injury, as much, and indeed more to their baggage than our own.

In consequence of the above, (and with a design to write you) I halted here to day, which I hope we shall usefully employ in drying our baggage, cleaning our arms, and putting ourselves in a posture of defence. Lieut. Wilkinson has experienced no inconvenience from his march by land with the Indians; and the event has proved the necessity of some officer accompanying them, as he informs me, he found it necessary to purchase some beeves for their consumption on the route, for which he drew on the superintendent of Indian affairs, and will write to you more particularly on the subject. They were absent from the boat four days, and had he not been with them, they would have supplied themselves by marauding, to the great offence of our *good* citizens.

I am informed, that a party of 40 Sacs were at Boon's Lick, above the Osage river, a few days since; but I by no means conceive [they were] on the route to intercept us, as the people pretend at this place.

Three days since, one of my men [Kennerman] complained of indisposition, and went on shore to march; he has never joined the party, and

the rear, and they had complained to me of being without shoes, leggins, &c. One of our Pawnees did not arrive until late; the other had communicated his suspicion to me that the Oto, who was in company, had killed him: he acknowledged that he proposed to him to take out their baggage, and return to St. Louis. The real occasion of his absence, however, was his having followed a large fresh trace up the Gasconade a considerable distance; but finding it led from the Missouri, he examined it and discovered horses to have been on it, he then left it, joined our's, and came in. This being generally the route taken by the Potowatomies, when they go to war against the Osage, it occasioned some alarm. Every morning we were awoke by the mourning of the savages, who commenced crying about daylight, and continued for the space of an hour. I made enquiry of my interpreter

---

from various reasons, I conceive has deserted. I have therefore enclosed an advertisement, which if the general will please to cause to be posted at St. Louis, Kaskaskias, and Lusk's Ferry on the Ohio, I conceive he will be caught.

I have written to Capt. Danl. Bissell on the occasion; but hope the general will enforce my request to that gentleman, as to his [Kennerman's] being brought to trial. I was much mortified at the event, not only on account of the loss of the man, but that my peculiar situation prevented me from pursuing him, and making him an example.

With respect to the Tetaus, the general may rest assured, I shall use every precaution previous to trusting them; but as to the mode of conduct to be pursued towards the Spaniards, I feel more at a loss, as my instructions lead me into the country of the Tetaus, part of which is no doubt claimed by Spain, although the boundaries between Louisiana and New Mexico, have never yet been defined, in consequence of which, should I encounter a party from the villages near Santa Fe, I have thought it would be good policy to give them to understand, that we were about to join our troops near Natchitoches, but had been uncertain about the head waters of the rivers over which we passed; but, that *now*, if the commandant approved of it, we would pay him a visit of politeness, either by deputation, or the whole party, but if he refused, [to] signify our intention of pursuing our direct route to the post below; but if not I

with respect to this, who informed me that this was a custom not only with those who had recently lost their relatives, but also with others who recalled to mind the loss of some friend, dead long since, and joined the other mourners purely from sympathy. They appeared extremely affected, tears ran down their cheeks, and they sobbed bitterly; but in a moment they dry their cheeks and they cease their cries. Their songs of grief generally run thus: "My dear father exists no longer: have pity on me, O Great Spirit! you see I cry forever; dry my tears and give me comfort." The warrior songs are thus: "Our enemies have slain my father (or mother); he is lost to me and his family; I pray to you, O Master of Life! to preserve me until I revenge his death, and then do with me as thou pleaseth." Distance 5 miles.[51]

---

flatter myself secure us an unmolested retreat to Natchitoches.[52] But if the Spanish jealousy, and the instigation of domestic [de Lisa] traitors should induce them to make us prisoners of war, (in time of peace) I trust to the magnanimity of our country for our liberation, and a due reward to their opposers, for the insult and indignity offered their national honor. However, unless they give us ample assurances of just and honorable treatment, according to the custom of nations in like cases, I would resist, *even* if the inequality was as great as at the affair of Bender [Russia], or the streights of Thermopylae.

Will you pardon the foregoing as the enthusiasm of a youthful mind, yet, not althogether impressed by the dictates of prudence.

I hope the general will be persuaded, that with his son, I shall act as I would to a brother, endeavoring in all cases to promote his honor and prosperity.[53]

I am, dear general,
Your sincere friend,
And obedient humble servant,
(Signed)   Z. M. PIKE

General J. Wilkinson.

N.B. In consequence of indisposition & c. lieut. Wilkinson will steer one boat and I the other.

26th July, Saturday.—We commenced at 5 o'clock to ferry the Indians over the Gasconade, and left the entrance of this river half past 6 o'clock in the afternoon. Met five Frenchmen, who informed us that they had just left the Osage river, and that it was so low they could not ascend it with their canoe. We wrote letters and sent them back by them. Dr. Robinson, Baroney, Sparks, and all the Indians encamped about one league above us. Killed one bear, two deer, one otter, three turkies, and one racoon. Distance 15 miles.

27th July, Sunday.—We embarked at half past five o'clock, and arrived at the Indians' camp at 7 o'clock. They had been alarmed the day before, and in the evening sent men back in the trace, and some of the chiefs sat up all night. Breakfasted with them. About half past three o'clock encamped in sight of the Osage river. There being every appearance of rain, we halted thus early in order to give the Indians time to prepare temporary camps and to secure our baggage. I went out to hunt, and firing at a deer, near two of the Indians who were in the woods, they knew the difference of the report of my rifle from their guns, were alarmed, and immediately retired to camp. Distance 13 miles.

Pike's letter of the 26th read:

"DEAR GENERAL:
   I HALT a moment, in order to say we have arrived thus far all safe, although our savages complain much of fatigue, &c.
   The bearer had been sent by Mr. Sangonet [Charles Sanguinet Sr.] to examine the Osage river, and reports that they could not get their canoes up the river more than 60 miles: if so, we have a bad prospect before us; but go we will, if God permits. . . . We have been detained several days by the Indians."

Pike's chart sets to rest Coues' doubts as to this camp of the 26th and proves his guess correct, namely, near Chamois, Osage Co. Oddly enough, Coues objected to the names Pike (or Nau) gives the Auxvasse rivers hereabouts and begs that they be called in plain English Big and Little Muddy. Pike's recovered charts show that he did call and map them thus in 1806. Pike shows a nest of islands near Portland, Calloway Co. known as Portland Island and a confusion of shallows and sand bars.

28th July, Monday.—Embarked at half past 5 o'clock, and at half past 10 arrived in the Osage river, where we stopped, discharged our guns, bathed, &c. We then proceeded on about six miles, where we waited for and crossed the Indians to the west shore, and then proceeded on to the first island and encamped on the west side. Sans Oreille, and four or five young men only, coming up, the rest encamping some distance behind. Killed one deer and one turkey. Distance 19 miles.

29th July, Tuesday.—All the Indians arrived very early and the Big Soldier, whom I had appointed the officer to regulate the march, was much displeased that Sans Oreille and the others had left him, and said for that reason he would not suffer any woman to go in the boat, and by that means separate the party; but in truth it was from jealousy of the men whose women went in the boats. He began by flogging one of the young men and was about to strike Sans Oreille's wife, but was stopped by him and told that he knew he had done wrong, but that the women were innocent. We then crossed them and embarked at half past eight o'clock. About twelve

---

July 27. This camp was on the Missouri below the mouth of Loose or Bear Creek which Pike calls "Bear River." The nearest modern town is Medora. The largest island passed in this day's march was St. Aubert island. Bear Creek island is just above camp. Pike was naturally rather careless in his placing of these islands, for they are quite unimportant.

Coues, relying on an excessive estimate of mileage in the *Journal,* placed the camp several miles too far west, at the site of "the old French village Côte sans Dessein, so called from the celebrated long narrow ledge of rocks of the same name immediately above"—Coues, II, 369 n. 21.

July 28. Leaving the Missouri, the party proceeded up the Osage to camp according to Coues "in Cole Co., past two small tributaries known as Caddy and Sandford creeks, and not far above Maries r." (page 371 n. 22.) this camp is Pike's nearest approach to Jefferson City, the largest place in this region.

July 29. Continuing up the Osage, Pike had more annoying experiences with his Indian wards. They were forever squabbling among themselves but he firmly and justly kept them in hand.

o'clock we found the Indians rafting the river, when the first chief of the Little Osage, called Tuttasuggy (or the Wind), told me that the man whom the Big Soldier struck had not yet arrived with his wife, "but that he would throw them away." As I knew he was extremely mortified at the dissensions which appeared to reign amongst them, I told him by no means,—that one of my boats should wait for the woman and her child, but that the man might go to the devil, as a punishment for his insubordination.

I then left Baroney with one boat, and proceeded with the other. We were called ashore by three young Indians, who had killed some deer, and on putting them on board, gave them about one or two gills of whiskey, which intoxicated all of them. It commenced raining about one o'clock, and continued incessantly for three hours, which obliged us to stop and encamp. One of our men (Miller) lost himself, and did not arrive until after dark. Killed five deer, one turkey, and one racoon. Distance 14 miles.

30th July, Wednesday.—After the fog dispersed I left lieutenant Wilkinson with the party to dry the baggage, and I went with Dr. Robinson and Bradley. About two o'clock we returned, set sail, and having passed the first rapid about three miles, encamped on the eastern shore. Killed three deer. Distance 5 miles.

31st July, Thursday.—We embarked early, and passed several rapids pretty well. Dined with the Indians. Two of them left us in the morning for the village, and they all had an idea of doing the same, but finally concluded otherwise. One of the Osages, who had left the party for the village, returned

---

Camp 13 was in present Cole county; Coues had difficulty in locating this camp, for the *Journal's* only indication was that the day's march was fourteen miles, and the Nau map omitted any mark for it.

July 30. This camp was at the point of the bend now enclosing St. Thomas, Cole Co. Pike was about one mile south of the present hamlet of Osage Bluff. Coues incorrectly placed him three miles lower down, near Proft's Creek (page 372, n. 24). Pike's Charts here show little tracings of streams which it is impossible to identify.

and reported that he had seen and heard strange Indians in the woods. This we considered as merely a pretext to come back. I this day lost my dog, and the misfortune was the greater, as we had no other dog who would bring anything out of the water: this was the dog Fisher presented to me at Prairie des Cheins. Killed three deer and one turkey. Distance 18 miles.

1st August, Friday.—It having rained all night, the river appeared to have risen about six inches. We spread out our baggage to dry, but it continuing to rain, by intervals, all day, the things were wetter at sun-down than in the morning. We rolled them up, and left them on the beach. We sent out two hunters in the morning, one of whom killed three deer; all the Indians killed three more—Total six.

2nd August, Saturday.—The weather cleared up. The loading being spread out to dry, Dr. Robinson, myself, Bradley, Sparks, and Brown went out to hunt. We killed four deer; the Indians two. Having reloaded the boats, we embarked at 5 o'clock, and came about two miles.[54] The river rose, in the last twenty-four hours, four inches.

3rd August, Sunday.—Embarked early, and wishing to save [make the most of] the fresh, I pushed hard all day. Sparks was lost, and did not arrive until night. We encamped about 25 paces from the river, on a sand-bar.[55] Near day I heard the sentry observe that the boats had better be brought in, when I got up and found the water within a rod of our tent, and before I could get all our things out it had reached the tent. Killed nine deer, one wild cat, one goose, and one turkey. Distance 18 miles.

July 31. Rowing on up the Osage, Pike made eighteen miles to encamp about one mile below present Humphrey Creek and four miles above Big Tavern Creek. A place called St. Elizabeth, Miller Co., is now two or three miles east of the spot. Of a large cave marked on Pike's chart Coues says: "There was more than one cave or 'tavern' in the bluff near the creek . . . where the early Osage boatmen used to put up." Coues was at a loss in guessing the site of this day's camp, for camp marks were scarce on the map, but his location, "a little above Big Tavern Cr.," was a good one.

4th August, Monday.—We embarked early, and continued on for some time, not being able to find a suitable place to dry our things, but at length stopped on the east shore. Here we had to ferry the Indians over a small channel which we did not before observe; all of them, however, not arriving, we put off and continued our route. Finding our progress much impeded by our mast I unshipped it and stripped it of its iron, and, after lieutenant Wilkinson had carved our names on it, set it adrift, followed by the yards. This mast had been cut and made at Pine Creek, Upper Mississippi. After proceeding some miles, we found the Indians on the west shore, they having rafted the river. We stopped for them to cook, after which we proceeded on. The navigation had become very difficult from the rapidity of the current, occasioned by the rise of the water, which rose one foot in an hour. Killed two deer. Distance 10 miles. Rainy.

5th August, Tuesday.—We lay by this day, in order to give the Indians an opportunity to dry their baggage. Dr. Robinson and myself accompanied by Mr. Henry, went out to hunt; we lost the latter about two miles from camp. After hunting some time on the west shore, we concluded to raft the river, which we effected with difficulty and danger, and hunted for some time, but without success. We then returned to the party and found Mr. Henry, who had been lost, had arrived one hour before us: he had met one of the soldiers who brought him in. Today in our tour I passed over a remarkably large rattlesnake, as he lay curled up, and trod so near him as to touch him with my foot, he drawing himself up to make room for my heel.

August 4. On August 4, impeded by rapid currents occasioned by a rise of the water, Pike made only two miles. The record on Pike's Chart No. 32 for this day agrees with the actual geography in regard to courses and ends, but not in regard to tributaries. There is no creek corresponding in size and position to that on which Pike located camp 18. Little Gravois Creek was the only one of any size from the north passed this day, and it is shown in the bight of the bend three or four miles below. There is, however, a much smaller unnamed creek falling into the Osage at the place Pike indicates. Perhaps it was on this that he camped. If this supposition be true, he was about two miles below the junction of Miller, Camden, and Morgan

Dr. Robinson, who followed me, was on the point of treading on him, but by a spring avoided it. I then turned round and touched him with my ram-rod, but he shewed no disposition to bite, and appeared quite peaceable. The gratitude which I felt towards him for not having bit me induced me to save his life. Killed four deer. River rises thirteen inches. Rain continues.

6th August, Wednesday.—We embarked at half past eight o'clock, it having cleared off and had the appearance of a fine day. Passed Gravel river on the west. About three miles above this river the Indians left us and informed me, by keeping a little to the south and west, they would make in 15 miles what would be at least 35 miles for us. Dr. Robinson, Mr. Henry, and serjeant Ballenger accompanied them. Killed two deer. Distance 13 miles.[56]

7th August, Thursday.—Not being detained by the Indians, we are *for once* enabled to embark at a quarter past five o'clock. The river having fell, since yesterday morning, about four feet, we wish to improve every moment of time previous to its entire fall. We proceeded extremely well, passed the Saline river on the east and encamped opposite *La Belle Roche* on the west shore. This day we passed many beautiful cliffs on both sides of the river, saw a bear and wolf swimming the river. I employed myself part of the day in translating into French a talk of general Wilkinson to the Cheveux Blanche. Distance 21 miles.

---

counties. Coues placed him in nearly the same position by use of the recorded mileage and the Nau map. The latter, however, threw the editor off by indicating its site on the south, instead of the north, bank.

August 7. Pike camped tonight in the sharp bend three or four miles below the mouth of the Niangua River. Nearby is the present town of Damsel, Camden Co. The bluff opposite camp is the "La Belle Roche" mentioned. Only one of the two creeks charted on this long day's journey can be identified. That is Grand Anglaise Creek, fifty yards wide, the higher of the two. On the Nau map Pike called this stream G. Gravel R.

8th August, Friday.—We embarked 20 minutes past five o'clock. Found the river had fallen about two feet during the night. At the confluence of the Youngar with the Osage river we breakfasted. Encamped at night on a bar. Distance 21 miles.

9th August, Saturday.—We embarked at five o'clock, and at half past six o'clock met the Indians and our gentlemen. They had met with nothing extraordinary. They had killed in their excursion seven deer and three bear. We proceeded to an old wintering ground, where there were eight houses, which were occupied last winter by————, who had not been able to proceed any higher for want of water. Passed the Old Man's Rapids, below which, on the west shore, are some beautiful cliffs. Dined with the Indians, after which we passed Upper Gravel river on the west, Pottoe river on the east. Sparks went out to hunt, and did not arrive at our encampment, nor did the Indians. Distance 25 miles.

———————

August 8. Continuing up the Osage past its confluence with the Niangua River, Pike made another good day's journey, halting for the night opposite the mouth of Bolinger, or Bollinger, Creek, on which are now located the Osage Iron Works, Camden Co. The river called Youngar in the *Journal* and Yungar on the chart is the Niangua River, a tributary of some size. Linn Creek joins the Osage just below. On it is the town of Linn Creek, the seat of Camden Co. Coues put the 21st camp around the bend about four miles too high. (Page 376, n. 31.)

August 9. Pike made what he estimated as twenty-five miles. He was rejoined by the Indians after their short cut about the mouth of Huff or Jenkins Branch, which they had probably followed down after crossing the divide. Pike navigated the Old Men's or Old Man's Rapid. He passed a trace from the north (Wells Branch) a stream which he called Upper Gravel River, now known as Proctor Creek, and another stream which he called Pottatoe River or Rainey Creek.

In note 32 on pages 376–7, Coues became very involved in the identification of these streams and did not have his usual good luck in his guesses. The Nau map marked the camp considerably below the two labeled by Pike "P. R.," but the *Journal* mentioned passing it, namely "Pottoe r." on that day. Coues believed the map, saying that "by no stretch can we get Pike past Pottoe r. of the text"—an unfortunate conclusion, for Pike's chart clearly agrees with the *Journal* in placing camp two miles above that river. Coues' mistake was due to his confusion concerning the modern

10*th August, Sunday.*—Embarked a quarter past five o'clock, when the sun shone out very clearly; but in fifteen minutes it began to rain, and continued to rain very hard until one o'clock. Passed the Indians, who were encamped on the west shore, about a half a mile, and halted for them. They all forded the river but Sans Oreille, who brought his wife up to the boats, and informed me that Sparks had encamped with them, but left them early to return in search of us. We proceeded after breakfast. Sparks arrived just at the moment we were embarking. The Indians traversing the country on the east had sent Sparks with Sans Oreille. About two o'clock A. M. [P. M.] split a plank in the bottom of the batteaux. Unloaded and turned her up, repaired the breach, and continued on the route: by four o'clock found the Indians behind a large island: we made no stop, and they followed us. We encamped together on a bar, where we proposed halting to dry our corn, &c. on Monday. Killed four deer. Distance 18 1-2 miles.

---

representative of "P.R.," "Pottoe r.," or "Pottatoe river." He thought that it meant Deer Creek instead of Rainey Creek.

August 10. Pike proceeded without any important incident and that night encamped together with the Indians on a bar. He was about a mile above Duroc, Benton County, about six miles below where Coues put him (page 377 n. 33). The tributaries passed this day need identification. The lowest is Buffalo Creek, the only stream of any size meeting the river at the bend, but it is shown too far south on Pike's chart. This is "Francis" river of the Nau map. The next stream, coming in from the south, is Deer Creek or Beaver Creek. This is the "Cardinal" river of the Nau map. Farther upstream the map shows the little run, nameless on the United States Geological Survey quadrangle, on which the twenty-third camp was located. On Pike's chart 31 this creek is shown again and lettered "Cave Creek." It is not, however, the "Cave Creek" of the Nau map which explains Coues' confusion.

Pike's traverse of the Osage is given in the northeast corner of his chart 31. His camp was distant from the present town of Warsaw, Benton Co., about three miles in a straight line, or seven miles following the river as Pike did. Warsaw, the seat of the county, and much the largest town along here, is on a branch line of the Missouri Pacific. If it had existed in Pike's day he would have chartered it in the bend three miles below Grand River and opposite the large island which he does chart, Warsaw Island.

11*th August, Monday.*—We continued here to dry our corn and baggage. This morning we had a match at shooting: the prize offered to the successful person was a jacket and a twist of tobacco, which I myself was so fortunate as to win; I made the articles, however, a present to the young fellow who waited on me. After this, taking Huddleson with me, I went out to hunt: after travelling about twelve miles we arrived at the river, almost exhausted with thirst. I here indulged myself by drinking plentifully of the water, and was rendered so extremely unwell by it, that I was scarce capable of pursuing my route to the camp. On arriving opposite it, I swam the river, from which I experienced considerable relief. The party informed me they had found the heat very oppressive, and the mercury, at sun-down, was at 25° Reaumer [88° Farenheit]. This day, for the first time, I saw trout west of the Allegheny mountains. Reloaded our boats, and finished two new oars which were requisite.

12*th August, Tuesday.*—Previously to our embarkation, which took place at half past five o'clock, I was obliged to convince my red brethren that, if I protected them, I would not suffer them to plunder my men with impunity, for the chief had got one of my lads' tin cups attached to his baggage, and notwithstanding it was marked with the initials of the soldier's name, he refused to give it up. On which I requested the interpreter to tell him, "that I had no idea that he had purloined the cup, but supposed some other person had attached it to his baggage; but that, knowing it to be my soldier's, I requested him to deliver it up, or I should be obliged to take other measures to obtain it." This had the desired effect; for I certainly should have put my

---

Pike was less careful than usual here in plotting tributaries. He left out one of the largest, Turkey Creek. The ones he did remember, however, when he drew his chart that evening, can be recognized. "Vermillion" River is present Vermillion or Cole Camp Creek. West Creek is the small unnamed run four miles above. Deep Creek is Little Tebo or Little Tebeau Creek, heading near the town of Lincoln. Grand River is the only one properly named. It is a stream of considerable size with tributaries reaching up west into Kansas and north almost to Kansas City. The two large islands shown near the 24th camp are Wright's and Halloway.

Coues made two errors here, trivial in themselves, but more important when he inserted them both in the text (page 379):

1). Following the Nau map, he placed camp on the east instead of the west bank;

threats into execution from this principle, formed from my experience during my incourse with Indians, *that if you have justice on your side, and do not enforce it, they universally despise you.* When we stopped for dinner, one of my men [Sparks] took his gun and went out; not having returned when we were ready to re-embark, I left him. Passed the Indians twice when they were crossing the river. Passed some very beautiful cliffs on the west shore; also Vermillion and Grand rivers, the latter of which is a large stream, and encamped at the [Pomme de Terre].

Immediately after our encampment a thunder storm came on, which blew overboard my flag-staff and a number of articles of my clothing, which were on top of the cabbin, and sunk them immediately. Being much fatigued, and the bank difficult of ascent, lay down in the cabin, without supper and slept all night. It continued to rain. The man I left on shore arrived on the opposite bank in the night, having killed two deer; but was obliged to leave the largest behind. Finding he was not to be sent for, he concealed his gun and deer, and swam the river. Distance 24 miles.[57]

13th August, Wednesday.—It continued to rain. In the morning sent a boat over for Spark's gun and deer. Embarked at half past 9 o'clock. Stopped to dine at two o'clock. During the time we halted, the river rose over the flat bar, on which we were: this, if we had no other proof, would convince us we were near the head of the river, as the rain must have reached it. We made almost a perfect circle, so that I do not believe we were, at night, three miles from where we encamped last night. This day, for the first time, we have prairie hills. Distance 13 miles.

---

2). He refused to believe Pike's statement that on August 12 the party passed Vermillion River; so he corrected "Vermillion" River to read Little Tabeau. "Vermillion" River, on the contrary, rightly refers to present "Vermillion" or Cole Camp Creek. Coues' mistake was the result of his two previous ones. He first decided among his other errors of note 33 that present Vermillion Creek was Francis r. of the Nau map. Francis River, on the contrary, as has been noted above, refers to Buffalo Creek, ten miles downstream. Coues then placed camp number 23 above instead of below Vermillion Creek. Of course by Coues' interpretation, Pike could not have passed Vermillion Creek August 12; he was already fourteen miles above it.

On this day, of course unknown to him, Lieutenant Pike was promoted to a Captaincy.

14th August, Thursday.—Embarked at half past five o'clock. Passed the *Park*, which is ten miles round, and not more than three quarters of a mile across, bearing from S.5° E. to due N. At its head we breakfasted, and just as we were about to put off we saw and brought to a canoe manned with three engagees of Mr.————, who informed us that the Little Osage had marched a war party against the Kans, and the Grand Osage a party against our citizens on the Arkansaw river. Wrote by them to the general and all friends. Gave the poor fellows some whiskey and eight quarts of corn, they having had only two turkies for four days. We left them and proceeded, passing on our east some of the largest cedars I ever saw. Came on very well in the afternoon, and encamped on an island above Turkey island. Distance 28 miles.

15th August, Friday.—We embarked at five o'clock, and at eight o'clock met the Indians and the gentlemen who accompanied them. Found all well. They had been joined by their friends and relatives from the village, with horses to transport their baggage. Lieutenant Wilkinson informed me that

———————

August 14. Embarking at half-past five, Pike passed an unusual park or open grove almost encircled by the Osage. He met a canoe manned by three *engagès* of Mr. Pierre Chouteau to whom he made presents. He proceeded for what he estimated to be twenty-five miles, and encamped on an island above Turkey Island. He now was near the northeast corner of St. Clair County and the southeast corner of Henry County. The creek from the south near Turkey island is Wright's, charted on the Nau map as "Buckeye Creek."

His letter of the 14th to General Wilkinson read as follows:

Park on the Osage river, 14th Aug. 1806[58]

DEAR SIR,

By Baptiste La Tulip, I send this letter, who informs me he bears letters to Chouteau, informing him that a party of *Little Osages* have marched to war against the Kansas; and a party of *Grand Osages* left the village expressly to make war on the white people on the Arkansaw. This latter step the White Hair did everything in his power to prevent, but could not. If true, what are we to think of our *bons amis,* the Osage?

But to————[Manuel de Lisa] must we ascribe the stroke against the *Kanses,* who I am informed sent a message to the Osage nation to *raze*

their meeting was very tender and affectionate—"Wives throwing themselves into the arms of their husbands, parents embracing their children, and children their parents, brothers and sisters meeting, one from captivity, the others from the towns—they, at the same time, returning thanks to the *Good God* for having brought them once more together;" in short, the *toute ensemble* was such as to make polished society blush, when compared with those savages, in whom the passions of the mind, either joy, grief, fear, anger, or revenge, have their full scope: why can we not correct the baneful passions, without weakening the good? Sans Oreille made them a speech, in which he remarked, "Osage, you now see your wives, your brothers, your daughters, your sons, redeemed from captivity. Who did this? was it the Spaniards? No. The French? No. Had either of those people been governors of the country, your relatives might have rotted in captivity, and you never would have seen them; but the Americans stretched forth their hands, and they are returned to you!! What can you do in return for all this goodness? Nothing: all your lives would not suffice to repay their goodness." This man had children in captivity, not one of whom were we able to obtain for him.

---

the Kanses village entirely. On this subject I intended to have been more particular, and substantiate it by proofs; but present circumstances seem to give credit to it. On my arrival at the village, most particular enquiry shall be made on the subject.

Yesterday morning lieutenant Wilkinson, the doctor the interpreter, and one soldier, marched with the Indians, as they were very apprehensive of an attack. The people in the canoe heard them crying and saw them on their march.

Nothing extraordinary has yet taken place on our route, except our being favored with a vast quantity of rain, which I hope will enable us to ascend to the village.

What face will the Indians receive us with? and to whom are we to ascribe their hostile disposition, unless the traitors of St. Louis?

Lieutenant Wilkinson is in very good health, and will lament his having missed this opportunity of assuring his parents of his love and affection.

I am, dear general,
Your obedient servant,

(Signed)   Z. M. Pike.

Gen. James Wilkinson.

The chief then requested that lieutenant Wilkinson and Dr. Robinson might be permitted to accompany them by land, which I consented to. Wrote a letter to the Cheveux Blanche, by lieutenant Wilkinson. When we parted (after delivering the Indians their baggage) Sans Orielle put an Indian on board, to hunt, or obey any other commands I might have for him. We stopped at eleven o'clock to dry our baggage. Found our biscuit and crackers almost all ruined. Put off at half past four o'clock, and encamped at three quarters past five o'clock.[59] Distance 15 1-2 miles.

16th August, Saturday.—We embarked at five o'clock and came on extremely well in the barge to a French hunting camp (evacuated), twelve miles to breakfast, the batteaux coming up late: we exchanged hands. About twelve o'clock passed the grand fork, which is equal in size to the one on which we pursued our route. Waited to dine at the rocks called the Swallow's Nest, on the west shore above the forks. The batteaux having gained nearly half an hour, the crews are convinced that it is not the boat, but men who make the difference: each take their own boat, after which we proceeded very well, the water being good and men in spirits. Saw an elk on the shore, also met an old man alone hunting, from whom we obtained no information of consequence. Encamped on the West shore at Mine river. Passed the

---

August 16. This day's journey Pike proudly recorded in the *Journal* as thirty-seven miles, and he hardly overestimated it, for the barge and the batteau were racing all day. Pike passed Weaubleau Creek, which he named Linden River on the original chart and Linn River on the Nau map. Pike's chart here contains much information. A stream from the south now called Bushy Creek, then two from the north, the upper being Gallinipper Creek. This today falls in just below Osceola, St. Clair Co. Pike's "grand Forks" is the confluence of the Osage and Sac rivers. Elk Creek just above is the present Salt Creek. Mine Creek or Saline is now called Little Monegaw Creek. Incidentally, besides calling this "Mine Creek or Saline" on the chart, Pike called it "Mine River" in the text and "Mine Cr." on the Nau map. Passing this creek of many names, Pike camped just above it. The Nau map and Coues erred slightly in locating this camp by putting it below, instead of above, Little Monegaw Creek. "The Belle [Bel] Oiseau [Osage chief] was killed by the Sacs in the year 1804, in a boat of Manuel de Liso [Lisa] when on his way down to Saint Louis, in order to join the first deputation of his nation who were forwarded to the seat of government by Governor Louis [Lewis]"—Pike. *An Account of Expeditions,* 125.

place where the chief, called the Belle [Bel] Oiseau, and others were killed. Distance 37 miles.

17th August, Sunday.—We embarked at five o'clock and came twelve miles to breakfast. At four o'clock arrived at ten French houses on the east shore, where was then residing a Sac, who was married to an Osage femme and spoke French *only*. We afterwards passed the position where Mr. Chouteau formerly had his fort, not a vestige of which was remaining, the spot being only marked by the superior growth of vegetation. Here the river bank is one solid bed of stone-coal, just below which is a very shoal and rapid ripple; from whence to the village of the Grand Osage is nine miles across a large prairie. We came about two miles above, and encamped on the west shore. This day the river has been generally bounded by prairies on both sides. Distance 41 1-2 miles.

18th August, Monday.—We put off at half past five o'clock. Stopped at nine o'clock to breakfast. Passed the second fork of the river at twelve o'clock, the right hand fork bearing N. about 30 yards wide, the left (the one we pursued) N. 60° W. and not more than 50 or 60 feet in width, very full of old trees, &c. but plenty of water. Observed the road where the chiefs and lieutenant Wilkinson crossed. We proceeded until one o'clock, when we were

---

August 17. Continuing his course up the Osage, the creeks Pike passed on this day are: Clear Creek from the left and an unnamed stream from the right, two more small tributaries from the left and right, and then Panther or Painter Creek from the right. After passing Panther Creek, Pike came upon the French houses on the south bank and, later, "passed the position where Mr. [Pierre] Chouteau formerly had his fort [Fort Carondelet]. After this weary day of rowing, Pike made camp opposite Ladies Branch, not far from the present towns of Popinsville, Prairie City and Schell City, Vernon Co.

August 18. Approaching the Osage villages, Pike left the main branch of the Osage, at what he called the second fork, following the Little Osage, past Muddy Creek, until further progress by boat was halted by drift. There he camped after sending to the villages for horses to transport his baggage.

Coues located this drift near some marshy ground opposite Horseshoe lake, basing his evident decision on the proximity of the drift to the forks of the Osage and Little Osage rivers, as shown by the Nau map (page 385 n. 42). Pike's chart, however, shows the drift as higher, about two or three miles above Coues' location, at a point where a

halted by a large drift quite across the river. Dispatched Baroney to the village of the Grand Osage, to procure horses to take our baggage nearer to the towns; unloaded our boats and in about two hours lieutenant Wilkinson with Tuttasuggy, arrived at our camp, the former of whom presented me an express from the general, and letters from my friends. The chiefs remained at our camp all night. I was attacked by a violent head-ache. It commenced raining, and continued with great force until day. Distance 19 1-4 miles.

---

little creek flows in from the south. The camp for August 19 was, therefore, about six miles southeast of the present Rich Hill, a considerable town in Bates County.

At the drift Pike was rejoined by Lieutenant Wilkinson, who, accompanying the Indians, had preceded his commanding officer and arrived at the villages. The latter described his reception as follows:

"We reached the village of Little Osages after a fatiguing and laborious march of six days across an arid prairie.

When within a mile of the town, the chief Tuttasuggy, or Wind, desired that a regular procession might be observed; he accordingly placed me between himself and his first warrior, and the ransomed captives followed by files. Half a mile from the village we were met by 180 horsemen, painted and decorated in a very fanciful manner; they were considered as a guard of honor, and on our approach opened to the right and left, leaving a sufficient space for us to pass through. A few yards in advance, on the right, I perceived 60 or more horsemen painted with blue chalk; when the chief observed them, he commanded a halt, and sent forward his younger brother Nezuma, or Rain that Walks, with a flag and silk handkerchief as a prize for the swiftest horseman. At a given signal they started off at full speed, the two foremost taking the flag and handkerchief, and the rest contenting themselves with having shown their agility and skill. As I entered the village I was saluted by a discharge from four swivels which the Indians had taken from an old fort [Fort Carondelet] erected by the Spaniards on the river, and passed through a crowd of nearly a thousand persons, part of whom I learned were of the Grand village. I was immediately, but with ceremony, ushered into the lodge of Soldier of the Oak, who, after having paid me some very handsome compliments, courteously invited me to eat of green corn, buffalo-meat, and water-melons about the size of a 24-pound shot, which, though small were highly flavored."—Coues, 540-1.

19*th August, Tuesday.*—We commenced very early to arrange our baggage, but had not finished at one o'clock, when the chief of the Grand Osage, and 40 or 50 men of his village, arrived with horses. We loaded and took our departure for the place where Manuel de Liza had his establishment, at which we arrived about four o'clock, and commenced pitching our encampment near the edge of the prairie, when I was informed that three men had arrived from St. Louis, sent by Manuel de Liza. I dispatched lieutenant Wilkinson to the village, with Baroney, who brought to camp the man who had charge of the others from St. Louis: he having no passport, I detained him until further consideration. Our reception by the Osage was flattering, and particularly by the *White Hair* and our fellow-travellers. This evening there arrived in the village of the Grand Osage an express from the Arkansaw, who brought the news that a boat, ascending that river, had

---

General Wilkinson's express of Aug. 6th was received here and read:

Cantonment Missouri, August 6th, 1806.[60]

SIR,

IN consequence of the receipt of the enclosed letters, I have thought proper to send you an express, to enable you to announce to the Osage the designs of their enemies, that they may take seasonable measures to circumvent them. You will not fail, in addition to the within talk, to enhance our paternal regard for this nation, by every proper expression; but are to keep clear of any conflict in which they may be involved, though you are to avoid the appearance of abandoning them. If it should be the Potowatomies' intention to carry their threat into execution. It is probably they will not attempt to make the blow before the falling of the leaves, and in the mean time the Osages should establish a chain of light scouts, along the coast of the Missouri, to ascertain with certainty the approach of their enemy.

It is reduced to a certainty that———[Manuel de Lisa] and a society of which he is the ostensible leader, have determined on a project to open some commercial intercourse with Santa Fe, and as this may lead to a connection injurious to the United States, and will, I understand, be attempted without the sanction of law or the permission of the executive: you must do what, consistently, you can to defeat the plan. No good can be derived to the United States from such a project, because the prosecution of it

been fired on, and had two white men killed and two wounded, and that the brother-in-law of the Cheveux Blanche, who happened to be on board, was also killed. This put the whole village in mourning.

20*th August, Wednesday.*—About twelve o'clock I dispatched Baroney for the chiefs of the Grand village, in order to give the general's parole to the Cheveux Blanche, also a young man to the village of the Little Osage. The Cheveux Blanche and his people arrived about three o'clock, and after

---

will depend entirely on the Spaniards, and they will not permit it, unless to serve their political, as well as their personal interests. I am informed that the ensuing autumn and winter will be employed in reconnoitering and opening a connection with the Tetaus, Panis, &c. that this fall, or the next winter, a grand magazine [storehouse] is to be established at the Osage towns, where these operations will commence; that————[Lisa] is to be the active agent, having formed a connection with the Tetaus. This will carry forward their merchandise within three or four days travel of the Spanish settlements, where they will deposit it, under a guard of 300 Tetaus.————[Lisa] will then go forward with four or five attendants, taking with him some jewelry and fine goods. With those he will visit the governor, to whom he will make presents, and implore his pity by a fine tale of sufferings which have been endured by the change of government: that they are left here, with goods to be sure, but not a dollar's worth of bullion, and therefore they have adventured to see him, for the purpose of praying his leave for the introduction of their property into the province. If he assents, then the whole of the goods will be carried forward; if he refuses, then————[Lisa] will invite some of his countrymen to accompany him to his deposit, and having there exposed to them his merchandise, he will endeavor to open a forced or clandestine trade; for he observes, the Spaniards will not dare to attack his camp. Here you have the plan, and you must take all prudent and lawful means to blow it up.

In regard to your approximation to the Spanish settlements, should your route lead you near them, or should you fall in with any of their parties, your conduct must be marked by such circumspection and discretion, as may prevent alarm or conflict, as you will be held responsible for consequences. On this subject I refer you to my orders [p. 57-60]. We have nothing new respecting the pending negotiations in Europe; but from colonel [T. H.] Cushing I understand the Spaniards below [down the Mississippi] are behaving now with great courtesy.

waiting some time for the *Wind* and his people, I just informed the chiefs that I had merely assembled them to deliver the parole of the general, and present the marks of distinction intended for the Cheveux Blanche and his son, hanging a grand medal around the neck of the latter. The packets committed to my charge for the relations of the deceased Osages, were then delivered to them, the widow making the distribution. It must be remarked

---

By the return of the bearer you may open correspondence with the secretary of war; but I would caution you against anticipating a step before you, for fear of deception and disappointment.[61] To me you may, and must, write fully and freely, not only giving a minute detail of every thing past worthy of note, but also of your prospects and the conduct of the Indians. If you discover that any tricks have been paid from St. Louis, you will give them to me with names, and must not fail to give particulars to the secretary of war, with names, to warn him against improper confidence and deception. Enclose your dispatch for me to colonel [T.] Hunt, and it will follow me by a party which I leave for the purpose. It is interesting to you to reach Nachitoches in season to be at the seat of government pending the session of congress; yet you must not sacrifice any essential object to this point. Should fortune favor you on your present excursion, your importance to our country will, I think, make your future life comfortable.

To shew you how to correct your watch by the quadrant, after it has been carefully adjusted, preparatory to your observing on the eclipses of the satellites of Jupiter, I send you a very simple plan, which you will readily understand; a bason of water, in some place protected from the motion of the air, will give you a fairer artificial horizon than Mercury. I think a tent, with a suitable aperture in the side of it would do very well. I have generally unroofed a cabin. Miranda has botched his business. He has lost his two schooners captured, and himself in the Leander returned to Jamaica.[62] The French have a squadron of four frigates at Porto Rico, and of five sail of the line with Jerome Bonaparte at Martinique. I consider them lost.

Your children have been indisposed; but Mrs. Pike writes you. She appears well. My regards to your associates, and may God protect you.

(Signed)   J. WILKINSON.

Lieutenant Pike.

that I had merely requested the Cheveux Blanche to come with his son, and receive the general's message; but instead of coming with a few chiefs, he was accompanied by 186 men, to all of whom we were obliged to give something to drink. When the council was over we mounted our horses and rode to the village, and halted at the quarters of the chief, where we were regaled with boiled pumpkins: then we went to two different houses, and were invited to many others, but declined, promising that I would pay them a visit, previous to my departure, and spend the whole day. We then returned to camp.

On August 19, Pike moved up to just below the confluence of the Little Osage and Marmiton rivers. There he established a permanent camp, which he named Camp Independence. Considering this an important site, he prepared nearby an observatory from which to take his bearings, both latitude and longitude, but his instruments were so inaccurate that he obtained no useful results. Camp Independence is shown twice on his chart. It was situated ideally, midway between the two northern towns of the Osage nations.

These Indians, whom Pike visited as the first objective of his expedition, were divided into three branches, the Grand Osages, the Little Osages, and the Arkansas branch. They are described by R. I. Holcombe as follows: "At the time of Pike's and Wilkinson's visit the Osages numbered about 4,000 souls, as follows: Big Osages, 1,694; Little Osages, 824; Chancers, or Arkansas band, 1,500. The head chiefs of the respective branches were White Hair, The Wind, and Big Track . . . The government may be described as an oligarchical republic, where the chiefs proposed and the people decided all public measures. . . .

"The men of the tribe were divided into two classes, warriors and hunters composing the first, and cooks and doctors the second. The doctors were also priests and magicians, and possessed great influence, supposed to have knowledge of deep mysteries, and to be wonderfully skilled in the use of medicines. The cooks were also of much importance, this class including all of the warriors, who, from age or other causes, were unable to join the war parties. The cooks also exercised the function of town-criers. . . .

"The lodges varied in length from 36 to 100 feet; they were not placed in rows or streets or with any regularity whatever, but were usually placed near one another. Pike says the Osage towns held more people in the same space of ground than any other places he ever saw.

"Physically the Osages of former days were said to be the finest specimens

After enquiring of White Hair if the men of Manuel de Liza had any ostensible object in view, he informed me that they had only said to him that they expected Manuel would be up to trade in the autumn. I concluded to take the deposition of [Jean] Baptiste Larme [Duchouquette] as to the manner in which he was employed by Manuel de Liza, and forward the same to Dr. Brown[65] and the attorney-general of Louisiana, and permit the men to return to St. Louis, as it was impossible for me to detach a party with them as prisoners.

---

of Western Indians. They were tall, erect, and dignified, and they were very agile and muscular. The average height of the men was over six feet. Old White Hair is said to have been nearly seven feet. They were considered by the Indians to the south and west of them as a brave warlike nation, but the northern nations, the Pottawatomies, Sacs, and Foxes, and the Iowas, held them in contempt, and really often whipped them two to one. The humane policy of the United States, in procuring treaties of amity between them and other tribes, and in inculcating upon them the divine precepts of the golden rule, practically made Quakers of them."[63]

In spite of Mr. Coues' statement: "But there is of course no question of the exact site of a village which stood for more than a century" (page 390, n. 45), the precise location of these villages is now made possible by the recovery of Pike's original charts. Coues and R. I. Holcombe, the best authorities, were both bewildered by the inaccuracy and ambiguity of the Nau map.

Coues' locations are as follows: Grand Osage Village, on the Little Osage River, where an eastward bend receives a creek from the south, about three miles below the confluence of the Little Osage and Marmiton; Little Osage Village, on the Little Osage River about six miles "higher up" (whether he meant six miles above Camp Independence or above the Grand Osage Village is not clear). To support these locations he referred the reader to R. I. Holcombe as though to one who had certain information (pages 386 n. 42 and 398, n. 45).

Holcombe, on the contrary, had no more information than Coues, but, instead of supporting, he contradicted, him. Holcombe's statement of the case is as follows: "From the map made by Gen. Pike, and partially from his description, the location of the Osage villages was in the northern part of this [Vernon] county, south of the Osage River. The Big or 'Grand' Osage village was below the mouth of the Marmiton a few miles; while the village of the Little Osage was on the west side of the Marmiton. The two villages seem to have been five or six miles apart, but their exact location cannot now be determined as Pike's map is far from accurate."[64]

21st August, Thursday.—In the morning White Hair paid us a visit, and brought us a present of corn, meat, and grease, and we invited him, his son, and son-in-law to breakfast with us, and gave his companions something to eat. I then wrote a number of letters to send by express, and enclosed the deposition of Larme. In the afternoon we rode to the village of the Little Osage, and were received by our fellow-travellers with true hospitality. Returned in the evening, when a tremendous storm of rain, thunder and lightning commenced, and continued with extraordinary violence until half past nine o'clock. It was with great difficulty we were enabled to keep our tents from blowing down. The place prepared for an observatory was carried away.

22nd August, Friday.—Preparing in the morning for the council, and committing to paper the heads of the subject on which I intended to speak. The chiefs of the Little Osage arrived about one o'clock, also the interpreter of

---

Holcombe and Coues agreed on the location for the Grand Osage, but disagreed on that for the Little Osage.

The locations of these disputed villages are twice shown accurately and clearly on Pike's chart and the exact site is marked by Pike's symbols.

The Grand Osage Village was nine miles, following the stream, above the point where Coues and Holcombe put it, on the north bank of the Marmiton River, where a large westward bend receives a stream from the east. It was at the foot of a noticeable butte rising one hundred feet above the prairie. The village of the Little Osage was on the north side of the river of that name six miles above its confluence with the Marmiton. It was a slight distance back from the river, on the east bank of the second tributary from the north, and thus very close to the present town of Arthur, Vernon Co. These locations harmonize with Pike's account in the *Journal,* as neither Coues' nor Holcombe's did.

The neighboring country seemed to Pike a paradise, and Holcombe, proud of his Vernon County, noted such passages and adds: "Could Gen. Pike revisit the northern part of this county now, he would, indeed, find it, as he imagined it would one day become, 'the seat of husbandry,' and, too, he would find the prairie farms of Blue Mound township "occupied by numerous herds of domestic animals,' including thoroughbred cattle and hogs."

Pike's letters describing these troublesome days, written the 28th, will be found on p. 97 *seq.*

the Grand Osage, who pretended to say that the Grand Osage had expected us at their village with the Little Osage. The Cheveux Blanche arrives with his chiefs. The ceremony of the council being arranged, I delivered them the general's *parole* forwarded by express. My reason for not delivering it until this time was, in order to have the two villages together, as it was equally interesting to both. After this I explained at large the will, wishes, and advice of their *Great Father,* and the mode which I conceived most applicable to carry them into effect.[66] The Cheveux Blanche replied in a few words, and promised to give me a full reply tomorrow. The Wind replied to the same amount; after which the Cheveux Blanche addressed himself to the Wind as follows;—"I am shocked at your conduct, Tuttasuggy, you who have lately come from the States, and should have been wise; but you led the redeemed captives, with an officer of the United States, to your village, instead of bringing them through my town in the first instance." To this the *Wind*

Pike's letters to Wilkinson read (App. to Pt. II, 40-42).

> *Camp Independence, near the Osage Towns,*
> *August* 28*th,* 1806.

Dear General,

You will no doubt be much surprised to perceive by the date of this letter, that we are still here; but we have been unavoidably detained by a variety of circumstances.

I had the happiness to receive your express the day of my arrival, the bearer having arrived the night before, and have attended particularly to its contents.

On the 19th inst. I delivered your *parole* to the Cheveux Blanche, and on the 21st held a grand council of both towns, and made the necessary communications and demands for horses, on the subject of making peace with the Kans, accompanying me to the Panis, down the Arkansaw, and if there was any *brave* enough to accompany me the whole voyage.

They requested one day to hold council in the villages previous to giving an answer. It was three before I received any; their determination was as follows:—From the *Grand Osage* village, or [that of] Cheveux Blanche we are accompanied by his son, and *Jean La Fon* [Fou], the second chief of the village, with some young men not known, and he furnishes us four horses.

made no reply, but left his seat shortly after under pretence of giving some orders to his young men. I conceived this reprimand intended barely to shew us the superiority of the one and inferiority of the other, and originated, in my opinion, from an altercation of lieutenant Wilkinson and the Cheveux Blanche, in which allusions were made by the former, on the friendly conduct of the *Little Chief,* (alias the Wind) when compared to that of the latter. I must here observe that when the chiefs and prisoners left me, accompanied by lieutenant Wilkinson, I did not know the geographical situation of the two villages, but conceived that, in going to the *Little Village,* they would pass by the *Grand Village,* and of course that lieutenant Wilkinson and the chief would arrange the affair properly.

The *Little Osage* sends the brother of the chief (whom I really find to be the third chief of the village) and some young men unknown, and furnishes *six* horses! ! This is their present promise, but four of the ten are yet deficient. With these I am merely capable of transporting our merchandise and ammunition. I shall purchase two more, for which I find we shall be obliged to pay extravagant prices.

I sincerely believe that the two chiefs, *White Hair* and *The Wind,* have exerted all their influence; but it must be but *little,* when they could only procure *ten* horses out of seven or eight hundred.

I have taken an exact survey of the river to this place, noting particular streams, &c. a protracted copy of which lieutenant Wilkinson forwards by this opportunity. Since our arrival here I have ascertained the variation of the compass to be 6° 30′ E. the latitude, by means of several observations, 37° 26′ 17″ N.; and by an observation of three different nights, obtained two immersions of Jupiter's satellites, which will enable us to ascertain every geographical object in view [error of about forty miles].

On the same night I arrived near the village, there was a Mr. Baptist Duchouquette, alias Larme, with two men, in a small canoe arrived and went immediately to the lodge of the White Hair, whose conduct, with that of our resident interpreter, appears (in my estimation) to have changed since I sent lieutenant Wilkinson to demand to see Baptist's passport, if he had one; if not, to bring him to camp—which was done.

23rd August, Saturday.—I expected to have reserved from the chiefs their answers to my demands; but received an express from both villages, informing that they wished to put them off until tomorrow. I then adjusted my instruments. Took equal altitudes and a meridional altitude of the sun, but, owing to flying clouds, missed the immersions of Jupiter's satellites.

24th August, Sunday.—Was nearly half the day in adjusting the line of collimation in the telescopic sights of my theodolite. It began to cloud before evening, and although the sky was not entirely covered, I was so unfortunate as to miss the time of an immersion and (although clear in the intermediate period) an emersion also. I was informed by Baroney that the Little Village had made up eleven horses for us. In the evening, however,

---

I detained him two days, until I had made an enquiry of White Hair, who said he had merely mentioned him that *Labardie* was coming with a quantity of goods. Finding I could substantiate nothing more criminal against him than his having entered the Indian boundaries without a passport, and not being able to send him back a prisoner, detained him sufficient time to alarm him, and then took his deposition (a copy of which is inclosed to the attorney-general), and wrote Dr. Brown on the occasion, and requested him to enter a prosecution against these men.

Barroney informs me that he has not the least doubt but——— [Lisa] was at the bottom of this embassy, although in the name of——— [Mr. Labardie], as after the arrival of Baptist, the Indians frequently spoke of———[Lisa] and declared, if he had come he could have obtained horses plenty.

Our interpreter, also (Maugraine), I do believe to be a perfect creature of———[Lisa]: he has almost positively refused to accompany me (although I read your order on the subject), alleging he was only engaged to interpret at this place, notwithstanding he went last year to the Arkansaw for Mr. Chouteau without difficulty. I have not yet determined on the line of conduct to be pursued with him, but believe, on his giving a positive refusal, I shall use military law. What the result will be is uncertain; but to be thus braved by a scoundrel, will be lessening the dignity of our government. He is married into a powerful family, and appears, next to the White

the interpreter, accompanied by the Son-in-law and son of the Cheveux Blanche, came to camp, and informed me that there were no horses to be got in the village of the Big Osage.[67]

25th August, Monday.—In the morning we were visited by the Cheveux Blanche and three or four of his chiefs, who were pleased to accord to my demands. He found much difficulty in informing me that, in all his village, he could only raise four horses, but that we should be accompanied by his son and son-in-law. I then expressed to him the difference of our expectations from the reality. He remained until after twelve o'clock, when I went to the Little Osage Village, and was received with great friendship by the chief. Remained all night at the house of Tuttasuggy. Took the census.

26th August, Tuesday.—Rose early and found my friends in council, which was merely relative to our horses. The chief then declared their

---

Hair, to have the most influence in the Grand [Osage] village. The general will please to observe that much of the foregoing rests on conjecture, and therefore will give it its due weight. But to him I not only write as my general, but as [to] a paternal friend, who would not make use of my open communications, when not capable of being substantiated by proofs.[68]

We have heard nothing of the Potowatomies; but should they come in a few days, they will meet with a warm reception, as all are ready to receive them.

Since my arrival here many Spanish medals have been shown me, and some commissions. All I have done on the subject is merely to advise their delivery below [at St. Louis], when they would be acknowledged by our government. Many have applied for permission to go to Saint Louis; none of which I have granted, except to the son of Sans Oreille, who goes down to make enquiry for his sister.

I have advanced our express some things on account, and forward his receipts; also, some trifles to Barroney, who I have found to be one of the

determination to me, and that he himself gave me one horse, and lent me eight more to carry our baggage to the Pawnees. Sold the old batteaux for 100 dollars, in merchandise, which I conceived infinitely preferable to leaving her to the uncertain safe-guard of the Indians. About this time we received the news that the party of Potowatomies were discovered to be near the towns. I gave them the best advice I was capable of giving, and then returned to our camp.

27th August, Wednesday.—Spent in arranging our baggage for the horses. Received four horses from the Little Village and two from the Big Village. In the evening lieutenant Wilkinson rode to the Grand Village. I observed two immersions of Jupiter's satellites.

28th August, Thursday.—Writing to the secretary at War and the general, and making arrangements for our departure. Visited by the Wind and Sans Oreille.

---

finest young men I ever knew in his situation, and appears to have entirely renounced all his Saint Louis connections, and is as firm an American as if born one: he of course is entirely discarded by the people of Saint Louis; but I hope he will not suffer for his fidelity.

On the chart forwarded by lieutenant Wilkinson is noted the census which I caused to be taken of the village of the *Little Osage;* that of the big one I shall likewise obtain—which are from actual enumeration. Lieutenant Wilkinson will (if nothing extraordinary prevents) descend the Arkansaw, accompanied by Ballenger and two men, as the former is now perfectly acquainted with the mode of taking courses and protracting his route, and the latter appears as if he had not the proper capacity for it, although a good dispositioned and brave man.

I am, dear sir,
Your obedient servant,
(Signed)   Z. M. Pike, Lt.

Gen. Wilkinson.

29th August, Friday.—Forenoon writing letters. In the afternoon Dr. Robinson and myself went to the Grand Village, at which we saw the great medicine dance. Remained at the village all night.

30th August, Saturday.—Returned to the camp after settling all my affairs at the town. Sealed up our dispatches and sent off the general's express. In the afternoon we were visited by the principal men of the Little

---

[Osage Towns], 29th August, 1806.[69]

DEAR SIR,

I WILL continue my communications, by relating that the *Wind* has come in and informed me that the other two horses which he promised have been withdrawn by their owners. He appeared really distressed, and I conceive I do him justice in believing that he is extremely mortified at the deceptions which have been passed on him.

It is with extreme pain I keep myself *cool* amongst the difficulties which those people appear to have a disposition to throw in my way; but I have declared to them that I should go on, even if I collected our tents and other baggage (which we will be obliged to leave together) and burn them on the spot.

I have sold the batteaux which I brought up (and which was extremely rotten) for 100 dollars, in merchandize, the price of this place; which I conceive was preferable to leaving her to destruction, as I am afraid I do the barge (for which I demanded 150 dollars), although I leave her under the charge of the *Wind* and shall report her to colonel [Thomas] Hunt.

I shall dispatch the express tomorrow, as he complains much of the detention, &c. and as I hope nothing worthy of note will occur at this place previous to our departure. I hope the general will believe me to be, and should this be my last report, to have been, his sincerely attached friend and

obedient servant,

(Signed)   Z. M. PIKE, Lt.

Gen. Wilkinson.

30th August, Osage Towns, 1806[70]

DEAR SIR,

I HAVE brought Mr. Noal, alias Maugraine, to reason, and he either goes himself or hires, at his expence, a young man who is here who speaks

Village and the chief, to whom I presented a flag, and made the donations which I conceived requisite to the different Indians, on account of horses &c.

31st August, Sunday.—Arranging our packs and loading our horses, in order to fit our loads, as we expected to march on the morrow. Up late writing letters.

———————

the Panis language, and in many other respects is preferable to himself; but he will be the bearer of the express to Saint Louis.

The Cheveux Blanche requested me to inform you that there is a murderer (an Osage) in his village, who killed a Frenchman on the Arkansaw; but owing to the great dissensions and schism of the Arkansaw faction, he is fearful to deliver up, without some of his friends having agreed to it, and his authority being strengthened by a *formal* demand from you, when he assures me he shall be brought down a prisoner. Indeed the Cheveux Blanche appears to be very delicately situated, as the village on the Arkansaw serves as a place of refuge for all the young and daring, and discontented; and added to which, they are much more regularly supplied with ammunition, and, should not our government take some steps to prevent it, they will ruin the Grand village, as they are at liberty to make war without restraint, especially on the nations who are to the west, and have plenty of horses. The chief says he was promised, at Washington, that these people should be brought back to join him; but, on the contrary, many of his village are emigrating there.

Owing to the difficulty of obtaining horses, Mr. Henry returns from this place. In descending the Mississippi I will request him to pay his respects to you.

I last evening took the census of the Grand village, and found it to be—Men, 502, Boys, 341; Women and Girls, 852; Total 1695; Lodges, 214.

The express waits, which I hope the general will accept as an excuse for this scrawl, having written him fully on the 28th and 29th inst.

I am, dear general,
Your ever sincere friend
and obedient servant,
(Signed)		Z. M. PIKE, Lt.

Gen. J. Wilkinson.

1st September, Monday.—Struck our tents early in the morning, and commenced loading our horses. We now discovered that an Indian had stolen a large black horse, which the Cheveux Blanche had presented to lieutenant Wilkinson. I mounted a horse to pursue him; but the interpreter sent to town, and the chief's wife sent another in its place. We left the place about twelve o'clock with fifteen loaded horses, our party consisting of two lieutenants, one doctor, two sergeants, one corporal, fifteen privates, two interpreters, three Pawnees, and four chiefs of the Grand Osage, amounting in all to 30 warriors and one woman. We crossed the Grand Osage fork and a prairie N. 80° W. five miles to the fork of the Little Osage. Joined by Sans Oreille and seven Little Osage, all of whom I equipped for the march. Distance 8 miles.

September 1. On September 1 Pike finally left the place, after the Indians had begun stealing back the horses. His party consisted then of thirty persons. He was later joined by Sans Oreille and seven Little Osage Indians. His map, continued on Chart No. 30, shows that from the villages of his allies, he travelled generally west over the prairie between the Little Osage and Marmiton rivers, dropping occasionally north to camp on the bank of the former. He continued thus into the present state of Kansas, to the source of the Little Osage river, where he camped slightly below the modern town of Little Osage, Vernon Co. Coues, misled by the trail marked on the Nau map, put the camp at the mouth of the Marmiton (page 593 n. 49). This mistake led to others in locating the camps of September 2nd and 3rd, for he deduced them from the mileages, starting with his base point too far east. The Nau map is entirely inaccurate for this stretch. It ran the Little Osage south instead of west, and it promiscuously scattered camp marks along—neither in sufficient number nor in the right places.

September 2. Pike, learning that Chouteau, the trader, had arrived at the villages, rode back to learn the news and to write a scrawl to the general and his friends. His party proceeded without him and encamped at the mouth of the little stream which now comes down from Rinehart, Vernon Co.

That Pike was impressed by the beauty and sublime extent of the prairie is attested by the legends he placed on his chart (No. 30) here: "Prairies boundless in view" and "Prairies which the eye assisted by the best glass could not compass." Pike, although effusive (when he had plenty of leisure), was not poetic. His comparison is hardly Shakespearian, but it does show that he was thrilled, and no ordinary sight thrilled him. The endless prairie at sunrise or sunset is breathtaking. Even soldier Pike, busy and weary with the day's marching and mapping, yielded to it.

2d September, Thursday.—Marched at six o'clock. Halted at ten o'clock, and two o'clock on the side of the creek, our route having been all the time on its borders. Whilst there I was informed by a young Indian that Mr. C. Chouteau had arrived at the towns. I conceived it proper for me to return, which I did, accompanied by Baroney, first to the Little Village; from whence we were accompanied by the *Wind* to the Big Village, where we remained all night at the lodge of the Cheveux Blanche. Mr. Chouteau gave us all the news; after which I scrawled a letter to the general and my friends.

3rd September, Wednesday.—Rose early, and went to the Little Village to breakfast. After giving my letters to Mr. Henry, and arranging my affairs, we proceeded, and overtook our party at two o'clock. They had left their first camp about four miles. Our horses being much fatigued, we concluded

---

September 3. Pike followed the trail of his party and rejoined them just four miles beyond Camp 2 on the bank of a small stream from the south. Coues located this camp in the vicinity of Hoover, a place two miles E of the inter-state line; or miles east of its correct site (page 394 n. 51). As a matter of fact it was considerably past Rinehart, and probably in the vicinity of Hoover, a place 2 miles E of the inter-state line; or perhaps just over this boundary, which here runs on a meridian of longitude (about 94° 37′). When he rested in encampment 3, Pike was in or was about to enter the N E portion of Bourbon County, Kansas, in the vicinity of the villages of Hammond, Fulton, and Barnesville. The two former of these are on the Kansas City, Fort Scott & Gulf R. R. Pike seems to have been about ten miles N N E of Fort Scott, the county seat of Bourbon, built in 1842.

From the point where Pike entered Kansas, it is now possible to trace his route across the present state to a point on the Republican Fork of the Kansas River, very near the middle of the northern boundary of the commonwealth. The task is not easy as has been proven by those who had only the slender threads of Pike's text as a guide. Pike's Indians took him a roundabout way by the Smoky Hill River. The whole country is flat, with a complicated river system. The explorer cut through it, incessantly crossing creeks and rivers, not one of which did he follow for any considerable distance after he left the Osage Basin.

His trace dotted on his map and camp positions are recognizable for the most part. The whole of his Kansan route would have been in the Missouri watershed had it not been for the northward extension of the Arkansas basin in the drainage of the Neosho and Vermilion Rivers. This Pike entered as soon as he left the Osage basin, crossed and quit before reaching the Smoky Hill river. His camp positions show his marches of September 5 to 17 as follows: September 5, on up the Little Osage

to remain all night. Sent out our red and white hunters, all of whom only killed two turkies. Distance 4 miles.

4th September, Thursday.—When about to march in the morning, one of our horses was missing, and we left Sans Oreille, with the two Pawnees, to search for him, and proceeded till about nine o'clock; then stopped until twelve o'clock, and then marched. In about half an hour was overtaken and informed that Sans Oreille had not been able to find our horse; on which we encamped,[71] and sent two horses back for the load. One of the Indians, being jealous of his wife, sent her back to the village. After making the necessary notes, Dr. Robinson and myself took our horses and followed the course of the little stream, until we arrived at the Grand river, which was distant about six miles. We here found a most delightful bason of clear water, of 25 paces diameter and about 100 in circumference, in which we bathed; found it deep and delightfully pleasant. Nature scarcely ever formed a more beautiful place for a farm. We returned to camp about dusk, when I was informed that some of the Indians had been *dreaming* and wished to return. Killed one deer, one turkey, one racoon. Distance 13 miles.

5th September, Friday.—In the morning our Little Osage came to a determination to return, and, much to my surprise, Sans Oreille among the rest! I had given an order on the chiefs for the lost horse to be delivered to Sans Oreille's wife, previously to my knowing that he was going back, but took from him his gun, and the guns from all the others also. In about five miles we struck a beautiful hill, which bears south on the prairie: its elevation I suppose to be 100 feet. From its summit the view is sublime to the east and south-east. We waited on this hill to breakfast, and had to send two

---

River; 6th, over divide to Arkansas waters of the Neosho River; 7th, approaching the Neosho; 8th, across this river; 9th, further along, south of it; 10th, across subdivide of Vermilion river basin; 11th, heading this river and across subdivide into Neosho basin again; 12th, across Cottonwood fork of the Neosho; 14th, further along this fork; 15th, across divide from these Arkansas to Missouri waters again; 16th, nearing Smoky Hill River; 17th, across this river (total distance from the Osage villages about 210 miles; by Pike's mileage of September 1-17, about 250 miles). The Kansas counties crossed were Bourbon, Allen, Woodson, Coffey, Lyon, Chase, Marion, Dickinson, and Saline.

September 6. Yesterday (the 5th) Pike travelled past the present site of Fulton,

miles for water. Killed a deer on the rise, which was soon roasting before the fire. Here another Indian wished to return and take his horse with him, which, as we had so few, I could not allow, for he had already received a gun for the use of his horse. I told him he might return, but his horse would go to the Pawnees. We marched, leaving the Osage trace, which we had hitherto followed, and crossed the hills to a creek which was almost dry. Descended it to the main river, where we dined. The discontented Indian came up, and put on an air of satisfaction and content. We again marched about six miles further, and encamped at the head of a small creek, about a half a mile from water. Distance 19 miles.

6th September, Saturday.—We marched at half past six o'clock and arrived at a large fork of the little Osage river, where we breakfasted. In the holes in the creek we discovered many fish, which, from the stripes on their bellies, and their spots, I supposed to be trout and bass: they were twelve inches long. This brought to mind the necessity of a net, which would have frequently afforded subsistence to the whole party. We halted at one o'clock and remained until four o'clock. Being told that we could not arrive at any water, we here filled our vessels. At five o'clock arrived at the dividing ridge, between the waters of the Osage and Arkansaw (alias White river), the dry branches of which interlock within 20 yards of each other. The prospect from the dividing ridge to the east and south-east is sublime. The prairie rising and falling in regular swells, as far as the sight can extend, produces a very beautiful appearance. We left our course, and struck down to the south-west on a small creek, or rather a puddle of water. Killed one deer. Distance 20 miles.

Bourbon Co. Today he crossed the dividing ridge between the Osage and the Arkansas drainage. Beyond the divide he dropped down to his camp on the upper tributary of Elm Creek, a branch of the Neosho River. The city of Iola, Allen Co., is now in the right angle of the junction of these two streams.

From Camp 6 to the Pawnee Village, Pike's route is difficult to recover (Chart No. 29). The paths followed no stream courses but crossed and recrossed them incessantly, advancing roughly perpendicular to the river system. Again Pike noted the magnificent view. He looked back as he crossed the dividing ridge to see the drab prairie rolling grandly away like the ocean.

7th September, Sunday.—We left this at half past six o'clock, before which we had a difficulty with the son of the chief, which was accommodated. At nine o'clock we came on a large fork and stopped for breakfast. Proceeded on and encamped on a fine stream, where we swam our horses, and bathed ourselves.[72] Killed four deer. Distance 15 miles.

8th September, Monday.—Marched early, and arrived at a grand fork of the White river. The Indians were all discontented: we had taken the wrong ford; but, as they were dispersed through the woods, we could not be governed by their movements. Previously to our leaving the camp, the son of the Cheveux Blanche proposed returning, and offered no other reason than that he felt too lazy to perform the route. The reason I offered to prevent his going was ineffectual, and he departed with his hunter, who deprived us of one horse. His return left us without any chief or man of consideration, except the son of the Belle Oiseau, who was but a lad. The former appeared to be a discontented young fellow, and filled with self pride: he certainly should have considered it as a honor to be sent on so respectable an embassy as he was. Another Indian, who owned one of our horses, wished to return with him, which was positively refused him; but fearing he might steal him, I contented him with a present. We marched, and made the second branch, crossing one prairie twelve miles, in which we suffered much with drought. Distance 22 miles.[73]

9th September, Tuesday.—Marched at seven o'clock, and struck a large creek at eleven miles distance.[74] On holding a council, it was determined to ascend this creek on the highest point of water, and then strike across to a large river of the Arkansaw. We ascended four miles and a half, and encamped.[75] Killed one cabrie [antelope], two deer, two turkies. Distance 12 miles.

10th September, Wednesday.—Marched early. Struck and passed the divide[76] between the *Grand* river and the Verdegris river. Stopped to breakfast on a small stream of the latter; after which we marched and encamped on the fourth small stream.[77] Killed one elk, one deer. Distance 21 miles.

11th September, Thursday.—Passed four branches and over high hilly prairies. Encamped at night on a large branch of Grand river.[78] Killed one cabrie, one deer. Distance 17 miles.

12th September, Friday.—Commenced our march at seven o'clock. Passed very ruff flint hills. My feet blistered and very sore. I stood on a hill, and in one view below me saw buffalo, elk, deer, cabrie, and panthers. Encamped on the main branch of Grand river, which had very steep banks and was deep.[79] Dr. Robinson, Bradley, and Baroney arrived after dusk, having killed three buffalo, which, with one I killed, and two by the Indians, made six; the Indians alledging it was the Kans' hunting-ground, therefore they would destroy all the game they possibly could. Distance 18 miles.

13*th September, Saturday.*—Late in marching, it having every appearance of rain. Halted to dine on a branch of Grand river. Marched again at half past two o'clock, and halted at five, intending to dispatch Dr. Robinson and one of our Pawnees to the village tomorrow. Killed six buffalo, one elk, and three deer. Distance 9 miles.[80]

14*th September, Sunday.*—The doctor and Frank (a young Pawnee) marched for the village at day-light; we at half past six o'clock. Halted at one o'clock. On the march we were continually passing through large herds of buffalo, elk and cabrie; and I have no doubt but one hunter could support 200 men. I prevented the men shooting at the game, not merely because of the scarcity of ammunition, but, as I conceived, the laws of morality forbid it also. Encamped at sunset on the main branch of White river hitherto called Grand river.[81] Killed one buffalo and one cabrie. Distance 21 miles.

15*th September, Monday.*—Marched at seven o'clock passed a very large Kans encampment, evacuated, which had been occupied last summer. Proceeded on to the dividing ridge, between the waters of the White river and the Kans.[82] This ridge was covered with a layer of stone, which was strongly impregnated with iron ore, and on the west side of said ridge we found spa springs. Halted at one' o'clock, very much against the inclination of the Osage, who, from the running of the buffalo, conceived a party of Kans to be near. Killed two buffalo. Distance 18 miles.

16*th September, Tuesday.*—Marched late, and in about four miles and a half distance, came to a very handsome branch of water, at which we stopped and remained until after two o'clock, when we marched and crossed two branches.[83] Encamped on the third. At the second creek a horse was discovered on the prairie, when Baroney went in pursuit of him on a horse of lieutenant Willkinson, but arrived at our camp without success. Distance 13 miles.

17*th September, Wednesday.*—Marched early and struck the main southeast branch of the Kans river:[84] at nine o'clock it appeared to be 25 or 30 yards wide, and is navigable in the flood seasons. We passed it six miles to a small branch to breakfast. Game getting scarce, our provision began to run low. Marched about two o'clock, and encamped at sun-down on a large branch.[85] Killed one buffalo. Distance 21 miles.

18*th September, Thursday.*—Marched at our usual hour, and at twelve o'clock halted at a large branch of the Kans, which was strongly impregnated with salt.[86] This day we expected the people of the village to meet us. We marched again at four o'clock. Our route being over a continued series of hills and hollows, we were until eight at night before we arrived at a small dry branch.[87] It was nearly ten o'clock before we found any water. Commenced raining a little before day. Distance 25 miles.

19*th September, Friday.*—It having commenced raining early, we secured our baggage and pitched our tents. The rain continued without any intermission the whole day, during which we employed ourselves in reading the Bible, Pope's Essays, and in pricking on our arms with India ink *some characters*, which will frequently bring to mind our forlorn and dreary situation, as well as the happiest days of our life. In the rear of our encampment was a hill, on which there was a large rock, where the Indians kept a continual sentinel, as I imagine, to apprise them of the approach of any party, friends or foes, as well as to see if they could discover any game on the prairies.

20*th September, Saturday.*—It appearing as if we possibly might have a clear day, I ordered our baggage spread abroad to dry; but it shortly after clouded up and commenced raining. The Osage sentinel discovered a buffalo on the prairies; upon which we dispatched a hunter on horseback in pursuit of him, also some hunters out on foot, and before night they killed three buffalo, some of the best of which we brought in and jerked or dried by the fire. It continued showery until afternoon, when we put our baggage again in a position to dry, and remained encamped. The detention of the doctor and our Pawnee ambassador began to be a serious matter of consideration.

21*st September, Sunday.*—We marched at eight o'clock, although every appearance of rain, and at eleven o'clock, passed a large creek remarkably salt. Stopped at one o'clock on a fresh branch of the salt creek. Our interpreter having killed an elk, we sent out for some meat, which detained us so late that I concluded it best to encamp where we were, in preference to running the risk of finding no water.[88] Lieutenant Wilkinson was attacked with a severe head head-ache and slight fever. One of my men had been attacked with a touch of the pleurisy on the 18th and was still ill. We were informed by an Osage woman that two of the Indians were conspiring to desert us in the night and steal some of our horses, one of whom was her husband. We engaged her as our spy. Thus were we obliged to keep ourselves on our guard against our own companions and fellow-travellers, men of a nation highly favored by the United States, but whom I believe to be a faithless set of poltrons, incapable of a great and generous action. Among them, indeed, there may be some exceptions.

In the evening, finding that the two Indians above mentioned had made all preparations to depart, I sent for one of them, who owned a horse and had received a gun and other property for his hire, and told him, "I knew his plans, and that if he was disposed to desert, I should take care to retain his horse; that as for himself, he might leave me if he pleased, as I *only* wanted *men* with us." He replied, "that he was a *man*, that he always performed his promises, that he had never said he would return, but that he would follow me to the Pawnee village, which he intended to do." He then brought his baggage and put it under charge of the sentinel, and slept by my fire; but notwithstanding I had him well watched. Killed one elk. Distance 10 miles.

22nd September, Monday.—We did not march until eight o'clock, owing to the indisposition of lieutenant Wilkinson. At eleven waited to dine. Light mists of rain, with flying clouds. We marched again at three o'clock, and continued our route twelve [two] miles to the first branch of the republican fork.[89] Met a Pawnee hunter, who informed us that the chief had left the village the day after the doctor arrived, with 50 or 60 horses and many people, and had taken his course to the north of our route; consequently we had missed each other. He likewise informed that the Tetaus [Comanches] had recently killed six Pawnees, the Kans had stolen some horses, and that a party of 300 Spaniards had lately been as far as the Sabine; but for what purpose unknown. Distance 11 miles.

23rd September, Tuesday.—Marched early and passed a large fork of the Kans river, which I suppose to be the one generally called Solomon's.[90] One of our horses fell into the water and wet his load. Halted at ten o'clock on a branch of this fork. We marched at half past one o'clock, and encamped at sun-down, on a stream where we had a great difficulty to find water. We were overtaken by a Pawnee, who encamped with us. He offered his horse for our use. Distance 21 miles.

24th September, Wednesday.—We could not find our horses until late, when we marched.[91] Before noon met Frank (who had accompanied Doctor Robinson to the village) and three other Pawnees, who informed us that the chief and his party had only arrived at the village yesterday, and had dispatched them out in search of us. Before three o'clock we were joined

PIKE'S DRAWING OF "BLUE MOUNTAIN" (PIKE'S PEAK)
(All who are acquainted with the view of Pike's Peak from the south will
recognize its long, wavy line as here seen from that standpoint. Pike's
drawing is unique and humorous for illustrating a "tenderfoot's" effort to
show the little foothills which obscure the Peak to the nearby spectator. The
artist does not want to neglect them, nor yet allow them to obstruct the
vision. He therefore lets them gently stand aside, to right and left—yet
higher than the Monarch itself!)

Photograph by H. L. Standley
PIKE'S PEAK FROM THE SOUTH
This view shows the intervening foothills which Pike made prominent
in his drawing.

FIG. 5: Pike's Drawing of "Blue Mountain" (Pike's Peak)
(All who are acquainted with the view of Pike's Peak from the south will
recognize its long, wavy line as here seen from that standpoint. Pike's drawing
is unique and humorous for illustrating a "tenderfoot's" effort to show the little
foothills that obscure the Peak to the nearby spectator. The artist does not want
to neglect them, nor yet allow them to obstruct the vision. He therefore lets them
gently stand aside, to right and left—yet higher than the Monarch itself!)

by several Pawnees: one of them wore a scarlet coat, with a small medal of general Washington, and a Spanish medal also. We encamped at sun-set on a middle sized branch, and were joined by several Pawnees in the evening, who brought us some buffalo meat.[92] Here we saw some mules, horses, bridles and blankets, which they obtained of the Spaniards. Few only had *breech cloths*, most being wrapped in buffalo robes, otherwise quite naked. Distance 18 miles.

25th September, Thursday.—We marched at a good hour, and in about eight miles struck a very large road on which the Spanish troops returned and on which we could yet discover the grass beaten down in the direction which they went.

When we arrived within about three miles of the village, we were requested to remain, as the ceremony of receiving the Osage into the towns was to be performed here. There was a small circular spot, clear of grass, before which the Osage sat down. We were a small distance in advance of the Indians. The Pawnees then advanced to within a mile of us, and halted, divided into two troops, and came on each flank at full charge, making all the gestures and performing the manœuvres of a real war charge. They then encircled us around, and the chief advanced in the centre and gave us his hand: his name was *Caracterish*.[93] He was accompanied by his two sons and a chief by the name of *Iksatappe*. The Osage were still seated; but the Belle Oiseau then rose and came forward with a pipe, and presented it to the chief, who took a whiff or two from it. We then proceeded on: the chief, lieutenant Wilkinson and myself in front; my serjeant, on a white horse, next with the colors; then our horses and baggage, escorted by our men, with the Pawnees on each side, running races, &c. When we arrived on the hill over the town we were again halted, and the Osage seated in a row, when each Pawnee who intended so to do presented them with a horse, gave a pipe to smoke to the Osage to whom he had made the present. In this manner were eight horses given. Lieutenant Wilkinson then proceeded on with the party to the river above the town, and encamped. As the chief had invited us to his lodge to eat, we thought it proper for one to go. At the lodge he gave me many particulars which were interesting to us, relative to the late visit of the Spaniards.[94] I went up to our camp in the evening, having a young Pawnee with me loaded with corn for my men. Distance twelve miles.

26th September, Friday.—Finding our encampment not eligible as to situation, we moved down on to the prairie hill,[95] about three-fourths of a mile nearer the village. We sent our interpreter to town to trade for provision. About three o'clock in the afternoon twelve Kans arrived at the village, and informed Baroney that they had come to meet us, hearing we were to be at the Pawnees village. We pitched our camp upon a beautiful eminence, from whence we had a view of the town, and all that was transacting.

In the evening Baroney, with the chief, came to camp to give us the news, and returned together.

27th September, Saturday.—Baroney arrived from the village about one o'clock, with Characterish[96] and three other chiefs, to all of whom we gave a dinner. I then made an appropriate present to each, after which lieutenant Wilkinson and myself accompanied them to town, where we remained a few hours, and returned. Appointed to-morrow for the interview with the Kans and Osage.

28th, September, Sunday.—Held a council of the Kans and Osage, and made them smoke of the pipe of peace. Two of the Kans agreed to accompany us. We received a visit from the chief of the village. Made an observation on an emersion of one of Jupiter's satellites.

29th September, Monday.—Held our grand council with the Pawnees, at which were present not less than 400 warriors, the circumstances of which were extremely interesting. The notes I took on my grand council held with the Pawnee nation were seized by the Spanish government, together with all my speeches to the different nations. But it may be interesting to observe here (in case they should never be returned) that the Spaniards had left several of their flags in this village; one of which was unfurled at the chief's door the day of the grand council, and that amongst various *demands* and *charges* I gave them, was, that the said flag should be delivered to me, and one of the United States flags' to be received and hoisted in its place. This probably was carrying the pride of nations a little too far, as there had so lately been a large force of Spanish cavalry at the village, which had made a great impression on the minds of the young men, as to their power, consequence, &c. which my appearance with 20 infantry was by no means calculated to remove. After the chiefs had replied to various parts of my discourse, but were silent as to the flag, I again reiterated the demand for the flag, "adding that it was impossible for "the nation to have two fathers; that they must either be "the children of the Spaniards or acknowledge their "American father." After a silence of some time, an old man[97] rose, went to the door, and took down the Spanish flag, and brought it and laid it at my feet, and then received the American flag and elevated it on the staff, which had lately borne the standard of his Catholic majesty. This gave great satisfaction to the Osage and Kans, both of whom, decidedly avow themselves to be under the American protection. Perceiving that every face in the council was clouded with sorrow, as if some great national calamity was about to befal them, I took up the contested colors, and told them "that as they had now shewn themselves dutiful children in acknowledging their great American father, I did not wish to embarrass them with the Spaniards, for it was the wish of the Americans that their red brethren should remain peaceably round their own fires, and not embroil themselves in any disputes between the white people: and that for fear the Spaniards might return there in force again. I returned them their flag, but with an injunction that it should never be hoisted during our stay." At this there was a general shout of applause and the charge particularly attended to.

30*th September, Tuesday.*—Remained all day at the camp but sent Baroney to town, who informed me on his return that the chief appeared to wish to throw great obstacles in our way. A great disturbance had taken place in the village, owing to one of the young Pawnees who lately came from the United States, (Frank) having taken the wife of an Osage and ran away with her. The chief, in whose lodge the Osage put up, was extremely enraged, considering it a breach of hospitality to a person under his roof, and threatened to kill Frank if he caught him.

1*st October, Wednesday.*—Paid a visit to town, and had a very long conversation with the chief, who urged every thing in his power to induce us to turn back. Finally, he very candidly told us that the Spaniards wished

---

On this date, Oct. 1st. Lieutenant Pike wrote Secretary of War Dearborn as follows:

Pawnee Republic, 1st Oct., 1806.[98]

SIR,

WE arrived here on the 25th ult. after a tedious march of 375 miles, the distance (as I conceive) being very much augmented by the Osages, who accompanied us, leading us too far to the south, owing to the great fear of the Kans. We suffered considerably with thirst, but our guns furnished us amply with buffalo meat.

We delivered in safety to the chief the two young Pawnees who had

to have gone further into our country, but he induced them to give up the idea—that they had listened to him and he wished us to do the same—that he had promised the Spaniards to act as he now did, and that we must proceed no further, or he must stop us by force of arms. My reply was, "that I had been sent out by our *great father* to explore the western country, to visit all his red children, to make peace between them, and turn them from shedding blood; that he might see how I had caused the Osage and Kans to

---

lately visited Washington, and caused to be explained to the nation, the parole which they bore from the president of the United States.

On our arrival, we found the Spanish and American flags both expanded in the village, and were much surprised to learn, that it was not more than three or four weeks, since a party of Spanish troops (whose number were estimated by the Indians of this town, at 300) had returned to Santa Fe; and further learnt that a large body of troops had left N. Mexico, and on their march had met with the villagers of the Pawnee Mahaws, who were on one of their semi-annual excursions; that they encamped together, and entered into a treaty, but after this the Pawnees raised their camp in the night, and stole a large portion of the Spaniards' horses. This circumstance induced them to halt on the Arkansaw with the main body of the troops, and to send forward the party who appeared at this village; who proposed to this chief to join a party of his warriors to their troops, march to and entirely destroy the village of the Pawnee Mahaws; this proposition he had prudence enough to reject, although at war with that nation. The Spanish officer informed him that his superior, who remained at the Arkansaw, had marched from Santa Fe, with an intention of entering into a treaty with the following nations of Indians, vis: the Kanses, the Pawnee Republic, the Grand Pawnees, Pawnee Loups, Otos, and Mahaws; and had with him a grand medal, commissions, and four mules for each; but by the stroke of the Pawnee Mahaws, the plan was disconcerted, except only as to this nation. The commissions are dated Santa Fe, 15th June 1806, and signed governor general, &c. &c. of New Mexico, and run in the usual style of Spanish commissions to savages, as far as I was capable of judging of their contents.

The chief further informed me, that the officer who commanded said party, was too young to hold councils, &c. that he had *only* come to open the road, but that in the spring his superior would be here, and teach the Indians what was good for them; and that they would build a

meet to smoke the pipe of peace together, and take each other by the hands like brothers; that as yet my road had been smooth, and a blue sky over our heads. I had not seen any blood in our paths; but he must know that the young warriors of his *great American father were not women* to be turned back by *words,* that I should therefore proceed, and if he thought proper to stop me, he could attempt it; but we were *men,* well armed, and would *sell our lives* at a dear rate to his nation—that we knew our *great father* would

---

town near them. In short, it appears to me to have been an expedition expressly for the purpose of striking a dread into those different nations of the Spanish power, and to bring about a general combination in their favor. Under these impressions, I have taken the earliest opportunity of reporting the infringement of our territory, in order that our government may not remain in the dark, as to the views of her neighbor. I effected a meeting at this place, between a few Kans and Osages, who smoked the pipe of peace and buried the hatchet, agreeably to the wishes of their great father; in consequence of which a Kans has marched for the Osage nation, and some of the latter propose to accompany the former to their village; whether this good understanding will be permanent, I will not take on me to determine; but at least, a temporary good effect has succeeded. From the Osage towns, I have taken the course and distances, by the route we came, marking each river or rivulet we crossed, pointing out the dividing ridges, &c. The waters which we crossed, were the head of the [Little] Osage, White [Neosho], and Verdigrise rivers, (branches of the Arkansaw) and the waters of the [Smoky Hill fork of the] Kans river. The latitude of this place, I presume, will be in about 39° 30′ N. and I hope to obtain every other astronomical observation, which will be requisite to fix its geographical situation beyond dispute. I expect to march from here in a few days, but the future prospects of the voyage are entirely uncertain, as the savages strive to throw every impediment in our way, agreeably to the orders received from the Spaniards. Being seated on the ground, and writing on the back of a book, I hope will plead my excuse for this scrawl.

I am, sir

With high respect,

Your obedient servant,

(Signed)   Z. M. Pike, Lt.

The hon. Henry Dearborn,
Secretary war department.

send our young warriors there to gather our bones and revenge our *deaths* on his people—when our spirits would rejoice in hearing our exploits sung in the war songs of our chiefs." I then left his lodge and returned to camp in considerable perturbation of mind.

2d October, Thursday.—We received advice from our Kans that the chief had given publicity to his idea of stopping us by force of arms, which gave serious reflections to me, and was productive of many singular expressions from my brave lads, which called for my esteem at the same time

---

Pike's letter to Wilkinson read:

Pawnee Republic, 2d Oct., 1806.[99]

DEAR GENERAL,

INCLOSED you have a copy of my letter from this place, to the secretary of war, in order, that should you think any communication on the contents necessary, you may have a perfect command of the information given the war department, and will be the more capable of illustrating the subject.

You will perceive by said communication, that we were led considerably out of our course by our guides, and in my opinion not less than 100 miles; this was entirely owing to the pusillanimity of the Osage, who were more afraid of the Kans, than I could possibly have imagined.

You will likewise perceive the council which took place between those nations (under our auspices) and its effects, but which I candidly confess, I have very little hopes will be productive of a permanent peace, as none of the principal men of either nation were present; but as both are anxious for a cessation of hostilities perhaps it may have the desired effect.

Two of the Kans chiefs have said they will pursue the voyage with me agreeably to my orders; I do not yet know whether they will descend the Arkansaw with lieut. Wilkinson, or continue on to Red river with me, but they have their own selection.

The general will no doubt be struck with some surprize, to perceive that so large a party of the Spanish troops have been so lately in our territory; no doubt at first you would conclude that it must have been militia; but when informed that their infantry was armed with muskets and bayonets, and had drums; that the men wore long mustaches and whiskers, which almost covered the whole of their faces; their cavalry armed with

that they excited my laughter. Attempted to trade for horses but could not succeed. In the night we were alarmed by some savages coming near our camp in full speed, but they retreated equally rapid, on being hailed with fierceness by our sentinels. This created some degree of indignation in my little band, and as we had noticed that all the day had passed without any traders presenting themselves, which appeared as if all intercourse was interdicted!! Writing to the secretary of war [pp. 115-117], the general &c.

---

swords and pistols, and that regular guards and patroles were kept by horse and foot, you may probably change your opinion.

The route by which they came, and returned, was by no means the direct one from Santa Fe, and why they should have struck so low down as the Grand Saline, unless they had an idea of striking at the village of the *Grand Pest:* or conceived the Saline in their territory, I cannot imagine.

On our arrival here, we were received with great pomp and ceremony, by about 300 men on horseback, and with great apparent friendship by the chief. The Osage (one chief and four warriors) were presented with eight horses, the Kans who arrived two days after, were also presented with horses. The day after, we assembled the four principal chiefs to dine, after which I presented the principal, with a double-barrel'd gun, gorget [ornamental neckband), and other articles, (this man wore the grand Spanish medal) and to the second the small medal you furnished me, with other articles; and to each of the others a gorget in their turn. Those presents I conceived would have a good effect, both as to attaching them to our government, and in our immediate intercourse.

At the council which was held a day or two afterwards, I presented them with merchandize (which at this place should be valued at $250) and after explaining their relative situation as to the Spanish and American governments, I asked on my part, *if they would assist us with a few horses,* a Tetau prisoner *who spoke Pawnee, to serve as an interpreter, an exchange of colors; and finally, for some of their chiefs to accompany us, to be sent to Washington.* The exchange of colors was the only request granted at the time; and for particular reasons (which lieut. Wilkinson related) I thought proper to return them to the chief; and after spending two or three anxious days, we were given to understand, that our requests could not be complied with in the other points, and were again strongly urged by the

3d October, Friday.—The intercourse again commenced. Traded for some horses. Writing for my express.

4th October, Saturday.—Two French traders arrived at the village in order to procure horses to transport their goods from the Missouri to the village. They gave us information that *captains Lewis and Clark*, with all

---

head chief, to return the way we came, and not prosecute our voyage any further; this brought on an explanation as to our views towards the Spanish government; in which the chief declared, that it was the intention of the Spanish troops to have proceeded further towards the Mississippi, but, that he objected to it, and they listened to him and returned; he therefore hoped we would be equally reasonable; but finding I still determined on proceeding, he told me in plain terms (if the interpreter erred not) that it was the *will of the Spaniards we should not proceed;* which not *answering,* he painted innumerable difficulties which he said lay in the way; but finding all his arguments had *no effect,* he said, "It was a pity," and was silent.

This day I sent out several of my party to purchase horses, but know not yet how we shall succeed, as the Kans have intimated an idea, that the chief will prohibit his people from trading with us.

The Pawnees and the Tetaus are at war; the latter killed six of the former in August last, consequently the effecting any communication with the Tetaus by means of this nation is impossible.

If God permits, we shall march from here in a few days, and at the Arkansaw I shall remain, until I build two small canoes for lieut. W.[ilkinson], (whose party will consist of Ballenger and two or three men, with three Osage). Those canoes will be easily managed, and in case of accident to one, the other will still be sufficient to transport their baggage.

I am informed, that in a few days he [Wilkinson] will meet French hunters, and probably arrive at the village of the *Grand Pest* in a fortnight; and as all the Osage nation are apprized of his descent, I conceive he will meet with no insurmountable difficulties.[100] The Tetaus are at open war with the Spaniards, so that could we once obtain an introduction, I conceive we should meet with a favorable reception. Yet how it is to be brought about, I am much at a loss to determine, but knowing that, at this *crisis* of *affairs,* an intimate connection with that nation, might be extremely serviceable to my *country,* I shall proceed to *find* them; in hopes

their people, had descended the river to St. Louis: this diffused general joy through our party. Our trade for horses advanced none this day.

5th October, Sunday.—Buying horses, preparing to march, and finishing my letters.

---

to find some means through the French, Osage and Pawnee languages, of making ourselves understood.

Any number of men (who may reasonably be calculated on) would find no difficulty in marching the route we came with baggage wagons, field artillery, and all the usual appendages of a small army; and if all the route to Santa Fe should be of the same description in case of war, I would pledge my life (and what is infinitely dearer, my honor) for the successful march of a reasonable body of troops, into the province of New Mexico.

I find the savages of this country less brave; but possessing much more duplicity, and by far a greater propensity to lying and stealing, then those I had to pass through in my last [Mississippi] voyage.

I am extremely doubtful if any chief of those nations, can be induced to prosecute the voyage with us, as their dread of the Tetaus, and the objections of the Pawnees, seems to outweigh every argument, and inducement to the contrary.

3d October—The Pawnee chief has induced the Kans to return to their villages, by giving them a gun and promising horses, with many frightful pictures drawn if they proceeded.

The Osages lent me five horses, which their people who had accompanied us were to have led back, but receiving fresh ones from the Pawnees, they would not be troubled with them. In fact, it was a fortunate circumstance, as four of the horses I obtained of the Osage, have such bad backs, they cannot proceed, and we will be obliged to leave them; and not purchasing here with facility, I would have been obliged to sacrifice some of our baggage. I therefore sent them a certificate for each horse, on the Indian agent below, which I hope the general will order him to discharge.

I know the general's goodness will excuse this scrawl, as he is well acquainted with the situation it must be written in, and at the same time, believe me to be his sincere friend and

Most obedient

Humble servant,

(Signed)   Z. M. PIKE, Lt.

General J. Wilkinson.

6*th October, Monday.*—Marched my express. Purchasing horses and preparing to march on the morrow.

7*th October, Tuesday.*—In the morning found two of our newly purchased horses missing. Sent in search of them: the Indians brought in one pretty early. Struck our tents and commenced loading our horses. Finding there was no probability of our obtaining the other lost one, we marched at two P. M. and as the chief had threatened to stop us by force of arms, we had made every arrangement to make him pay as dear for the attempt as possible. The party was kept compact, and marched on by a road round the village, in order that if attacked the savages would not have their houses to fly to for cover. I had given orders not to fire until within five or six paces, and then to charge with the bayonet and sabre, when I believe it would have cost them at least 100 men to have exterminated us (which would have been necessary) the village appeared all to be in motion. I galloped up to the lodge of the chief, attended by my interpreter and one soldier, but soon saw there was no serious attempt to be made, although many young men were walking about with their bows, arrows, guns and lances. After speaking to the chief with apparent indifference, I told him that I calculated on his justice in obtaining the horse, and that I should leave a man until the next day at 12 o'clock to bring him out. We then joined the party and pursued our route: when I was once on the summit of the hill which overlooks the village, I felt my mind as if relieved from a heavy burthen, yet all the evil I wished the *Pawnees* was that I might be the instrument in the hands of our government, to open their *ears* and *eyes* with a *strong hand*, to convince them of our power. Our party now consisted of two officers, one doctor, 18 soldiers, one interpreter, three Osage men and one woman, making 25 warriors. We marched out and encamped on a small branch, distant seven miles, on the same route we came in.[101] Rain in night.

8*th October, Wednesday.*—I conceived it best to send Baroney back to the village with a present, to be offered for our horse, the chief having suggested the propriety of the measure; he met his son and the horse with Sparks. Marched at ten o'clock, and at four o'clock came to the place where the Spanish troops encamped the first night they left the Pawnee village.[102] Their encampment was circular, and having only small fires round the circle to cook by. We counted 59 fires, now if we allowed six men to each fire, they must have been 354 in number. . . . We encamped in a large branch of the second fork of the Kans river.[103] Distance 18 miles.

9th October, Thursday.—Marched at eight o'clock, being detained until that time by our horses being at a great distance. At eleven o'clock we found the forks of the Spanish and Pawnee roads, and when we halted at twelve o'clock, we were overtaken by the second chief (or Iskatappe) and the American chief with one-third of the village. They presented us with a piece of bear meat. When we were about to march, we discovered that the dirk of the doctor had been stolen from behind his saddle; after marching the men the doctor and myself, with the interpreter, went to the chief and "demanded that he should cause a search to be made;" it was done, but when the dirk was found, the possessor asserted that he had found it on the road; I told him "that he did not speak the truth," and informed the chief that we never suffered a thing of ever so little value to be taken without liberty. At this time the prairie was covered with his men, who began to encircle us around, and lieutenant Wilkinson with the troops had gained half a mile on the road. The Indian demanded a knife before he would give it up, but as we refused to give any, the chief took one from his belt and gave him, took the dirk and presented it to the doctor, who immediately returned it to the chief as a present, and desired Baroney to inform him he now saw it was not the value of the *article* but the act we despise, and then galloped off. In about a mile we discovered a herd of elk which we pursued; they took back in sight of the Pawnees, who immediately mounted 50 or 60 young men and joined in the pursuit; then for the first time in my life, I saw animals slaughtered by the true savages, with their original weapons, bows and arrows; they buried the arrow up to the plume in the animal. We took a piece of meat and pursued our party: we overtook them and encamped within the Grand or Solomon Fork, which we crossed on the 23d September, (lower down) on our route to the Pawnees.[104] This was the Spanish encamping ground. In the evening two Pawnees came to our camp, who had not eaten for three days, two of which they had carried a sick companion whom they had left that day; we gave them supper, some meat and corn, and they immediately departed in order to carry their sick companion this seasonable supply. When they were coming into camp, the centinel challenged, it being dark; they immediately (on seeing him bring his piece to the charge) supposing he was about to fire on them, advanced to give him their hands, he, however, not well discerning their motions, was on the point of firing, but being a cool collected little fellow, called out that there were two Indians advancing on him, and [asking] if he should fire; this brought out the guard, when the poor affrighted savages were brought into camp, very much alarmed, for they had not heard of a white man's being within their country, and thought they were entering one of the camps of their own people. Distance 18 miles.

10*th October, Friday.*—Marched at seven o'clock and halted at twelve o'clock to dine. Were overtaken by the Pawnee chiefs, whose party we left the day before; who informed us the hunting party had taken another road, and that he had come to bid us good-by. We left a large ridge on our left, and at sun-down crossed it. . . . [105] From this place we had an extensive view of the southwest: we observed a creek at a distance, for which I meant to proceed. The doctor, interpreter, and myself, arrived at eight o'clock at night; found water and wood, but had nothing to eat.[106] Kindled a fire in order to guide the party, but they not being able to find the route, and not knowing the distance, encamped on the prairie without wood or water.

11*th October, Saturday.*—Ordered Baroney to return to find the party and conduct them to our camp. The doctor and myself went out to hunt, and on our return found all our people had arrived, except the rear guard, which was in sight. Whilst we halted five Pawnees came to our camp and brought some bones of a horse which the Spanish troops had been obliged to eat, at their encampment on this creek; we took up our line of march at twelve o'clock, and at sun-down the party halted on the saline.[107] I was in pursuit of buffalo and did not make the camp until near ten o'clock at night. Killed one buffalo. Distance 12 miles.

12*th October, Sunday.*—Here the Belle Oiseau and one Osage left us, and there remained only one man and woman of that nation—their reason for leaving us was that our course bore too much west, and they desired to bear more for the hunting ground of the Osage. In the morning sent out to obtain the buffalo meat, and laid by until after breakfast. Proceeded at eleven o'clock, and crossing the river two or three times, we passed two camps where the Spanish troops had halted. Here they appeared to have remained some days, their roads being so much blended with the traces of the buffalo that we lost them entirely. This was a mortifying stroke, as we had reason to calculate, that they had good guides, and were on the best route for wood and water. We took a south-west direction, and before night, were fortunate enough to strike their roads on the left, and at dusk, much to our surprise, struck the east fork of the Kans or La Touche de la Cote Bucanieus.[108] Killed one buffalo. Distance 18 miles.

13th October, Monday.—The day being rainy, we did not march until two o'clock, when it having an appearance of clearing off, we raised our camp, after which we marched seven miles and encamped on the head of a branch of the river we left.[109] Had to go two miles for water. Killed one cabrie.

14th October, Tuesday.—It having drizzled rain all night, and the atmosphere being entirely obscured, we did not march until a quarter past nine o'clock, and commenced crossing the dividing ridge between the Kans and Arkansaw rivers. Arrived on a branch of the latter at one o'clock; continued down it in search of water, until after dusk, when we found a pond on the prairie, which induced us to halt.[110] Sparks did not come up, being scarcely able to walk with rheumatic pains. Wounded several buffalo, but could get none of them. Distance 24 miles.

15th October, Wednesday.—In the morning road out in search of the south trace, and crossed the low prairie, which was nearly all covered with ponds,[111] but could not discover it. Finding Sparks did not arrive, sent two men in search of him, who arrived with him about eleven o'clock. At twelve o'clock we commenced our line of march, and at five o'clock, Dr. Robinson and myself left the party at a large creek[112] (having pointed out a distant wood to lieutenant Wilkinson for our encampment) in order to search some distance up it for the Spanish trace. Killed two buffalo and left part of our clothing with them, to scare away the wolves. Went in pursuit of the party. On our arrival at the creek appointed for the encampment, did not find them. Proceeded down it for some miles, and not finding them, encamped, struck fire, and then supped on one of our buffalo tongues.

16th October, Thursday.—Early on horseback; proceeded up the creek some distance in search of our party, but at twelve o'clock crossed to our two buffaloes; found a great many wolves at them, notwithstanding the precaution taken to keep them off. Cooked some marrow bones and again mounted our horses, and proceeded down the creek to their junction. Finding nothing of the party, I began to be seriously alarmed for their safety. Killed two more buffalo, and made our encampment and feasted sumptuously on the marrow bones. Rain in the night.

17th October, Friday.—Rose early, determining to search the creek to its source. Very hard rain, accompanied by a cold north-west all day. Encamped near night without being able to discover any signs of the party. Our sensations now became excruciating, not only for their personal safety, but the fear of the failure of the national objects intended to be accomplished by the expedition;[113] and our own situation was not the most agreeable, not having more than four rounds of ammunition each, and 400 miles in the nearest direction from the first civilized inhabitant; we, however, concluded to search for them on the morrow, and if we did not succeed in finding them, to strike the Arkansaw, where we were in hopes to discover some traces, if not cut off by the savages.

18th October, Saturday.—Commenced our route at a good time, and about ten o'clock, discovered two men on horse-back in search of us, (one my waiter;) they informed us the party was encamped on the Arkansaw, about three miles south of where we then were: this surprised us very much as we had no conception of that river being so near. On our arrival were met by lieutenant Wilkinson, who with all the party was greatly concerned for our safety. The Arkansaw, on the party's arrival, had not water in it six inches deep, and the stream was not more than 20 feet wide, but the rain of the two days covered all the bottom of the river, which in this place is 450 yards from bank to bank, which are not more than four feet in height, bordered by a few cotton-wood trees on the north side by a low swampy prairie, on the south by a sandy sterile desert at a small distance.[114] In the afternoon the doctor and myself took our horses and crossed the Arkansaw, in order to search for some trees which might answer the purpose to make canoes; found but one and returned at dusk. It commenced raining at 12 o'clock at night.

19th October, Sunday.—Finding the river rising rapidly, I thought it best to secure our passage over, we consequently made it good by ten o'clock, A. M. Rain all day. Preparing our tools and arms for labor and the chase on the morrow.

20th October, Monday.—Commenced our labor at two trees for canoes, but one proved too much doated. . . . Killed two buffalo and one cabrie. Discharged our guns at a mark, the best shot a prize of one tent and a pair of shoes. Our only dog was standing at the root of the tree, in the grass, and one of the balls, struck him on the head and killed him. Ceased raining about 12 o'clock.

21st October, Tuesday.—Doctor Robinson and myself mounted our horses, in order to go down the river to the entrance of the three last creeks, we had crossed on our rout, but meeting with buffalo, we killed four; also, one cabrie. Returned to camp and sent for the meat.

22nd October, Wednesday.—Having sat up very late last evening, expecting the sergeant, and party (who did not arrive) we were very anxious for them, but about 10 o'clock Bradley arrived and informed us, that they could not find the buffalo, which we had killed on the prairie, they all arrived before noon, and in the afternoon we scaffolded some meat and nearly compleated the frame of a skin Canoe, which we concluded to build; overhauled my instruments and made some rectifications preparatory to taking an observation &c.

23rd October, Thursday.—Dr. Robinson and myself, accompanied by one man, ascended the river with an intention of searching the Spanish trace; at the same time, we dispatched *Baroney* and our two hunters to kill some buffalo, to obtain the skins for canoes. We ascended the river, about 20 miles to a large branch on the right; just at dusk gave chase to a buffalo and was obliged to shoot nineteen balls into him, before we killed him. Encamped in the fork.

24th October, Friday.—We assended the right branch about five miles, but could not see any sign of the Spanish trace; this is not surprizing, as the river bears south west, and they no doubt kept more to the west from the head of one branch to another. We returned and on our way, killed some prairie squirrels or wishtonwishes, and nine large rattle snakes, which frequent their villages.[115] On our arrival, found the hunters had come in a boat, one hour, with two buffalo and one elk skin.

The letters of Pike and Wilkinson written here on the Arkansas follow:

[PIKE TO GENERAL WILKINSON][116]

Arkansaw, 24th Oct. 1806. *Latitude* 37° 44′ 9′′ *N.*

DEAR GENERAL,

OUR party arrived here on the 15th inst. myself and Dr. Robinson on the 19th, [18th] we having been out to seek the trace of the Spanish troops missed the party, and were not able to join them until the 4th [3rd] day.

The river being very regular, lieut. Wilkinson had calculated to proceed on the day following, on the most direct route for the Red river,[117] but shortly after my joining, a considerable rain fell and raised the river, and we have been ever since preparing wooden and skin canoes, for that gentleman and party to descend in.

The river is between three and four hundred yards in width; generally flat low banks, not more than two or three feet high, and the bed a sand bank from one side to the other.

25th October, Saturday.—Took an observation, passed the day in writing, and preparing for the departure of Lt. Wilkinson.

26th October, Sunday.—Delivered out a ration of corn by way of distinction of the Sabbath. Preparing for our departure.

The want of water will present the greatest obstacle to the progress of the party who descend the Arkansaw, as they have no cause to fear a scarcity of provision, having some bushels of corn on hand, and at their option to take as much dried meat as they think proper, hundreds of pounds of which are lying on scaffolds at our camp; and they are likewise accompanied by the choice of our hunters.

Under those circumstance, and those stated in my letter from the Pawnees, I can assert with confidence, there are no obstacles I should hesitate to encounter, although those inseparable from a voyage of several hundred leagues through a wilderness inhabited only by savages, may appear of the greatest magnitude to minds unaccustomed to such enterprizes.

Lieut. Wilkinson and party appear in good spirits, and shew a disposition which must vanquish every difficulty.

We were eight days travelling from the Pawnee village to the Arkansaw, (our general course S. 10° W.) several of which we lay by nearly half, owing to various circumstances: my course made it 150 miles, but could now march it in 120. Lieut. Wilkinson has copied and carries with him a very elegant protracted sketch of the route, noting the streams, hills, &c. that we crossed; their courses, bearings, &c. and should I live to arrive, I will pledge myself to shew their connexions, and general direction with considerable accuracy, as I have myself spared no pains in reconnoitering or obtaining information from the savages in our route.

From this point, we shall ascend the river until we strike the mountains, or find the Tetaus; and from thence bear more to the S. until we find the head of the *Red river,*[118] where we shall be detained for some time, after which nothing shall cause a halt until my arrival at Natchitoches.

I speak in all those cases in the positive mood, as, so far as lies in the compass of human exertions, we command the power; but I pretend not to surmount impossibilities, and I well know the general would pardon my anticipating a little to him.

The general will probably be surprized to find that the expences of the expedition will more than double the contemplated sum of our first calculations; but I conceived, the Spaniards were making such great exertions

27th October, Monday.—Delivered to lieutenant Wilkinson, letters for the general and our friends, with other papers, consisting of his instructions, traverse table of our voyage and a draught of our route, to that place complete; in order that if we were lost, and he arrived in safety; we might not

---

to debauch the minds of our savages, economy might be very improperly applied. And I likewise have found the purchase of horses to be attended with much greater expence than was expected at St. Louis. Those reasons, and when I advert to the expences of my two voyages, (which I humbly conceive might be compared with the one performed by captains Lewis and Clark) and the appropriations made for *theirs,* I feel a consciousness, that it is impossible for the most rigid to censure my accounts.[119]

I cannot yet say if I shall sacrifice my horses at Red River, but every exertion shall be made to save them for the public; some if in good condition would be fine ones, and average between fifty and sixty dollars. Should the fortune of war at length have honored me with a company, I hope the general will recollect his promise to me, and have my command attached to it; and on my arrival I shall take the liberty of soliciting his influence, that they may obtain the same, or similar rewards, to those who accompanied capt. Lewis, as I will make bold to say, that they have in the two voyages, incurred as great dangers, and gone through as many hardships.

I am, dear general,
Your ever attached friend,
And obedient servant,

(Signed)   Z. M. PIKE.

General J. Wilkinson.

N.B. Dr. Robinson presents his respectful compliments, and is sanguine in the success of our expedition.

[LIEUTENANT WILKINSON TO GENERAL WILKINSON][120]

Arkansaw River
27th Oct. 06.

My dear Parent,

In a few moments I enter by skin canoe to descend the river, and part with Mr. Pike—the prospect is not as favorable as I would wish, but as

have made the tour, without some benefit to our country. He took with him in corn and meat, 21 days provisions, and all the necessary tools, to build canoes or cabbins. Launched his canoes. We concluded, we would separate in the morning. He to descend and we to ascend to the mountains.

28*th October, Tuesday.*—As soon as possible, all was in motion, my party crossing the river to the north side, and lieutenant Wilkinson, launching his canoes of skins and wood. We breakfasted together, and then filed off; but I suffered my party to march, and I remained to see lieutenant Wilkinson

---

the Season of the year will admit; and I look forward to a pleasant voyage, tho it may be a tedious one, however I shall have the Satisfaction of handing you a correct survey of the Arkansaw and its waters.

My health is perfectly good, and my greatest care shall be to preserve it. I may now and then be a little wet, but I have a large store of thick winter cloathing, and a warm Tent. My coffee and tea is still on hand, as are all my herbs and medicines, none of which I have as yet used.

You must not look for me Till spring, as I am determined to acquire information of the country adjacent to the river.

Believe me your dutiful and affect. Son

James (rubric).

General Wilkinson.
[Addressed:] General or M^s. Wilkinson
for Lieut. Pike.   Natchitoches

[LIEUTENANT WILKINSON TO GENERAL WILKINSON][121]

Please to ask Mr. Pike for a Letter
I wrote him on the 27th relative to
the command

Arkansaw River
28th Oct. o6—
N.L. 37° 44′ 25″—

My Dear Sir,

I am now about undertaking a voyage, perhaps more illy equipd than any other Officer, who ever was on command, in point of stores, amunition, Boats and men.

sail, which he did at ten o'clock, having one skin canoe, made of four buffalo skins and two elk skins; this held three men besides himself and one
Osage. In his wooden canoe, were, one soldier, one Osage and their baggage; one other soldier marched on shore. We parted with "God bless you"
from both parties; they appeared to sail very well. In the pursuit of our
party, Doctor Robinson, Baroney, one soldier and myself, killed a brelau
and a buffalo, of the latter we took only his marrow bones and liver. Arrived
where our men had encamped, about dusk.[122] Distance 14 miles.

I have a small skin canoe, of 10 feet in length, with a wooden one of
the same length capable to carry one man and his baggage—not more I
believe. I have 5 men, whose strength is insufficient to draw up my skin
canoe to dry—and which must necessarily spoil. I have no grease to pay
the seams of my canoe, and was obliged to use my candles, mixd with
ashes, for the purpose. My men have no winter cloathing, and two of
them no Blankets. I must necessarily have the men wading half the day,
as the water opposite here is not ankle deep. I shall pass the Republican
pawnees, the most rascally nation I know—and perhaps meet with the
Pawnee pickeés a nation of whom I have considerable apprehension—and
meet in the course of 6 or 7 weeks the Osages and Arkansaws.

If I cannot proceed after I march Ten or Twelve days down, I shall
cross to the Kanses, or Osages, who hunt on the streams of the Arkansaw
and winter with them.

The river is now full of ice, so much so that I dare not put in my
canoes—last night we had a considerable fall of snow. I asked only for 6
men and could not get them.

Believe me, that I sacredly write the truth, with a coolness and deliberation I never before have done, and Believe
me Your sincerely affectionate, tho
Unhappy Son,
James B. Wilkinson (rubric).

[On the back of the letter:]
Lt. Pike will please to give this to
the Genl. only

General James Wilkinson.
Natchitoches
For Lt. Pike

29*th October, Wednesday.*—Marched after breakfast and in the first hours march, passed two fires, where twenty one Indians had recently encamped, in which party (by their paintings on the rocks) there were seven guns.[123] Killed a buffalo, halted, made fire and feasted on the choice pieces of meat. About noon discovered two horses feeding with a herd of buffalo; we attempted to surround them, but they soon cleared our fleetest coursers. One appeared to be an elegant horse; these were the first wild horses we had seen. Two or three hours before night, struck the Spanish road; and, as it was snowing, halted and encamped the party at the first woods on the bank of the river. The doctor and myself then forded it (the ice running very quick) in order to discover the course the Spaniards took, but owing to the many buffalo roads, could not ascertain it; but it evidently appeared that they

[LIEUTENANT WILKINSON TO LIEUTENANT PIKE][124]

Arkansaw River
Dr Sir,   26th Oc'tr 1806.
Your instructions relating to my descent of the Arkansaw, have been perused with attention, and as far as is in my power and the means given me shall strictly be complied with.

Before we separate and perhaps for ever, I have taken the liberty to propose a few questions, relative to the Equipment, and the *Command* you have given me. If you should think this a freedom, inconsistent with the principles of Subordination, or unprecedented, you will please to excuse the error and attribute it to ignorance, not to a want of respect for your Opinion, but to a want of confidence in my own.

1:st Whether do you consider my strength sufficient to enforce a due respect for our national Flag, from the many nations of Savages, I must necessarily meet on the voyage—Or,

2. Whether if an appeal to arms is requisite to repel an outrage offered, the efficient force of the Command would enable me to effect it? I speak of an outrage of a few,—for were many to make the attack, the consequence is obvious. OR,

3. Whether greater danger is not to be apprehended from the *Pawnee Pickeés* than any other Nation of Savages in *Louisiana,* not only owing

had waited here some time, as the ground was covered with horse dung, for miles around.[125] Returned to camp. The snow fell about two inches deep and then it cleared up. Distance 12 miles.

30th October, Thursday.—In the morning sent out to kill a buffalo, to have his marrow bones for breakfast, which was accomplished; after breakfast the party marched upon the north side, and the doctor and myself crossed with considerable difficulty (on account of the ice) to the Spanish camp, where we took a large circuit in order to discover the Spanish trace and came in at a point of woods; south of the river, where we found our party encamped. We discovered also that the Spanish troops had marked the river up,[126] and that a party of savages had been there not more than three days before. Killed two buffalo. Distance 4 miles.

---

to their intercourse with the Mexicans proper, *but to their friendship* for the Spaniards, *who have regular Factors amongst* them, and whose interest it is, to keep us in ignorance of the intrinsic value of the Salines of the Arkansaw—and which nation I must pass, and may probably see—Or

4. Whether greater danger is not to be apprehended from the meeting *with stragling bands of different nations, inimical to each other, and coursing a tract of country, through which they always make their hostile Sallies,* then meeting a Grand and powerful Nation, within its own undisputed Territory, and headed by its Chieftan.

The Pusilanimity of the Republican Pawnees is so well known, that no confidence can be placed in them, and should I meet any of that Nation, I shall calculate their purpose to be villanous and take measures accordingly.

I am of the Opinion that a traverse of the Arkansaw, and a Geographical sketch of the adjacent country, is an object of as much importance to our Executive, as one of Red River, its confluent streams and country, and at the other present moment perhaps more so, as Cap. Sparks and other Officers have ascended to its Source, or are now making the Survey.

To comply with the wish, intention, spirit and letter of the Generals order and your own, I cannot hurry down the river, without making the required observations; but the quantity of *Public ammunition allowed* me, renders it indispensably necessary to use every exertion to expedite

31*st October, Friday*.—Fine day—marched at three quarters past nine o'clock, on the Spanish road. Encamped, sun an hour high, after having made sixteen miles.[127] We observed this day a species of chrystilization on the road (when the sun was high) in low places where there had been water settled, on tasting it found it to be salt; this gave in my mind some authenticity to the report of the prairie being covered for leagues. Discovered the trace of about twenty savages who had followed our road; and horses going down the river. Killed one buffalo, one elk, one deer.

---

my progress. If any accident should happen to my *shackling* and *patched canoes*, could I form an other with a *common felling ax, and hatchet*, so as to take advantage of the present rise of the water—and what shelter would I have to protect my men from the weather, in case I should winter on the river. You will pardon me Sir, when I say, Justice would *give 5 men one Tent*, in preference to giving 13 men three, when 12 are allowed 2 only.

You will excuse me Sir, when I observe, that your reflections, when at the source of red river, would be more pleasant, when you considered, that by the gift of a *Broad ax, adz and drawing knife* (of which you have two and *more setts*) you prevented a Friend and Brother soldiers wintering without stores or anything comfortable, altho you might be detained a few days longer, than you would, had you refused those articles. I will conclude with observing, that if you *would add Stout* to my command (who you informed me is a ruff carpenter) I should not anticipate the difficulties I now do, or dread wintering without cabbins, and should feel satisfied within my own mind of the possibility of effecting every thing required.

For the many marks of Friendship I have experienced during our march, receive Sir my most sincere thanks, and wishes for your happiness and prosperity.

With Sentiments of high respect, esteem and attachment
I remain
Your obd. Ser[i].

Lieut. Z. M. Pike   James B. Wilkinson Lt. (rubric).

1st November, Saturday.—Marched early, just after commencing our line, heard a gun on our left; the doctor, Baroney and myself being in advance, and laying on the ground waiting for the party; a band of Cabrie came up, amongst our horses, to satisfy their curiosity; we could not resist the temptation of killing two, although we had plenty of meat. At the report of the gun they appeared astonished, and stood still until we hallowed at them to drive them away. Encamped in the evening on an island,[128] upon using my glass to observe the adjacent country, I observed on the prairie a herd of horses;

[On the back of this letter is the following:]

On the Inclosed letter I will only remark that I furnished a Tent, Broad Ax, Adz and Drawing Knife and that Lt. Wilkinson had with him 19 lb powder 39 lb Lead and Ball, with 4 Doz. Cartridges, when my whole party had not more than 35 lb of powder, 40 lb of Lead and 10 Doz Cartridges;[129] also that one of his men was a Carpenter by profession and another a mill wright. As to His observations as it respects the Indians, they require a different Notice.

Pike.

[Address:]   Lieut. Z. M. Pike
Present.

The parties which now separate consist of Wilkinson's detachment of six, namely, Wilkinson, Ballanger, Boley, Bradley, Huddleston and Wilson, and Pike's party of sixteen; the role of that party reads:

Z. M. Pike	John H. Robinson
William E. Meek	John Brown
John Sparks	Jeremiah Jackson
Jacob Carter	Thomas Dougherty
William Gorden	Patrick Smith
Baroney Vasquez	Theodore Miller
Hugh Menaugh	John Mountjoy
Alexander Roy	Freegift Stoute

doctor Robinson and Baroney, accompanied me to go and view them; when within a quarter of a mile, they discovered us, and came immediately up near us, making the earth tremble under them (this brought to my recollection a charge of cavalry). They stopt and gave us an opportunity to view them, among them there were some very beautiful bays, blacks and greys, and indeed of all colours. We fired at a black horse, with an idea of creasing him, but did not succeed; they flourished round and returned again to see us, when we returned to camp.

2d November, Sunday.—In the morning for the purpose of trying the experiment, we equipped six of our fleetest coursers with riders and ropes, to noose the wild horses if in our power, to come among the band. They stood until they came within forty yards of them, neighing and whinnowing, when the chase began, which we continued about two miles, without success. Two of our horses ran up with them; we could not take them. Returned to camp, I have since laughed at our folly, for taking the wild horses, in that manner, is scarcely ever attempted, even with the fleetest horses, and most expert ropers, (see my account of wild horses, and the manner of taking them in my dissertations on the province of Texas.)[130] Marched late. River turned to north by west.[131] Hills change to the north side. Distance 13 1-2 miles. Killed one buffalo.

3d November, Monday.—Marched at ten o'clock passed numerous herds of buffalo, elk, some horses &c. all travelling south. The river bottoms, full of salt ponds; grass similar to our salt meadows. Killed one buffalo. Distance 25 1-2 miles.

4th November, Tuesday.—This day brought to our recollection, the fate of our countrymen at [Fort] Recovery [Ohio]; when [General Arthur St. Clair was] defeated by the Indians, in the year '91. In the afternoon discovered the north side of the river to be covered with animals; which, when we came to them proved to be buffalo cows and calves. I do not think it an exaggeration to say there were 3,000 in one view. It is worthy of remark, that in all the extent of country yet crossed, we never saw one cow, and that now the face of the earth appeared to be covered with them. Killed one buffalo. Distance 24 1-2 miles.[132]

5th November, Wednesday.—Marched at our usual hour; at the end of two miles, shot a buffalo and two deer and halted, which detained us so long that we foolishly concluded to halt the day and kill some cows and calves, which lay on the opposite side of the river. I took post on a hill, and sent some horsemen over, when a scene took place which gave a lively representation of an engagement. The herd of buffalo being divided into separate bands covered the prairie with dust, and first charged on the one side then to the other, as the pursuit of the horsemen impelled them: the report and smoke from the guns, added to the pleasure of the scene, which in part compensated for our detention.

6th November, Thursday.—Marched early, but was detained two or three hours by the cows, which we killed. The cow buffalo, was equal to any meat I ever saw, and we feasted sumptuously on the choice morsels. I will not attempt to describe the droves of animals we now saw on our route; suffice it to say, that the face of the prairie was covered with them, on each side of the river; their numbers exceeded imagination. Distance 16 miles.[133]

7th November, Friday.—Marched early. The herbage being very poor, concluded to lay by on the morrow, in order to recruit our horses, killed three cow buffalo, one calf, two wolves, one brelaw. Distance 18 miles.[134]

8th November, Saturday.—Our horses being very much jaded and our situation very eligible, we halted all day, jerked meat, mended mockinsons, &c.

9th November, Sunday.—Marched early. At twelve o'clock, struck the Spanish road, (which had been on the outside of us) which appeared to be considerably augmented, and on our arrival, at the camp, found it to consist of 96 fires, from which a reasonable conclusion might be drawn. that there were from 6 to 700 men. We this day found the face of the country considerably changed; being hilly, with springs: passed numerous herds of buffalo and some horses. Distance 27 miles.[135]

10th November, Monday.—The hills increased, the banks of the river, covered with groves of young cotton wood; the river itself much narrower and crooked. Our horses growing weak, two gave out, being [bring] then [them] along empty, cut down trees at night, for them to browze on. Killed one buffalo. Distance 20 miles.

11th November, Tuesday.—Marched at the usual hour. Passed two old, and one last summer, camps which had belonged to the savages, and we suppose Tetaus [Comanches]. Passed a Spanish camp where it appeared they remained some days as we conjectured to lay up meat, previously to entering the Tetau country, as the buffalo evidently began to grow much less numerous. Finding the impossibility of performing the voyage in the time proposed, I determined to spare no pains to accomplish every object even should it oblige me to spend another winter, in the desert. Killed one buffalo, one brelaw. Distance 24 miles.[136]

12*th November, Wednesday.*—Was obliged to leave two horses, which entirely gave out. Missed the Spanish road. Killed one buffalo. Distance 20 miles.[137]

13*th November, Thursday.*—We marched at the usual hour. The river banks begin to be entirely covered with woods on both sides, but no other specie than cotton wood. Discovered very fresh signs of indians, and one of our hunters informed me, he saw a man on horseback, ascending a ravine on our left. Discovered signs of war parties ascending the river. Wounded several buffalo. Killed one turkey, the first we have seen since we left the Pawnees.[138]

14*th November, Friday.*—In the morning, doctor Robinson, one man and myself, went up the ravine, on which the man was supposed to have been seen, but could make no important discovery. Marched at two o'clock; passed a point of red rocks and one large creek.[139] Distance 10 miles.

15*th November, Saturday.*—Marched early. Passed two deep creeks[140] and many high points of the rocks;[141] also, large herds of buffalo. At two o'clock in the afternoon I thought I could distinguish a mountain to our right, which appeared like a small blue cloud; viewed it with the spy glass, and was still more confirmed in my conjecture, yet only communicated it to doctor Robinson, who was in front with me, but in half an hour, they appeared in full view before us.[142] When our small party arrived on the hill they with one accord gave three *cheers* to the *Mexican mountains.* Their appearance can easily be imagined by those who have crossed the Alleghany; but their sides were whiter, as if covered with snow, or a white stone. Those were a *spur* of the grand western chain of mountains, which divide the waters of the Pacific from those of the Atlantic oceans, and it divided the waters which empty into the bay of the Holy Spirit, from those of the Mississippi; as the Alleghany does, those which discharge themselves into the latter river and the Atlantic. They appear to present a natural boundary between the province of Louisiana and New Mexico and would be a defined and natural boundary. Before evening we discovered a fork on the south side bearing S. 25° W. and as the Spanish troops, appeared to have borne up it, we encamped on its banks, about one mile from its confluence, that we might make further discoveries on the morrow.[143] Killed three buffalo. Distance 24 miles.

16*th November, Sunday.*—After asserting [ascertaining] that the Spanish troops had ascended the right branch or main river; we marched at two o'clock P. M.[144] The Arkansaw appeared at this place to be much more navigable, than below, where we first struck it and for any impediment I have yet discovered in the river, I would not hesitate to embark in February at its mouth and ascend to the Mexican mountains, with crafts properly constructed. Distance 11 1-2 miles.

17th November, Monday.—Marched at our usual hour, pushed with an idea of arriving at the mountains, but found at night, no visible difference in their appearance, from what we did yesterday: one of our horses gave out and was left in a ravine, not being able to ascend the hill: but I sent back for him and had him brought to the camp. Distance 23 1-2 miles.[145]

18th November, Tuesday.—As we discovered fresh signs of the savages, we concluded it best to stop and kill some meat, for fear we should get into a country where we could not kill game. Sent out the hunters; I walked myself, to an eminence from whence I took the courses to the different mountains, and a small sketch of their appearance. In the evening, found the hunters had killed without mercy, having slain 17 buffalo and wounded at least 20 more.

19th November, Wednesday.—Having several buffalo brought in, gave out sufficient to last this month. I found it expedient to remain and dry the meat, as our horses were getting very weak, and the one died which was brought up on the 18th. Had a general feast of marrow bones; 136 of them, furnishing the repast.

20th November, Thursday.—Marched at our usual hour; but as our horses's loads were considerably augmented by the death of one horse and the addition of 900 lbs. of meat, we moved slowly,[146] and made only 18 miles. Killed two buffalo and took some choice pieces.

21st November, Friday.—Marched at our usual hour, passed two Spanish camps, within three miles of each other.[147] We again discovered the tracks of two men, who had ascended the river yesterday. This caused us to move with caution; but at the same time, increased our anxiety to discover them. The river was certainly as navigable here (and I think much more so,) than some hundred miles below, which I suppose arises from its flowing through a long course of sandy soil, which must absorb much of the water, and render it shoaler below than above, near the mountains. Distance 21 miles.

22nd November, Saturday.—Marched at our usual hour, and with rather more caution than usual. After having marched about five miles on the prairie, we descended into the bottom, the *front only*, when Baroney cried out *Voila un Savage*, when we observed a number running from the woods towards us, we advanced to them and on turning my head to the left, I observed several running on the hill, as it were to surround us; one with a stand of colors. This caused a momentary halt; but perceiving those in front, reaching out their hands, and without arms we again advanced, they met us with open arms, crouding round, to touch and embrace us. They appeared so anxious that I dismounted my horse, and in a moment, a fellow had mounted him and was off. I then observed the doctor and Baroney were in the same predicament. The indians were embracing the soldiers; after some time tranquility was so far restored, (they having returned our horses all safe) as to enable us to learn they were a war party, from the grand Pawnees, who had been in search of the Tetaus; but not finding them were now on their return. An unsuccessful war party on their return home, are always ready to embrace an opportunity, of gratifying their disappointed vengeance, on the first persons whom they meet. Made for the woods and unloaded our horses; when the two partizans endeavored to arrange the party; it was with great difficulty that they got them tranquil, and not until there had been a bow or two, bent on the occasion. When in some order, we found them to be sixty warriors, half with fire arms, and half with bows, arrows, and lances. Our party was sixteen total. In a short time they were arranged in a ring and I took my seat between the two partizans; our colors were placed opposite each other, the utensils for smoaking &c. were paraded on a small seat before us; thus far all was well. I then ordered half a carrot of tobacco, one dozen knives, 60 fire steels and 60 flints to be presented them. They demanded ammunition, corn, blankets, kettles &c. all of which they were refused, notwithstanding the pressing instances of my interpreter, to accord to some points. The pipes yet lay unmoved, as if they were undetermined whether to treat us as friends or enemies; but after some time we were presented with a kettle of water, drank, smoked, and eat together. During this time doctor Robinson was standing up, to observe their actions, in order that we might be ready to commence hostilities as soon as them. They now took their presents and commenced distributing them, but some malcontents, threw them away, by way of contempt. We began to load our horses, when they encircled us and commenced stealing every thing they could. Finding it was difficult to preserve my pistols; I mounted my horse when I found myself frequently surrounded during which some were endeavoring to steal the pistols: The doctor was equally engaged in another quarter, and all the soldiers in their positions; in taking things from them one having stolen my tomahawk, I informed the chief, but he paid no respect, except to reply that *"they were pitiful,"*[148] finding this, I determined to protect ourselves, as far as was in my power, and the affair began to take a serious aspect. I ordering my men to take their arms, and separate themselves from the savages at the same time declaring to them, I would *kill* the first man who touched our baggage. On which they commenced filing off immediately; we marched about the same time and found, they had made out to steal one sword, tomahawk, broad axe, five canteens, and sundry other small articles. After our leaving them; when I reflected on the subject, I felt myself sincerely mortified, that the smallness of my number obliged me thus to submit to the insults of a lawless banditti, it being the first time ever a savage took any thing from me, with the least appearance of force. After encamping at night[149] the doctor and myself went about one mile back, and way laid the road, determined in case we discovered any of the rascals pursuing us to steal our horses, to kill two at least; but after waiting behind some logs until some time in the night, and discovering no person, we returned to camp. Distance 17 miles, killed two buffalo and one deer.

23rd November, Sunday.—Marched at ten o'clock; at one o'clock came to the third fork on the south side[149A] and encamped at night in the point of the grand forks.[150] As the river appeared to be dividing itself into many small branches and of course must be near its extreme source, I concluded to put the party in a defensible situation; and ascend the north fork, to the high point of the blue mountain, which we conceived would be one days march, in order to be enabled from its pinical, to lay down the various branches and positions of the country. Distance 19 miles. Killed five buffalo.

24th November, Monday.—Early in the morning cut down 14 logs, and put up a breast work, five feet high on three sides and the other was thrown on the river. After giving the necessary orders for their government, during my absence, in case of our not returning. We marched at one o'clock with an idea

---

November 24. Arriving a mile or so past the mouth of Fountain Creek to a horseshoe bend in the Arkansas at Pueblo, Colo., where the stream and its banks would aid in defense, Pike set his men to work cutting logs and building a breast-work for a stockade. To historians, however, it is more important than its size would indicate. Mr. Coues discussed it and its location without the benefit of Pike's chart.

of arriving at the foot of the mountain; but found ourselves obliged to take up our nights lodgings under a single cedar, which we found in the prairie, without water and extremely cold. Our party besides myself consisted of doctor Robinson, privates Miller and Brown. Distance 12 miles. [Map p. 145.]

25th November, Tuesday.—Marched early, with an expectation of ascending the mountain, but was only able to encamp at its base, after passing over many small hills covered with cedars and pitch pines. Our encampment was on a creek where we found no water for several miles from the mountain, but near its base, found springs sufficient. Took a meridional observation, and the altitude of the mountain. Killed two buffaloes. Distance 22[151] miles.

This permits us to fix its position more definitely; the charts show the location twice, once on the upper center of Chart 24 and once on the right center of No. 23 (p. 145). In both diagrams the fort is placed on a prominent tongue of land almost surrounded by the first bend of the river west of the mouth of Fountain Creek. The river no longer makes this prominent bend; its course has been changed by floods and construction. Early maps of Pueblo, however, do show the bend. Mr. Frank Yale of the Colorado Fuel & Iron Company has traced for me, on company maps, the course of the river as far back as 1872. Its course at that time corresponded very well with that shown by Pike. The bend in question included the land for one or two blocks on each side of Santa Fé Avenue from Ilex Street, South Pueblo, to River Street, Pueblo. Pike's fort, the first American log structure, perhaps, in present Colorado, and probably the first structure, in the state to fly the American flag, was on Santa Fé Avenue near the Denver and Rio Grande Railway crossing. Pike took the latitude of the site of this camp as 37° 40′ 31′′, or slightly more in error than when he was on the Arkansas on October 24th. An Act of the Colorado Legislature, establishing a memorial for Pike on the site of his Conejos fort (Note 218) states that the American flag first flew in Colorado at that point. It is not constructive to quibble on such points, but only to state the facts. We have seen that the Republic's flag was displayed six or so miles below the mouth of the Huerfano at the Pawnee parley on the Arkansas on November 22nd (p. 140). There is small doubt that the flag flew here over the log hut at Pueblo; its presence offered a legal security in case of any insult shown the party by passing redmen not to be discounted; but Pike does not state the fact, as in the case of the Conejos structure.

Pike and Robinson, with two equally ill-equipped soldiers, now started north, Monday the 24th, on their historic march toward "the N. mountain" (Pikes Peak) as Pike calls it. The Nau map, accompanying all previous editions of Pike's *Journal,*

26th November, Wednesday.—Expecting to return to camp that evening, we left all our blankets and provisions, at the foot of the mountain. Killed a deer of a new species, and hung his skin on a tree with some meat. We commenced ascending, found it very difficult, being obliged to climb up rocks, sometimes, almost perpendicular; and after marching all day, we encamped in a cave, without blankets, victuals or water. We had a fine clear sky, whilst it was snowing at the bottom. On the side of the mountain, we found only yellow and pitch pine. Some distance up we found buffalo, higher still the new species of deer and pheasants.

---

was too vague and inaccurate to be useful in tracking the party on this trip to the Peak which will forever bear the leader's name, and which, because of its accessibility has been called the best known mountain in the world. Study of Pike's map, here reproduced (p. 145), helps considerably in fixing the route taken, and adds some items of information of moment.

Crossing the Arkansas, the party started up the west bank of Fountain Creek, tyro-like expecting to gain the mountain's base after a brisk walk. Finding that the stream's course bore more to the east than was to his liking, Pike, illustrating a very poor sense of plainsmanship, left the stream in order to steer straight toward "ye N[orth] Mountain"—oblivious of the commonsense fact that the large stream thus abandoned could only come from the great, snow-covered mountain mass which was the party's objective. Gaining thus the divide between Fountain and Turkey creeks, the day's march found Pike still on the prairie, with a lone cedar to camp under. On the day following, so far from ascending the Peak as expected, Pike merely gained the base of foothills on upper East Turkey Creek where springs were found, possibly on the Penrose or Jordan ranches at base of "Mount Miller" (Note 153). Nor were the novitiates in Rocky Mountain climbing more successful on the 26th, so far as gaining their altered objective, for now only the summit before them (probably "Mount Miller") represented the height of their ambition. Caching everything of weight in order to make a quick trip to the top of the mountain, the thrice-deceived men found a night must be spent in a mountainside cave with no comfort except their fire. The difficulty of the ascent is illustrated in the fact that camp was made within but one hour's march of the top. That animals were met in the upward journey make it seem likely that on the hill's summit lay good pasturage from which the snow was driving them down into the safer valleys. "Mount Miller" is known for its fine forage lands on the summit.

27th November, Thursday.—Arose hungry, dry, and extremely sore, from the inequality of the rocks, on which we had lain all night, but were amply compensated for toil by the sublimity of the prospects below. The unbounded prairie was overhung with clouds, which appeared like the ocean in a storm; wave piled on wave and foaming, whilst the sky was perfectly clear where we were. Commenced our march up the mountain, and in about one hour arrived at the summit of this chain: here we found the snow middle deep; no sign of beast or bird inhabiting this region. The thermometer which stood at 9° above 0 [+ 52° Fahr.] at the foot of the mountain, here fell to 4° below 0 [+ 23° Fahr.]. The summit of the Grand Peak, which was entirely bare of vegetation and covered with snow, now appeared at the distance of 15 or 16 miles from us, and as high again as what we had ascended, and would have taken a whole day's march to have arrived at its base, when I believe no human being could have ascended to its pinical.

Here then, on Thanksgiving Day, 1806, Zebulon Pike gazed from the "summit of this chain" upon the giant mass sixteen miles away which will carry his name down through the centuries. Considering that the plain on which the Peak stood was estimated at 8000 feet in elevation, instead of 6000, Pike (on December 3) did not figure out the height of Pike's Peak with much inaccuracy; he placed it at 18,581 instead of 14,110, showing an error of 2,671 feet, not counting the wrong estimate of the altitude of the plains at its foot. With better instruments, ones which had not suffered from rough riding on horses' backs. Pike might have succeeded better (Note 160).

Coues' suggestion that Black (or Blue) Mountain was Pike's objective is ruled out by the fact that Pike's Peak is not visible from that summit; while from nearby "Mount Miller"—so named by Dr. Lloyd Shaw, a local Pike authority—the Peak is visible. The name is that of one of Pike's two soldiers who accompanied him and the Doctor up from the Arkansas—Theodore Miller. It is typical of the callous criticism of Pike that his mistake in estimating the Peak's altitude has not been tested by the experience of others. Pike misjudged the altitude of the base of the Peak 2000 feet; Major Long's party of scientists in 1819 misjudged it 3000 feet. Long's estimate of the height of the Peak was 11,506½, or 2700 feet short of the fact; while Pike's estimate was 4471 in excess of the truth. The Theodore Miller, thus appropriately honored by Dr. Shaw was, also, as will appear, one of the two soldiers who accompanied Pike on the toilsome trip toward Tennessee Pass when the Arkansas River was reached near Buena Vista.

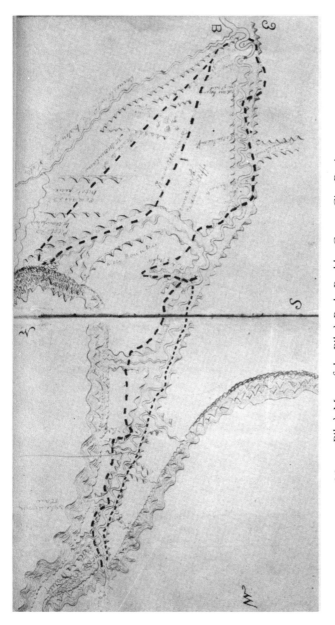

MAP 2: Pike's Map of the Pike's Peak–Pueblo–Canon City Region

The line of Pike's march is indicated by the faintly dotted line, which has been touched up to make it more visible. For detailed analysis of Pike's advance in this section see *Journal* entries from Nov. 25, forward. The line of smallest dots is that of Malgares Spanish Column on the south bank of the Arkansas. From the present site of Pueblo, Colorado, ("B") Pike's "Trace to ye N. Mountain" shows his pathway toward Pike's Peak; while "Trace returning" shows his return route. From the same site ("E") begins his track up the Arkansas to present Canon City.

This with the condition of my soldiers who had only light overalls on, and no stockings, and every way ill provided to endure the inclemency of the region; the bad prospect of killing anything to subsist on, with the further detention of two or three days, which it must occasion, determined us to return. The clouds from below had now ascended the mountain and entirely enveloped the summit on which rests eternal snows. We descended by a long deep ravine with much less difficulty than contemplated. Found all our baggage safe, but the provisions all destroyed. It began to snow, and we sought shelter under the side of a projecting rock, where we, all four, made a meal on one partridge, and a piece[152] of deer's ribs, the ravens had left us, being the first we had eaten in that 48 hours.

28th November, Friday.—Marched at nine o'clock. Kept straight down the creek to avoid the hills.[153] At half past one o'clock shot two buffalo, when we made the first full meal we had made in three days. Encamped in a valley under a shelving rock. The land here very rich, and covered with old Tetau camps.

30th November, Sunday.—Marched at eleven o'clock, it snowing very fast, but my impatience to be moving would not permit my lying still at that camp. The doctor, Baroney and myself, went to view a Tetau encampment, which appeared to be about two years old; and from their having cut down so large a quantity of trees[154] to support their horses, conclude there must have been at least one thousand souls: passed several more in the course of the day; also one Spanish camp.[155] Distance 15 miles.[156] Killed two deer. This day came to the first cedar and pine.

1st December, Monday.—The storm still continuing with violence, we remained encamped; the snow by night one foot deep; our horses being obliged to scrape it away, to obtain their miserable pittance, and to increase their misfortunes, the poor animals were attacked by the magpies, who attracted by the scent of their sore backs, alighted on them, and in defiance of their wincing and kicking, picked many places quite raw; the difficulty of procuring food rendered those birds so bold as to light on our mens arms and eat meat out of their hands. One of our hunter's out but killed nothing.

2d. December, Tuesday.—It cleared off in the night, and in the morning the thermometer stood at 17 below 0 [-2° Fahr.), (Reaumer) [Reaumeure] being three times as cold as any morning we had yet experienced. We killed an old buffalo on the opposite side of the river, which here was so deep as to swim horses.[157] Marched and found it necessary to cross to the north side, about two miles up, as the ridge joined the river. The ford was a good one, but the ice ran very bad, and two of the men got their feet froze before we could get accommodated with fire &c. Secured some of our old buffalo and continued our march. The country being very rugged and hilly, one of our horses took a freak in his head and turned back, which occasioned three of our rear guard to lay out all night; I was very apprehensive they might perish on the open prairie. Distance 13 miles.[158]

3rd December, Wednesday.—The weather moderating to 3 below 0 [+ 25° Fahr.], our absentees joined, one with his feet frozen, but were not able to bring up the horse; sent two men back on horseback. The hardships of last voyage[159] had now began, and had the climate only been as severe as the climate then was, some of the men must have perished, for they had no winter clothing; I wore myself cotton overalls, for I had not calculated on being out in that inclement season of the year. Dr. Robinson and myself, with assistants, went out and took the altitude of the north mountain [Pike's Peak] on the base of a mule;[160] after which, together with Sparks, we endeavored to kill a *cow* but without effect. Killed two bulls, that the men might use pieces of their hides for mockinsons. Left Sparks out. On our return to camp found the men had got back with the strayed horse, but too late to march.

4th December, Thursday.—Marched about five; took up Sparks who had succeeded in killing a cow. Killed two buffalo and six turkies. Distance 20 miles.[161]

5th December, Friday.—Marched at our usual hour. Passed one very bad place of *falling* rocks; had to carry our loads.[162] Encamped on the main branch of the river, near the entrance of the south mountains.[163] In the evening walked up to the mountain. Heard 14 guns at camp during my absence, which alarmed me considerably; returned as quickly as possible, and found that the cause of my alarm was their shooting turkies. Killed two buffalo and nine turkies. Distance 18 miles.

6th December, Saturday.–Sent out three different parties to hunt the Spanish trace, but without success.[164] The doctor and myself followed the river into the mountain, which was bounded on each side by the rocks of the mountain, 200 feet high, leaving a small valley of 59 or 60 feet.[165] Killed two buffalo, two deer, one turkey.

7th December, Sunday.—We again dispatched parties in search of the trace; one party discovered it on the other side of the river, and followed it into the valley of the river at the entrance of the mountain, where they met two parties who were returning from exploring the two branches of the river, in the mountains: of which they reported, to have ascended until the river was merely a brook, bounded on both sides with perpendicular rocks, impracticable for horses ever to pass them; they then recrossed the river to the north side, and discovered (as they supposed) that the Spanish troops had ascended a dry valley to the right—on their return they found some rock salt, samples of which were brought me. We determined to march the morrow to the entrance of the valley; there to examine the salt, and the road. Killed one wild cat.

8*th December, Monday*.—On examining the trace found yesterday, conceived it to have been only a reconnoitering party, dispatched from the main body, and on analysing the rock salt, found it to be strongly impregnated with sulphur. There were some very strong sulphurated springs at its foot. Returned to camp;[166] took with me Dr. Robinson and Miller, and descended the river, in order to discover certainly, if the whole party had came by this route. Descended about seven miles on the south side. Saw great quantities of turkies and deer. Killed one deer.

9*th December, Tuesday*.—Before we marched, killed a fine buck at our camp as he was passing. Found the Spanish camp about four miles below, and from every observation we could make, conceived they had all ascended the river. Returned to camp, where we arrived about two o'clock. Found all well; would have moved immediately, but four men were out reconnoitering. Killed three deer.

10*th December, Wednesday*.—Marched and found the road over the mountain to be excellent.[167] Encamped on a dry ravine. Obliged to melt snow for ourselves and horses; and as their was nothing else for the latter to eat, gave them one pint of corn each. Killed one buffalo.

11*th December, Thursday*.—Marched at ten o'clock, and in one mile struck a branch of the Arkansaw, on which the *supposed* Spaniards had encamped, where there was both water and grass. Kept up this branch, but was frequently embarrassed as to the trace; at three o'clock P. M. having no sign of it, halted and encamped,[168] and went out to search it; found it about one mile to the right. Distance 15 miles.

12*th December, Friday*.—Marched at 9 o'clock. Continued up the same branch as yesterday. The ridges on our right and left, appeared to grow lower, but mountains appeared on our flanks, though the intervals covered with snow. Owing to the weakness of our horses, made only 12 miles.[169]

13*th December, Saturday.*—Marched at the usual hour and passed large springs, and the (supposed) Spanish camp; and at twelve o'clock, a dividing ridge,[170] and immediately fell on a small branch running N. 20° W. There being no appearance of wood, we left it, and the *Spanish Trace* to our right, and made for the hills to encamp. After the halt I took my gun and went out to see what discovery I could make, and after marching about two miles north, fell on a river 40 yards wide, frozen over;[171] which after some investigation, I found run north east, this was the occasion of much surprise, as we were taught to expect to have met with the branches of the Red river, which should run south east.[172] Quere. Must it not be the head waters of the river Platte? If so the Missouri must run much more west, than is generally represented; for the Platte is a small river by no means presenting an expectation of so extensive a course.[173] Distance 18 miles. One horse gave out and was left.

14*th December, Sunday.*—Marched. Struck the river,[174] ascended it four miles, and encamped on the north side. The prairie being about two miles wide, was covered at least six miles (on the banks of the river) with horse dung and the marks of indian camps, which had been [occupied] since the cold weather, as was evident by the fires which were in the centre of the lodges; the sign made by their horses was astonishing, and would have taken a thousand horses some months.[175] As it was impossible to say which course the Spaniards pursued, amongst this multiplicity of signs, we halted early, and discovered that they or the savages had ascended the river. We determined to persue them,[176] as to the geography of the country, had turned out to be so different from our expectation; we were some what at a loss which course to pursue, unless we attempted to cross the snow cap't mountains, to the south east of us which was almost impossible.[177] Bursted one of our rifles, which was a great loss, as it made three guns which had bursted, and the five which had been broken on the march, and one of my men was now armed with my sword and pistols. Killed two buffalo.

15*th December, Monday.*—After repairing our guns, we marched, but were obliged to leave another horse. Ascended the river, both sides of which were covered with old Indian camps, at which we found corn cobs; this induced us to believe that those savages although erratic [nomadic], must remain long enough in one position to cultivate this grain, or obtain it of the Spaniards; from their sign they must have been extremely numerous, and possessed vast numbers of horses. My poor fellows suffered extremely with cold, being almost naked. Distance 10 miles.[178]

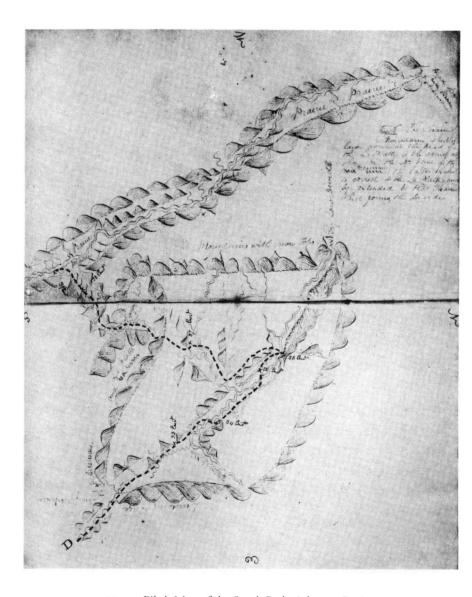

MAP 3: Pike's Map of the South Park–Arkansas Region
The line of Pike's march shows his approach from the southeast to the
South Platte at "Eleven Mile Canon"; thence up the Platte and doubling
back to gain Trout Creek Pass to the supposed "Red River"—the Arkansas,
just below Buena Vista, Colorado. Note the three instances of insertion of
"Red River," all of them crossed out when Pike learned the truth.

16th December, Tuesday.—Marched up the river about two miles and killed a buffalo. When finding no road up the stream, we halted and dispatched parties different courses; the doctor and myself ascending high enough to enable me to lay down the course of the river into the mountains. From a high ridge we reconnoitered the adjacent country, and concluded putting the *Spanish trace* out of the question, and to bear our course south west, for the head of Red river. One of our party found a large camp, which had been occupied by at least 3000 Indians, with a large cross in the middle. Quere. Are those people Catholics?

December 16th. Pike's camp (No. 36) of this date may well be remembered as one of the significant camps of his trip. His Chart No. 21 was fashioned from the height nearby. To the west the valley of the South Platte descends from what Pike terms on the chart "Very low Divide," namely, Hoosier Pass (alt. 11,526). Hard by are the peaks Lincoln, Quandry, Bross, Sherman and Democrat, ranging from an altitude of 14,000 to 14,276. To the east lay the Puma Hills, the Tarryalls and the Platte River range, called by Pike "Dividing ridge Last of the Arkansaw"—over which he had come from present Canon City by way of Four Mile (Oil) Creek. To the south and southwest, the direction he now determined to search for Red River, Pike saw two openings, Weston's Pass (alt. 11,676) at the head of Little South Platte, and Trout Creek Pass, both passageways famous for trails to and from South Park and used by red men and white for centuries; the former, Weston's, has for us, however, in this connection particular significance. Through it came the Indian-Spanish trail from "Rio Colorado" ("Colorado of the West") to the Platte rivers (North and South) and which lead (by either of those waterways) to the far-famed buffalo hunting grounds of the Yellowstone and its tributaries, Big Horn, Powder and Tongue.[179] Somewhere Pike had picked up the rumor of a Red River and a Yellowstone ("Pierre Jaun") in, or beyond, this South Park country. This enigma, which has puzzled so many editors and led to scoffing remarks directed toward Pike, is explained simply and instantly by properly correlating the above facts. A Red River did lie beyond South Park—the Rio Colorado of the Gulf of California; up this stream and Grand River, its tributary, only a short march over the Continental Divide, by way of Rabbit Ear or Muddy passes, put the huntsman down on the head of the North Platte running almost straight north to present Casper, Wyo.—within a half a days' march of the buffalo hunting-ground *par excellence* of the West in Big Horn, Johnson and neighboring counties of Wyoming. In actual practice in the days of the "Mountain Men" the North Platte and Powder (one chief Yellowstone tributary) were as one river. In fact the two may have

17th December, Wednesday.—Marched, and on striking a left hand fork of the river we had left, found it to be the main branch; ascended it some distance, but finding it to bear too much to the north, we encamped about two miles from it, for the purpose of benefitting by its water. Distance 15 miles.

18th December, Thursday.—Marched and crossed the mountain which lay south-west of us, in a distance of seven miles, arrived at a small spring; some of our lads observed, they supposed it to be Red river, to which I then gave very little credit. On entering a gap in the next mountain, came past an excellent spring which formed a fine creek, which we followed through narrows in the mountains for about six miles; found many evacuated camps of indians the latest yet seen, after pointing out the ground for the encampment, the doctor and myself went on to make discoveries (as was our usual custom,) and in about four miles march we struck (what we supposed to be Red river) which here was about 25 yards wide, ran with great rapidity

---

been considered as one. These streams must always be remembered as routes of trails, never from the navigation standpoint. Pike confused the rumor of the Red River of the West (Colorado) with the Red River of Texas; and the trail of Indian and Spanish buffalo-runners to the Yellowstone, with the Yellowstone River itself. If he had any reason for thinking a Spanish Trace was to be found in or near present South Park, other than merely because he had lost one at the mouth of the Royal Gorge, it was a Spanish Trace down either the North or South Platte—for the latter no doubt was, also, a route to the buffalo grounds of Wyoming. Such a trace up the South Platte would, likewise, have led to the Red River of the West, the Colorado. It is, then, to a lack of knowledge of this region, as the buffalo-runners knew it, that one must attribute Pike's curious mistake; numerous contemporaries like Perrin du Lac, Bradbury, Cutler and James re-echo it.

On December 16th the decision to look to the southwest for Red River was reached and, marching down the South Platte on the 17th, to near Hartzell's, at the confluence of the Little South Platte and High Creek, Pike ascended the former. Above the mouth of Agate Creek he found the course trended too much to the north; he then crossed the Little South Platte midway between Agate Creek and Long's Gulch and camped in that Gulch, two miles south of the Little Platte. On the day following (18th) the party followed the old San Juan road and modern highway over Trout Creek Pass and camped on that creek four miles above its junction with the Arkansas. Scouting in advance, as was their habit, Pike and Robinson descended the creek and discovered the river supposed to be the Red.

and was full of rocks. We returned to the party with the news, which gave general pleasure. Determined to remain a day or two in order to examine the [river's] source. Distance 18 miles. Snowing.

19*th December, Friday.*—Marched down the creek near the opening of the prairie, and encamped, sent out parties hunting, &c. but had no success. Still snowing and stormy, making preparations to take an observation.

20*th December, Saturday.*—Having found a fine place for pasture on the river sent our horses down to it with a guard, also three parties out a hunting, all of whom returned without success. Took an observation. As there was no prospect of killing any game, it was necessary that the party should leave that place, I therefore determined that the doctor and Baroney should descend the river in the morning; that myself and two men would ascend and the rest of the party descend after the doctor until they obtained provision and could wait for me.

What the present writer believes to have been the mistakes of previous editors in interpreting Pike's experiences from now on to his capture are due to failure properly to correlate his successive and perfectly logical series of geographical mistakes. In order to see the logic of them one must take his stand in Pike's shoes and conceive exactly his orientation.

Because it was reduced in volume by snow and ice, and because of the giant cliffs (Royal Gorge), Pike, on the present site of Canon City on December 10th, deemed Four Mile Creek the main "head" of the Arkansas. He did not believe that the river came down the mighty crevass. That the main road went up Four Mile was an additional deceptive factor.

Coming out of South Park now, upon a river which he never thought could be accommodated by the Royal Gorge, Pike believed he had found the river lying south of the Arkansas—the Red. It is vital to recognize Pike's complete misunderstanding and error at this point. Lacking his charts (19, 20 and 21), previous writers have been handicapped. On them we find six entries relating to divides which mention "Red River." On No. 21 we find the divide between the South Platte and "red river" indicated—with "red river" crossed out and "Arkansaw" written above it. On the same chart we find a divide between the South Platte and Four Mile Creek marked: "La Platte and Red river"; the words "Red river" are crossed, but nothing is substituted for them. On the same chart, at the head of the Arkansas, near Twin Lakes, we find the words: "Head of Red River": the last two words are crossed out and "Arkansaw" substituted. On Chart 20 we find written across the mountain

21st December, Sunday.—The doctor and Baroney marched; the party remained for me to take a meridional observation; after which we separated. Myself and the two men who accompanied me (Mountjoy and Miller) ascended 12 miles and encamped on the north side, the river continuing close to the north mountain and running through a narrow rocky channel and in some places not more than 20 feet wide and at least 10 feet deep. Its banks bordered by yellow pine, cedars, &c.

22nd December, Monday.—Marched up thirteen miles, to a large point of the mountain from whence we had a view at least 35 miles [upper Arkansas watershed], to where the river entered the mountains, it being at that place not more than ten or fifteen feet wide, and properly speaking, only a *brook*;

---

divide south of the Arkansas: "Divide of Red River & the Arkansaw." No substitutions are indicated. On Chart No. 19 we also find: "Divide between red River & the Arkansaw," no word being scratched out.

We now have before us the development of Pike's misunderstandings of his surroundings. But because he once said (p. 74), in a spirit of youthful bravado, that if he was captured he would pretend confusion as to his whereabouts, commentators and editors have surmised, in every tone of ridicule and unbelief, that Pike was consciously prevaricating in order to cover up his real purpose. These sheets of paper on which Pike drew his maps, after their long repose in Mexico, are interesting indeed, with their reiterated proof that Pike had meticulously corrected on them every error of which he was conscious.

Hailing with enthusiasm the discovery of the "Red (Arkansas) River" December 18th, the party marched to it and camped on the morrow. Despite the rigor of the weather, the ill-clad condition of all and the uncertainty of provisions, Pike now did the one thing which squared with his chief aim and ambition—divided the party and proceeded to explore the stream's headwaters. His doing this certainly gives the lie to Mr. Coues' flippant raillery about his preferring to break Spanish heads than explore "the head of any river" (Note 176). Departing upstream on the 21st, Pike passed the present site of Buena Vista, Chaffee Co. and, going on under the summits of the famous Collegiate Range, camped that night with his two companions between Fisher and Riverside. On the 22nd he explores thirteen miles further, to the vicinity of Twin Lakes. Viewing the uplifting valley of the "Red" (Arkansas) as it approaches Tennessee Pass, with its dwindling watercourse, he was assured that he was gazing at its very head, as, in truth, he was.

Beyond the heights where Leadville now stands (the Continental Divide) Pike

from this place after taking the course, and estimating the distance we returned to our camp of last evening. Killed one turkey and a hare.

23rd December, Tuesday.—Marched early, and at two o'clock, P. M. discovered the trace of the party on the opposite side of the river; forded it, although extremely cold and marched until some time in the night, when we arrived at the second nights encampment of the party. Our cloathing was frozen stiff, and we ourselves were considerably benumbed.

24th December, Wednesday.—The party's provision extending only to the 23d, and their orders being not to halt until they killed some game, and then wait for us: consequently they might have been considerably advanced. About 11 o'clock, met doctor Robinson on a prairie, who informed me that

---

saw the clouds which overhung valleys unknown to him but vaguely represented by geographers as the heads of the Rio Colorado; and, beyond a range not the Continental Divide was the head of some Missouri tributary. Pike's map made at the time (p. 150) carries no sign of these speculations. The only words thereon are "Head of ye Red River Arkansaw," with "Red River" crossed out; and a paragraph on the margin to the effect that the Platte's headwaters lie in the same range as those of the Arkansas.

Those who have indulged in sarcasm for the entry at this point on Nau's map of the words: "Yellow Stone River. Branch of the Missouri," can bear in mind that Pike's original map bore no such legend. The information recorded came, therefore, from an outside source; doubtless from some of the many Spanish maps, used, perhaps by Humboldt (whether he gave appropriate credit to those authorities or not!) and all mapmakers of the time. The basis of such maps is found in the documents in *Original Narratives of Early American History,* particularly, *Spanish Explorers* and *Spanish Exploration.* While criticizing Pike, appropriate blame should be attributed to the incorrectness of all sources at his command—and he had nothing to give him correct information. In fact it is the rare map which, today, depicts the tangle of rivers south of the Arkansas in New Mexico with any accuracy. Crossing Raton Pass one finds, first, the heads of the Cimarron, an Arkansas tributary. Then come the heads of the Canadian (like the Mora), also an Arkansas tributary. Below these come the heads of the Pecos, a Rio Grande tributary. Humboldt, who complained of Pike's borrowing from him might have complained more acutely at the ignorance of the mapmaker from whom he (Humboldt) borrowed the idea that the only rivers met south of the Ratons were the Mora and upper Pecos which united to form the Pecos! Not showing any Cimarron or Canadian at all! Some one

he and Baroney had been absent from the party two days without killing any thing, (also without eating,) but that over night, they had killed four buffalo, and that he was in search of the men; and suffered the two lads with me to go to the camp where the meat was, as we had also been nearly two days without eating. The doctor and myself pursued the trace and found them encamped on the river bottom. Sent out horses for the meat, shortly after Sparks arrived and informed us he had killed four cows. Thus from being in a starving condition we had 8 beeves in our camp. We now again found ourselves all assembled together on Christmas Eve, and appeared generally to be content, although all the refreshment we had to celebrate that day with, was buffalo meat, without salt, or any other thing whatever. My little excursion up the river was in order to establish the geography of the courses of the (supposed) Red River, as I knew well the indefatigable

---

"inspired" Pike or Nau to show, across the divide from the Arkansas the "Rio de Piedro Amerette del Missouri" on the Nau map. Was it more heinous for Pike to copy this idea from someone in 1810 than for Humboldt in 1811 to draw the Pecos where the Cimarron and Canadian ought to have been shown? Yet Pike is criticized while no one exploits Humboldt's mistakes! Now, if a tributary of the Missouri lay in the western Colorado Rockies north of the Platte (which Pike found) it must have been a branch of the next highest large Missouri tributary—the Yellowstone. Was it not likely that geographers confused the North Platte and Powder and drew them as a single stream? So far as the trappers were concerned they were just that, from the standpoint of the river trail to the north. Perrin du Lac showed a connection between the Platte and a "Riviere de Santa Fé," as noted (Note 34). Pike certainly did not originate the "Yellow Stone" myth; but candor requires us to say that, in map and title-page, he made an inexcusable amount of capital out of the "fact"; for that we must blame his very genuine jealousy of Lewis and Clark; for it made him seem the discoverer (approximately) of *the source of the river* which Lewis and Clark had made famous, the Yellowstone.

Returning from the Twin Lakes region, Pike occupied his campsite of the 21st and continued the descent of the Arkansas; finding the trail of the main party, he camped that night below Chalk Creek near Brown Creek, without provisions. On the 24th the party was reunited on the prairie above present-day Salida, Colo.

As we come to Pike's description of this historic Christmas Eve and Day, 1806, the first thus celebrated, perhaps, by Americans in Colorado, if not the entire upper Arkansas Valley, we are not able to decide how much the tale was

researches of doctor Hunter, Dunbar and Freeman, had left nothing unnoticed in the extent of their voyage up said river, I determined that its upper branches should be equally well explored; as in this voyage I had already ascertained the sources of the [Little] Osage, and White [Neosho] Rivers, (been round the head of the Kans) [Smoky Hill River] and on the head waters of the [South] Platte.

25th December, Thursday.—It being stormy weather and having meat to dry; I concluded to lie by this day. Here I must take the liberty of observing that in this situation, the hardships and privations we underwent, were on this day brought more fully to our mind. Having been accustomed to some degree of relaxation, and extra enjoyments; but here 800 miles from the frontiers of our country, in the most inclement season of the year; not one person clothed for the winter, many without blankets, (having been obliged

---

embellished by the author before being sent to the printer in 1810. One is free to make of it what he can. In the case of the present writer the impression is firm that the diary was little altered. When Pike's book came out his patron, Wilkinson, was under a cloud and Pike was known as Wilkinson's protégé and had been accused of connivance with him. While scornfully refuting the implication,[180] Pike did not make his book a defence; and his plain tale while showing errors of judgment, mistakes and misjudgments at the same time is quite lacking in the histrionics which his experiences at the time would have excused. Lewis and Clark knew nothing of such terrible hardships as were endured by Pike and his men. For instance, on the 25th Pike, speaking of the party's distance from "the frontiers of our country" as 800 miles, would hardly have been criticized for mentioning the great length of the journey accomplished up to that date, namely, 1700 miles as shown on Pike's traverse tables—approximately the length of the outgoing route of Lewis and Clark.

Pike's Christmas camp, with its unexpected bounty which averted starvation, was on the north bank of the Arkansas just below the mouth of Squaw Creek, as proven by his chart, and not above that stream (as Mr. Coues surmised) in Beaver Canon. Now, among other reflections common to the season, Pike again refers significantly to the ambition which prompted his expedition. Here he speaks definitely of the purpose of his "little excursion" up the supposed "Red River" (Arkansas) toward its headwaters, and echoes the hope that his work may rank him with, or above, those who had explored the river's lower stretches under much more fortunate circumstances. That work of Dunbar, Freeman and Sibley, previously mentioned,

to cut them up for socks, &c.) and now laying down at night on the snow or wet ground; one side burning whilst the other was pierced with the cold wind: this was in part the situation of the party whilst some were endeavoring to make a miserable substitute of raw buffalo hide for shoes &c. I will not speak of diet, as I conceive that to be beneath the serious consideration of a man on a voyage of such nature. We spent the day as agreeably as could be expected from men in our situation. Caught a bird [parakeet] of a new species, having made a trap for him.

26th December, Friday.—Marched at two o'clock and made 7 1-2 miles to the entrance of the mountains. On this piece of prairie the river spread ["Big Bend" at Salida] considerably, and formed several small Islands, a large stream [Little Arkansas] enters from the south. As my boy and some others were sick, I omitted pitching our tent in order that they might have it [for covering]; in consequence of which we were completely covered with snow on top, as well as that part on which we lay.

27th December, Saturday.—Marched over an extreme rough road, our horses received frequent falls and cut themselves considerably on the rocks. From there being no roads of buffalo, or sign of horses, I am convinced that neither those animals, nor the aborigines of the country, ever take this route, to go from the source of the river out of the mountains, but that they

---

had given the world something of the topography and correlation of the passageways of the Red, Black and Ouachita rivers. Dunbar's report[181] was an important document for its day; but it must have seemed inconsequential to Pike in comparison with his reconnaissance of the Little Osage, Neosho, Smoky Hill, South Platte and upper "Red" (Arkansas), although his reference thereto could hardly have been phrased with more seemly modesty. He would hardly have been criticized for stating outright that the trials endured by him, and the value of the information secured by his work, was far and away more important than that secured by every rival, Lewis and Clark alone excepted. The story of this Christmas very little comports with the "breaking Spanish heads" theory. Every movement of Pike's shows an orderly development of a plan based upon a definite fund of information and misinformation. Not one single act conforms with theory that a military-political purpose dominated his deportment.

Leaving the Christmas camp the party, on the morrow, passed the present site

must cross one of the chains to the right [Poncha Pass] or left, and find a smoother tract to the lower country. Was obliged to unload our horses and carry the baggage at several places. Distance 12 1-2 miles.[182]

28*th December, Sunday.*—Marched over an open space[183] and from the appearance before us, concluded we were going out of the mountains, but at night encamped[184] at the entrance of the most perpendicular precipices on both sides, through which the river ran and our course lay. Distance 16 miles.

29*th December, Monday.*—Marched but owing to the extreme rugged-ness of the road, made but five miles.[185] Saw one of a new species of animals on the mountains; ascended it to kill him, but did not succeed. Finding the impossibility of getting along with the horses, made one sled, which with the men of three horses, carries their load.

30*th December, Tuesday.*—Marched: but at half past one o'clock; were obliged to halt[186] and send back for the sled loads, as they had broken it and could not proceed owing to the waters running over the ice. Distance 8 miles. Crossed our horses twice on the ice.

31*st December, Wednesday.*—Marched; had frequently to cross the river on the ice, horses falling down, we were obliged to pull them over on the ice. The river turned so much to the north [Coaldale to Cotopaxi], as almost induced us to believe it was the Arkansaw. Distance 10 3-4 miles.

---

of Salida, Colo., and the mouth of the South Arkansas which here enters the main stream, draining the Poncha Pass country—with its very easy road toward the San Luis Valley, Taos and Santa Fé. If Pike had known of it—known (as some hold) that he was on the Arkansas instead of the Red—that route would have saved him that looking into the face of death in frozen Royal Gorge. Referring to the fact mentioned on another page, the proof that Pike knew of the "direct" road to Santa Fé (p. 119), it is surely not assuming too much to say that he must have been very uncertain about all other routes; although, as pointed out, the routes south from the Arkansas by way of the Timpas or the Huerfano very likely were known as "indirect" pathways to New Mexico. Being convinced (soon after leaving the present site of Great Bend, Kan.) that the season was too far advanced to permit him to return that season (p. 137-138), and having no winter clothing for himself or his men, and knowing the direct road which his alleged "spy" mission would compel him to take, why did Pike ignore it, and all such minor routes as the one now passed at Salida?

1st January 1807, *Thursday.*—The doctor and one man marched early, in order to precede the party until they should kill a supply of provision. We had great difficulty in getting our horses along, some of the poor animals having nearly killed themselves falling on the ice. Found on the way one of the mountain rams which the doctor and Brown had killed and left in the road. Skinned it with horns &c. At night ascended a mountain [Spikebuck], and discovered a prairie ahead about eight miles [mesa n. e. of Parkdale], the news of which gave great joy to the party.

2d January, *Friday.*—Laboured all day, but made only one mile, many of our horses much wounded in falling on the rocks. Provision growing short, left Stoute and Miller with two loads, to come on with a sled on the ice, which was on the water in some of the coves. Finding it almost impossible to proceed any further with the horses by the bed of the river, ascended the mountain and immediately after were again obliged to descend an almost perpendicular side of the mountain; in effecting which, one horse fell down the precipice, and bruised himself so miserably, that I conceived it mercy to cause the poor animal to be shot. Many others were nearly killed with falls received: left two more men with loads and tools to make sleds. The two men we had left in the morning had passed us.

3d January, *Saturday.*—Left two more men to make sleds and come on. We pursued the river, and with great difficulty made six miles by frequently cutting roads on the ice, and covering it with earth, in order to go round precipices &c.[187] The men left in the morning encamped with us at night, but those of the day before, we saw nothing off. This day two of the horses became senseless, from the bruises received on the rocks, and were obliged to be left.

4th January, *Sunday.*—We made the prairie about three o'clock, when I detached Mr. Baroney and two soldiers with the horses, in order to find some practicable way for them to get out of the mountains light [unloaded]; I then divided the others into two parties of two men each, to make sleds and bring on the baggage. I determined to continue down the river alone, until I could kill some sustenance, and find the two men who left us on the 2d inst. or the doctor and his companion, for we had no provision, and every one had then to depend on his own exertion for safety and subsistance. Thus we were divided into eight different parties, vis. 1st. The doctor and his companion; 2d. The two men with the first sled; 3d. The interpreter and the two men with the horses; 4th. Myself; 5th. 6th. 7th. and 8th. two men each with sleds at different distances; all of whom except the last, had orders, if they killed any game, to secure some part in a conspicuous place, for their companions in the rear. I marched on about five miles on the river, which was one continued fall through a narrow channel and immense cliffs on the both sides. Near night I came to a place where the rocks were perpendicular on both sides, and no ice (except a narrow border) on the water.[188] I began to look about, in order to discover which way the doctor and his companion had managed, and to find what had become of the two lads with the first sled, when I discovered one of the latter climbing up the side of the rocks; I called to him; he and his companion immediately joined me; they said they had not known whether we were before or in the rear; that they had eaten nothing for the last two days, and that this night they had intended to have boiled a deer skin to subsist on. We at length discovered a narrow ravine, where was the trace of the doctor and his companion; as the water had ran down it and frozen hard, it was one continued sheet of ice; we ascended it with the utmost difficulty and danger, loaded with the baggage. On the summit of the first ridge we found an encampment of the doctor, and where they had killed a deer, but they had now no meat. He afterwards informed me that they had left the greatest part of it hanging on a tree, but supposed the birds had destroyed it. I left the boys to bring up the remainder of the baggage, and went out in order to kill some subsistence: wounded a deer, but the darkness of the night approaching, could not find him, when I returned, hungry, weary and dry, and had only snow to supply the calls of nature. Distance 8 miles.

5th January, Monday.—I went out in the morning to hunt, whilst the two lads were bringing up some of their loads still left at the foot of the mountain. Wounded several deer, but was surprised to find I killed none, and on examining my gun, discovered her bent, owning as I suppose, to some fall on the ice, or rocks; shortly after received a fall, on the side of a hill, which broke her off by the breach; this put me into *desespoir*, as I calculated on it, as my grandest resource for great part of my party; returned to my companions sorely fatigued and hungry; I then took a double barrelled gun and left them, with assurances that the first animal I killed, I would return with part for their relief. About ten o'clock rose [breasted] the highest summit of the mountain,[189] when the unbounded space of the prairies again presented themselves to my view, and from some distant peaks,

I immediately recognized it to be the outlet of the Arkansaw, which we had left nearly one month since! This was a great mortification, but at the same time I consoled myself with the knowledge I had acquired of the source of the La Platte and Arkansaw rivers, with the river to the north west, supposed to be the Pierre Jaun,[190] which scarcely any person but a madman would ever purposely attempt to trace any further than the entrance of those mountains, which had hitherto secured their sources from the scrutinizing eye of civilized man.

I arrived at the foot of the mountain, and bank of the river, in the afternoon, and at the same time discovered on the other shore, Baroney with the horses; they had found quite an eligible pass, and had killed one buffalo and some deer. We proceeded to our old camp, which we had left the 10th of December, and re-occupied it. Saw the traces of the doctor and his companion, but could not discover their retreat.

This was my birth-day, and most fervently did I hope never to pass another so miserably. Distance 7 miles. Fired a gun off as a signal for the doctor.

6th January, Tuesday.—Dispatched the two soldiers back with some provision to meet the first lads, and assist them on, and the interpreter a hunting. About eight o'clock the doctor came in, having seen some of the men. He had been confined to the camp for one or two days, by a vertigo which proceeded from some berries he had eaten on the mountains. His companion brought down six deer, which they had at their camp; thus we again began to be out of danger of starving. In the afternoon, some of the men arrived, and part were immediately returned with provisions, & c. Killed three deer.

7th January, Wednesday.—Sent more men back to assist in the rear, and to carry the poor fellows provisions; at the same time kept Baroney and one man hunting. . . . Killed three deer.

8th January, Thursday.—Some of the different parties arrived. Put one man to stocking my rifle; others sent back to assist up the rear. Killed two deer.

9th January, Friday.—The whole party was once more joined together, when we felt comparatively happy, notwithstanding the great mortifications I experienced at having been so egregiously deceived as to the Red river. I now felt at considerable loss how to proceed, as any idea of services at that time from my horses were entirely preposterous; thus after various plans formed and rejected, and the most mature deliberation, I determined to build a small place for defence and deposit,[191] and leave part of the baggage, horses, my interpreter and one man, and with the balance, our packs of Indian presents, ammunition, tools &c. on our backs, cross the mountains on foot, find the Red river, and then send back a party to conduct their horses and baggage by the most eligible route we could discover, by which time the horses would be so recovered as to be able to endure the fatigues of the march. In consequence of this determination, some were put to constructing the block houses, some to hunting, some to taking care of horses, &c. &c. I, myself, made preparations to pursue a course of observations, which would enable me to ascertain the latitude and longitude of that situation, which I conceived to be an important one. Killed three deer.

10*th January, Saturday.*—Killed five deer; took equal altitudes; angular distances of two stars, &c. but do not now recollect which. Killed three deer.

11*th January, Sunday.*—Ascertained the latitude and took the angular distances of some stars. Killed four deer.

12*th January, Monday.*—Preparing the baggage for a march by separating it, &c. Observations continued.

13*th January, Tuesday.*—Weighed out each man's pack. This day I obtained the angle between sun and moon, which I conceived the most correct way I possessed of ascertaining the longitude, as an immersion and emersion of Jupiter's satellites could not now be obtained. Killed four deer.

14*th January, Wednesday.*—We marched our party, consisting of 18 [12] soldiers, the doctor and myself, each of us carrying 45lb. and as much provision as he thought proper, which, with arms, &c. made on an average, 70lbs. leaving Baroney and one man, Patrick Smith.

We crossed the first ridge (leaving the main branch of the river to the north of us.) and struck on the south fork, on which we encamped, intending to pursue it thro' the mountains, as its course was more southerly.[192]

The doctor killed one deer. Distance 13 miles.

15*th January, Thursday.*—Followed up this branch and passed the main ridge, of what I term the Blue Mountains.[193] Halted early. The doctor, myself, and one hunter, went out with our guns, each killed a deer, and brought them into camp. Distance 19 miles.

16*th January, Friday.*—Marched up the creek all day. Encamped early as it was snowing.[194] I went out to hunt, but killed nothing. Deer on the hill; the mountains lessening. Distance 18 miles.

17*th January, Saturday.*—Marched about four miles, when the great White Mountain[195] presented itself before us, in sight of which we had been for more than one month, and through which we supposed lay the long sought Red river. We now left the creek on the north of us,[196] and bore away more east, to a low place in the mountains.[197] About sun-set we came to the edge of a prairie, which bounded the foot of the mountain, and as there was no wood or water where we were, and the woods from the skirts of the mountains appeared to be at no great distance, I thought proper to march for it; in the middle of said prairie, crossed the creek, which now bore east. Here we all got our feet wet. The night commenced extremely cold. When we halted at the woods, at eight o'clock, for encampment;[198] after getting fires made, we discovered that the feet of nine of our men were frozen, and to add to the misfortune, of both of those whom we called hunters among the number. This night we had no provision. Reaumer's thermometer stood at 18 1-2° below 0 [-10 Fahr.]. Distance 28 miles.

18th January, Sunday.—We started two of the men least injured [hunting]; (the doctor and myself who fortunately were untouched by the frost) also went out to hunt something to preserve existence, near evening we wounded a buffalo with three balls, but had the mortification to see him run off notwithstanding. We concluded it was useless to go home to add to the general gloom, and went amongst some rocks where we encamped and sat up all night; from the intense cold it was impossible to sleep. Hungry and without cover.[199]

19th January, Monday.—We again took the field and after crawling about one mile in the snow, got to shoot eight times among a gang of buffalo, and could plainly perceive two or three to be badly wounded, but by accident they took the wind of us, and to our great mortification all were able to run off. By this time I had become extremely weak and faint, being the fourth day, since we had received sustenance; all of which we were marching hard and the last night had scarcely closed our eyes to sleep. We were inclining our course to a point of woods determined to remain absent and die by ourselves rather than to return to our camp and behold the misery of our poor lads, when we discovered a gang of buffalo coming along at some distance. With great exertions I made out to run and place myself behind some cedars and by the greatest of good luck, the first shot stopped one, which we killed in three more shots; and by the dusk had cut each of us a heavy load with which we determined immediately to proceed to the camp in order to relieve the anxiety of our men, and carry the poor fellows some food. We arrived there about 12 o'clock, and when I threw my load down, it was with difficulty I prevented myself from falling;

I was attacked with a giddiness of the head, which lasted for some minutes. On the countenances of the men was not a frown, nor a desponding eye; but all seemed happy to hail their officer and companions, yet not a mouthful had they eat for four days. On demanding what was their thoughts, the sergeant replied, on the morrow the most robust had determined to set out in search of us; and not return unless they found us, or killed something to preserve the life of their starving companions.

20*th January, Tuesday.*—The doctor and all the men able to march, returned to the buffalo to bring in the balance of the meat.

On examining the feet of those who were frozen we found it impossible for two of them to proceed, and two others only without loads by the help of a stick. One of the former was my waiter, a promising young lad of twenty whose feet were so badly frozen, as to present every probability of loosing them.

The doctor and party returned towards evening loaded with the buffalo meat.

21*st January, Wednesday.*—This day, separated the four loads, we intended to leave and took them at some distance from the camp, where we secured [cached] them. I went up to the foot of the mountain to see what prospect there was of being able to cross it, but had not more than fairly arrived at its base, when I found the snow four or five feet deep; this obliged me to determine to proceed and cotoyer [skirt] the mountain to the south, where it appeared lower, and until we found a place where we could cross.

22*nd January, Thursday.*—I furnished the two poor lads who were to remain with ammunition and made use of every argument in my power to encourage them to have fortitude to resist their fate; and gave them assurance of my sending relief as soon as possible.

We parted, but not without tears. We pursued our march, taking merely sufficient provisions for one meal in order to leave as much as possible for the two poor fellows, who remained (who were John Sparks and Thomas Dougherty.)[200] We went on eight miles and encamped on a little creek,[201] which came down from the mountains; at three o'clock went out to hunt, but killed nothing. Little snow.

23*rd January, Friday.*—After shewing the sergeant a point to steer for, the doctor and myself proceeded on ahead in hopes to kill something, as we were again without victuals. About one o'clock it commenced snowing very hard, we retreated to a small copse of pine where we constructed a camp[202] to shelter us, and as it was time the party should arrive, we sallied forth to search them. We separated, and had not marched more than one or two miles, when I found it impossible to keep any course without the compass, continually in my hand, and then not being able to see more than 10 yards. I began to perceive the difficulty even of finding the way back to our camp and I can scarcely conceive a more dreadful idea than remaining on the wild, where inevitable death must have ensued. It was with great pleasure I again reached the [copse of pine] camp, where I found the doctor had arrived before me. We lay down and strove to dissipate the idea of hunger, and our misery by the thoughts of our far distant homes and relatives. Distance 8 miles.

24th January, Saturday.—We sallied out in the morning and shortly after perceived our little band, marching through the snow (about two and a half feet deep,) silent and with downcast countenances. We joined them and learnt that they finding the snow to fall so thickly that it was impossible to proceed; had encamped about one o'clock the preceding day. As I found all the buffalo had quit the plains, I determined to attempt the traverse of the mountain,[203] in which we persevered, until the snow became so deep, it was impossible to proceed; when I again turned my face to the plain and for the first time in the voyage found myself discouraged; and the first time I heard a man express himself in a seditious manner; he exclaimed, "that it was more than human nature could bear, to march three days without sustenance, through snows three feet deep, and carry burthens only fit for horses" &c. &c.

As I knew very well the fidelity and attachment of the majority of the men, and even of this poor fellow, (only he could not endure fasting) and that it was in my power to chastise him, when I thought proper, I passed it unnoticed for the moment, determined to notice it at a more auspicious time. We dragged our weary and emaciated limbs along, until about 10 o'clock. The doctor and myself who were in advance discovered some buffalo on the plain, when we left our loads, and orders on the snow to proceed to the nearest woods to encamp.[204] We went in pursuit of the buffalo, which were on the move.

The doctor who was then less reduced than myself, ran and got behind a hill and shot one down, which stopped the remainder. We crawled up to the dead one and shot from him as many as twelve or fourteen times among the gang; when they removed out of sight. We then proceeded to butcher the one we had shot; and after procuring each of us a load of the meat, we marched for the camp, the smoke of which was in view. We arrived at the camp to the great joy of our brave lads, who immediately feasted sumptuously, after our repast I sent for the lad who had presumed to speak discontentedly in the course of the day, and addressed him to the following effect: "*Brown*, you this day presumed to make use of language which was seditious and mutinous; I then passed it over, pitying your situation and attributing it to your distress, rather than your inclination, to sow discontent among the party. Had I reserved provisions for ourselves, whilst you were starving; had we been marching along light and at our ease, whilst you were weighed down with your burden; then you would have had some pretext for your observations; but when we were equally hungry, weary, emaciated and charged with burden, which I believe my natural strength is less able to bear, than any man's in the party; when we are always foremost in breaking the road, reconnoitering and the fatigues of the chace; it was the height of ingratitude in you, to let an expression escape which was indicative of discontent; your ready compliance and firm perseverance, I had reason to expect, as the leader of men and my companions, in miseries and dangers. But your duty as a soldier called on your obedience to your officer, and a prohibition of such language, which for this time, I will pardon, but assure you, should it ever be repeated, by instant *death*, I will revenge your ingratitude and punish your disobedience. I take this opportunity like wise to assure you, soldiers generally of my thanks for obedience, perseverance and ready contempt of every danger, which you have generally evinced; I assure you nothing shall be wanting on my part, to procure you the rewards of our government and gratitude of your countrymen."[205]

They all appeared very much affected, and retired with assurances of perseverance in duty &c. Distance 9 miles.

25th January, Sunday.—I determined never again to march with so little provision on hand; as had the storm continued one day longer, the animals would have continued in the mountains, and we should have became so weak as not to be able to hunt, and of course have perished.

The doctor went out with the boys, and they secured three of the buffalo; we commenced bringing in the meat, at which we continued all day.

26th January, Monday.—We marched, determining to cross the mountains, leaving Menaugh[206] encamped with our deposit, after a bad day's march,[207] through snows, some places three feet deep; we struck on a brook which led west, which I followed down, and shortly came to a small run, running west; which we hailed with fervency as the waters of the Red river.[208] Saw some sign of elk. Distance 14 miles.

28th January, Wednesday.—Followed down the ravine and discovered after some time that there had been a road cut out, and on many trees were various hieroglyphicks painted;[209] after marching some miles, we discovered through the lengthy vista at a distance, another chain of mountains[210] and nearer by at the foot of the White mountains, which we were then descending, sandy hills. We marched on the outlet of the mountains, and left the sandy desert to our right; kept down between it and the mountain. . . . When we encamped,[211] I ascended one of the largest hills of sand, and with my glass could discover a large river,[212] flowing nearly north by west, and south by east, through the plain[213] which came out of the third chain of [San Juan] mountains, about N. 75° W. the prairie between the two mountains bore nearly north and south. I returned to camp with the news of my discovery. The sand hills extended up and down at the foot of the White mountains, about fifteen miles, and appeared to be about five miles in width.

Their appearance was exactly that of the sea in a storm, (except as to color) not the least sign of vegetation existing thereon. Distance 15 miles.

29th January, Thursday.—Finding the distance too great to attempt crossing immediately to the river, in a direct line, we marched obliquely to a copse of woods, which made down a considerable distance from the mountains.[214] Distance 17 miles. Saw sign of horses.

30th January, Friday.—We marched hard, and arrived in the evening on the banks (then supposed Red river) of the Rio del Norte.[215] Distance 24 miles.

31st January, Saturday.—As there was no timber here we determined on descending until we found timber, in order to make transports to descend the river with, where we might establish a position that four or five might defend against the insolence, cupidity and barbarity of the savages, whilt the others returned to assist on the poor fellows who were left behind, at different points.[216] We descended 18 miles, when we met a large west branch, emptying into the main stream, up which about five miles, we took up our station.[217] Killed one deer. Distance 18 miles.

1st February, Sunday.—Laid out the place for our works,[218] and went out hunting.

2d February, Monday.—The doctor and myself went out to hunt, and with great difficulty, by night, killed one deer, at the distance of seven or eight miles from camp, which we carried in.

3d February, Tuesday.—Spent in reading &c.

4th February, Wednesday.—Went out hunting, but could not kill any thing. One of my men killed a deer.

5th February, Thursday.—The doctor and myself went out to hunt, and after chasing some deer for several hours, without success, we ascended a high hill, which lay south of our camp, from whence we had a view of all the prairie and rivers to the north of us; it was at the same time one of the most sublime and beautiful inland prospects ever presented to the eyes of man. The prairie lying nearly north and south, was probably 60 miles by 45.

The main river bursting out of the western mountain, and meeting from the north-east, a large branch, which divides the chain of mountains, proceeds down the prairie, making many large and beautiful islands, one of which I judge contains 100,000 acres of land, all meadow ground, covered with innumerable herds of deer; about six miles from the mountains which cross the prairie, at the south end, a branch of 12 steps wide, pays its tribute to the main stream from the west course. Due W. 12°. N. 75°. W. 6°. Four miles below is a stream of the same size, which enters on the east; its general

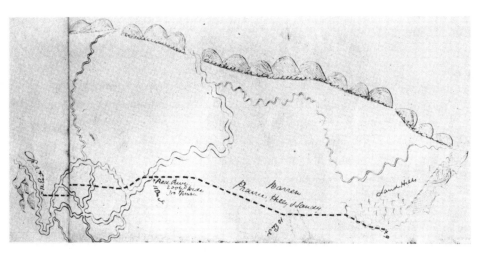

Map 4: Pike's Map of the San Luis Valley Section
This shows Pike's line of march from the "Sand Hills" to "Red River" (Rio Grande) and south to his post on Conejos. His Charts 17 and 18 do not go together perfectly, as the discrepancy in his line of march shows where it crosses the branches of the Rio Grande. The entry "Red River" marks Pike's crossing place of the Rio Grande, four miles below Alamosa, Colorado.

course is N. 65°.E. up which was a large road;[219] from the entrance of this down, was about three miles, to the junction of the west fork, which waters the foot of the hill on the north, whilst the main river wound along in meanders on the east. In short, this view combined the sublime and beautiful; the great and lofty mountains covered with eternal snows, seemed to surround the luxuriant vale, crowned with perennial flowers, like a terrestrial paradise, shut out from the view of man.

6th February, Friday.—The doctor having some pecuniary demands in the province of New Mexico, conceived this to be the most eligible point for him to go in, and return previous to all my party having joined me from the Arkansaw, and that I was prepared to descend to Natchitoches: he therefore this day made his preparations for marching tomorrow.[220] I went out hunting, and killed a deer at three miles distance, which, with great difficulty I brought in whole.

We continued to go on with the works of our stockade or breast work, which was situated on the north bank of the west branch, about five miles from its junction with the main river and was on a strong plan.

7th February, Saturday.—The doctor marched alone for Santa Fe, and as it was uncertain whether this gentleman would ever join me again, I at that time, committed the following testimonial of respect for his good qualities to paper, which I do not, at this time, feel any disposition to efface. He has had the benefit of a liberal education, without having spent his time as too many of our gentlemen do in colleges, viz. in skimming on the surfaces of sciences, without ever endeavouring to make themselves masters of the solid foundations, but Robinson studied and reasoned; with these qualifications he possessed a liberality of mind too great ever to reject an hypothesis because it was not agreeable to the dogmas of the schools; or adopt it, because it had all the eclat of novelty—his soul could conceive great actions, and his hand was ready to achieve them; in short, it may truly be said that nothing was above his genius, nor anything so minute that he conceived it entirely unworthy of consideration. As a gentleman and companion in dangers, difficulties and hardships, I in particular, and the expedition, generally, owe much to his exertions. In the evening I dispatched corporal Jackson, with four men, to re-cross the mountains, in order to bring in the baggage left with the frozen lads, and to see if they were yet able to come on. This detachment left me with four men only; two of which had their feet frozen; they were employed in finishing the stockade, and myself to support them by the chase.

8*th February, Sunday.*—Refreshing my memory as to the French grammar, and overseeing the works.

9*th February, Monday.*—Hunting, &c.

10*th February, Tuesday.*—Read and labored at our works.

11*th February, Wednesday.*—Hunting. Killed three deer.

12*th February, Thursday.*—Studying.

13*th February, Friday.*—Hunting.

14*th February, Saturday.*—Crossed the river and examined the numerous springs, which issued from the foot of the hill, opposite to our camp, which were strongly impregnated with mineral qualities, as not only to keep clear of ice previous to their joining the main branch, but to keep open the west fork until its junction with the main river, and for a few miles afterwards, whilst all the other branches in the neighborhood were bound in the adamantine chains of winter.

15*th February, Sunday.*—Reading, &c. Works going on.

16*th February, Monday.*—I took one man and went out hunting, about six miles from the post, shot and wounded a deer. Immediately afterwards, discovered two horsemen rising the summit of a hill, about half a mile to our right. As my orders were to avoid giving alarm or offence to the Spanish government of New Mexico, I endeavoured to avoid them at first, but when we attempted to retreat, they persued us at full charge, flourishing their lances, and when we advanced, they would retire as fast as their horses could carry them; seeing this we got in a small ravine, in hopes to decoy them near enough to oblige them to come to a parley, which happened agreeably to our desires, as they came on hunting us with great caution; we suffered them to get within 40 yards, where we had allured them, but were about running off again, when I ordered the soldier to lay down his arms and walk towards them; at the same time standing ready with my rifle to kill either, who should lift an arm in an hostile manner; I then hollowed to them, that we were Americans, and friends, which were almost the only two words I knew in the Spanish language; when with great signs of fear they came up, and proved to be a Spanish dragoon and a civilized Indian, armed after their manner, of which we see a description in the *Essai Militaire.* We were jealous of our arms on both sides, and acted with great precaution. They informed me that was the fourth day since they had left Santa Fe; that Robinson had arrived there, and was received with great kindness by the governor. As I knew them to be spies, I thought proper to inform them merely, that I was about to descend the river to Natchitoches. We sat here on the ground a long time, and finding they were determined not to leave me, we rose and bid them adieu, but they demanded where our camp was; and finding they were not about to leave us, I thought it most proper to take them with me, thinking we were on Red river, and of course in the territory claimed by the United States.

We took the road to my fort, and as they were on horseback, they travelled rather faster than myself; they were halted by the sentinel, and immediately retreated much surprised. When I came up I took them in, and then explained to them, as well as possible, my intentions of descending the river to Natchitoches, but at the same time told them that if governor Allencaster would send out an officer with an interpreter, who spoke French or English, I would do myself the pleasure to give his excellency every reasonable satisfaction as to my intentions in coming on his frontiers. They informed me that on the second day they would be in Santa Fe, but were careful never to suggest an idea of my being on the Rio del Norte.[221] As they concluded [speaking], I did not think as I spoke; they were very anxious to ascertain our numbers, &c.; seeing only five men here, they could not believe we came without horses, &c. To this I did not think proper to give them any satisfaction, giving them to understand we were in many parties, &c.

17th February, Tuesday.—In the morning, our two Spanish visitors departed, after I had made them some trifling presents, with which they seemed highly delighted. After their departure, we commenced working at our little work, as I thought it probable the governor might dispute my right to descend the Red river, and send out Indians, or some light party to attack us; I therefore determined to be as much prepared to receive them as possible. This evening the corporal and three of the men arrived, who had been sent back to the camp of the frozen lads. They informed me that two men would arrive the next day; one of which was Menaugh, who had been left alone on the 27th January, but that the other two, Dougherty and Sparks, were unable to come. They said that they had hailed them with tears of joy, and were in despair when they again left them, with the chance of never seeing them more. They sent on to me some of the bones taken out of their feet, and conjured me by all that was sacred, not to leave them to perish far from the civilized world. Ah! little did they know my heart, if they could suspect me of conduct so ungenerous. No! before they should be left, I would for months have carried the end of a litter, in order to secure them, the happiness of once more seeing their native homes; and being received in the bosom of a grateful country.

Thus those poor lads are to be invalids for life, made infirm at the commencement of manhood and in the prime of their course, doomed to pass the remainder of their days in misery and want; for what is the pension? not sufficient to buy a man his victuals! what man would even lose the smallest of his joints for such a trifling pittance.[222]

18*th February, Wednesday.*—The other two boys arrived; in the evening I ordered the sergeant and one man to prepare to march to-morrow for the Arkansaw, where we had left our interpreter, horses, &c. to conduct them on, and on his return to bring the two lads who were still in the mountains.

19*th February, Thursday.*—Sergeant William E. Meek, marched with one man, whose name was Theodore Miller, and I took three other men to accompany him out some distance, in order to point out to him a pass in the mountain, which I conceived more eligible for horses than the one we had come. I must here remark the effect of habit, discipline and example in [the fact of] two soldiers soliciting a command of more than 180 miles over two great ridges of mountains covered with snow, inhabited by lands [bands] of unknown savages [who were], in the interest of a nation [Spain], with whom we were not on the best understanding; and to perform this journey, each had about 10 pounds of venison; only let me ask what would our soldiers generally think, on being ordered on such a tour, thus equipped? yet those men volunteered it, with others and were chosen; for which they thought themselves highly honored; we accompanied them about six miles, pointed out the pass alluded to, in a particular manner, but the corporal [later] reported that the new one which I obliged him to take was impassable, having been three days in snows nearly middle deep.

We then separated and having killed a deer, sent one of the men back to the fort with it. With the other two, I kept on my exploring trip down the river on the east side, at some leagues from its banks, intending to return up it; at nine o'clock at night, encamped on a small creek which emptied into the river by nearly a due east course.

20*th February, Friday.*—We marched down the river for a few hours, but seeing no fresh sign of persons, or any other object to attract our attention took up our route for the fort; discovered the sign of horses and men on the shore. We arrived after night and found all well.

21*st February, Saturday.*—As I was suspicious that possibly some party of

Indians might be harboring round, I gave particular orders to my men, if they discovered any people to endeavor to retreat undiscovered but if not, never to run, and not to suffer themselves to be disarmed or taken prisoners but conduct whatever party discovered them, if they could not escape to the fort.

22nd February, Sunday.—As I began to think it was time we received a visit from the Spaniards or their emisaries, I established a look out guard on the top of a hill all day and at night a sentinel in a bastion on the land side; studying, reading &c. Working at our ditch to bring the river round the works.

23rd February, Monday.—Reading, writing &c. the men at their usual work, &c.

24th February, Tuesday.—Took one man with me and went out on the Spanish road hunting; killed one deer and wounded several others; and as we were a great distance from the fort, we encamped near the road all night. Saw several signs of horses.

25th February, Wednesday.—Killed two more deer when we marched for our post. Took all three of the deer with us, and arrived about 9 o'clock at night, as much fatigued &c. as ever I was in my life. Our arrival dissipated the anxiety of the men, who began to be apprehensive we were taken or killed by some of the savages.

26th February, Thursday.—In the morning was apprized by the report of a gun, from my lookout guard; of the approach of strangers. Immediately after two Frenchmen arrived.

My sentinel halted them and ordered them to be admitted after some questions; they informed me that his excellency governor Allencaster had heard it was the intention of the Utah Indians, to attack me; had detached an officer with 50 dragoons to come out and protect me, and that they would be here in two days. To this I made no reply; but shortly after the party came in sight to the number of, I afterwards learnt 50 dragoons and 50 mounted militia of the province, armed in the same manner, viz: Lances, escopates and pistols. My sentinel halted them at the distance of about 50 yards. I had the works manned. I thought it most proper to send out the two Frenchmen to inform the commanding officer that it was my request he should leave his party in a small copse of woods where he halted, and that I would meet him myself in the prairie, in which our work was situated. This I did, with my sword on me only. When I was introduced to Don Ignatio Saltelo and Don Bartholomew Fernandez, two lieutenants, the former the commandant of the party. I gave them an invitation to enter the works, but requested the troops might remain where they were; this was complied with, but when they came round and discovered that to enter, they were obliged to crawl on their bellies over a small draw-bridge, they appeared astonished but entered without further hesitation.

We first breakfasted on some deer, meal, goose and some biscuit (which the civilized indian who came out as a spy) had brought me, After breakfast the commanding officer addressed me as follows: "Sir, the governor of New Mexico, being informed you had missed your route, ordered me to offer you, in his name, mules, horses, money, or whatever you may stand in need of to conduct you to the head of Red river; as from Santa Fe to where it is sometimes navigable, is eight days journey and we have guides and the routes of the traders to conduct us." "What, said I, (interrupting him) is not this the Red river," No sir! the Rio del Norte." I immediately ordered my flag to be taken down and rolled up, feeling how sensibly I had committed myself, in entering their territory, and was conscious that they must have positive orders to take me in.

"He now" added "that he had provided one hundred mules and horses, to take in my party and baggage and how anxious his excellency was to see me at Santa Fe." I stated to him, the absence of my sergeant, the situation of the balance of the party and that my orders would not justify my entering into the Spanish territory. He urged still further until I began to feel myself a little heated in the argument and told him in a peremptory style, I would not go until the arrival of my sergeant with the balance of the party. He replied that there was not the least restraint to be used, only that it was necessary his excellency should receive an explanation of my business on his frontier, but that I could go now, or on the arrival of my party; but that if none went in at present he should be obliged to send in for provisions, but that if I would now march, he would leave an Indian interpreter and an escort of dragoons to conduct the sergeant into Santa Fe. His mildness induced me to tell him that I would march, but must leave two men, in order to meet the sergeant and party, to instruct him as to coming in, as he never would come without a fight, if not ordered.

I was induced to consent to the measure, by conviction, that the officer had positive orders to bring me in, and as I had no orders to commit hostilities, and indeed had committed myself, although innocently, by violating their territory, I conceived it would appear better to shew a will to come to an explanation than to be any way constrained; yet my situation was so eligible, and I could so easily have put them at defiance, that it was with great reluctance I suffered all our labor to be lost without once trying the efficacy of it.

My compliance seem to spread general joy through their party as soon as it was communicated, but it appeared to be different with my men, who wished to have a little *dust* (as they expressed themselves) and were likewise fearful of treachery.

My determination being once taken, I gave permission for the Spanish lieutenant's men to come to the outside of the works, and some of mine to go out and see them; when the hospitality and goodness of the Creoles and Metifs began to manifest itself by their producing their provision and giving it to my men, covering them with their blankets, &c.

After writing orders to my sergeant, and leaving them with my corporal and one private, who was to remain, we sallied forth, mounted our horses, and went up the river about 12 miles, to a place where the Spanish officers had made a camp deposit, from whence we sent down mules for our baggage, &c.

Z. M. PIKE, Captain,

1st United States Battalion Infantry.

Washington City, January, 1808.

Captain Pike was now taken to Santa Fé and Mexico, and the story of his experiences is related in *An Account of Expeditions*, 205–277 and appendixes thereto. Our purpose here is accomplished by giving only his summary of those Mexican experiences in his two letters to General Wilkinson of April 20th and July 5th, which follow. Pike's *Mexican Tour* journal appears in the following chapter.

Being hindered by the polite formalities of his Spanish hosts, although handsomely treated, except for the trickery respecting his papers which were held in Mexico, Pike made the best use of his eyes and ears that any closely watched "guest" could have done, and acquired quite as much information about the country, its resources and strength, as if (as he states) "he had been sent for that purpose." The critics who have espoused the "spy" theory of his expedition have made, of course, as much out of this as possible. But the material had to be handled gingerly by them—for it has proved a two-edged sword. No evidence was ever found that he connived with anyone who might have furthered any Burr-Wilkinson plot. On the other hand Pike reported all his findings to our government. Dr. Robinson, his faithful friend and comrade, fought four years with Mexican rebels against Spain, winning a brigadier-general's epaulettes. Critics have essayed to make a point of Pike's early denial to Spanish authorities that Robinson belonged to his party. Officially, the "white lie" was a truth; for his services as physician he had been allowed to accompany the expedition and to share and share alike with its members. Pike fully explained that he feared that difficulties in which the Doctor was embroiled would be increased by a plain statement of his relation to Pike's company; its leader, attempting to do a friendly act that in nowise would injure the Spaniards, denied Robinson's relations. Pike later fully explained this by letter to the Spanish authorities.[223] But, of course, having prejudged Pike as a crook, critics gave no more credit to the explanation than to anything else Pike wrote which discredited their "spy" theory.

At the earliest moment possible, April 20th, Pike addressed General Wilkinson and, after a brief statement of his experiences, expressed the hope that he could obtain the appointment as one of the commissioners to adjust the boundary line between Spain and the United States. It is to be noted that he does this before hearing of Wilkinson's being entangled in the Burr episode and even before reporting adequately the results of his expedition. This very little comports with the appropriate actions of such an agent, as the advocates of the "spy" theory claim Pike to have been. As such, he would be expected to report in full and await orders—not ask for an appointment that might shift his activities far from the field where his patron desired and needed them. At no point does the "spy" explanation either account for what Pike does, interpret any of his actions or square with anything he wrote or said.

His two important letters to General Wilkinson of April and July follow:
[PIKE TO WILKINSON][224]

Chihuahua, 20th April, 1807.

My Dear General,

Never did I sit down to address you with a heart so oppressed with anxiety and mortification; but knowing the uncertainty which must exist as to the fate of myself and party, I conceive it proper to attempt a communication, although I think it extremely uncertain, owing to the difficulty of the route, if it should ever come to hand, or at least, previous to my arrival at the territories of the United States, owing to various circumstances which are not to be communicated in a letter. I was detained in the mountains of Mexico until the month of January, and in February found myself with eight of my party *only,* on the head branches of the

Rio del Norte, which I then conceived to be the sources of the Red River, our information making the latter extend the whole distance between the former and the Arkansaw, although its sources are some hundred miles below either of the others.

Here I was encountered by two officers and 100 men, who bore orders from the governor of New Mexico, to cause me and my party to march to the capital of said province; but his request was in the most polite style, and in fact, the commanding officer assured me there was not the *least constraint,* but that his excellency desired a conference, and that I then should be conducted by the most direct route, to the navigable part of the Red river, from whence I could immediately descend to Nachitoches. Although dubious of the *faith* of the invitation, and in a situation from whence I could have defended myself as long as my provision lasted, or until I might probably have escaped in the night, yet knowing the pacific intentions of our government, and the particular instructions of my general, as to my conduct in case of a rencounter with a body of Spanish troops, I conceived it most proper to comply with the demand and repair to Santa Fe; and, as the balance of my party who remained in the mountains, were, many of them, invalids, and not in a situation to be able to return, I conceived it most proper to leave orders for them to follow, accompanied by an escort of Spanish troops left for that purpose.

On my arrival in Santa Fe, his excellency governor Allencaster informed me it was necessary that I should immediately march to Chihuahua, province of Biscay, in order to present myself to his excellency the commandant-general N. Salcedo, for further orders. This being so different from what I had been taught to expect, that I demanded of governor Allencaster, in a written communication, to know if I was to consider myself and party as prisoners of war? He replied in the negative. We marched on the following day, and arrived at this place on the 2d instant, from whence, I am informed by the general, I shall march, on the arrival of the remainder of my party, for Nachitoches.

I must here acknowledge myself and party under infinite obligations to the friendship and politeness of all the Spanish officers, and in a particular manner to the commandant-general of those provinces.

Should the politics of our country make it necessary to augment the army previous to my arrival, I hope the general will approve of my aspiring to a considerable promotion in the new corps. Should the line of demarcation be amicably adjusted between the United States and Spain, I hope to obtain the appointment of one of the commissioners, as I make bold to assert that, with respect to the arrangements necessary, and a knowledge of the country through which the line must pass, I am better instructed than any other officer of my age in our service; and, if joined to a colleague of profound astronomical knowledge, we could surmount every difficulty. I likewise beg leave to suggest to your excellency that I conceive the information I hold of considerable consequence in the determination of the line of limits, and that (if it be not already determined) I can throw considerable light on the subject.

I hope your excellency will be pleased to forward orders for me to Nachitoches, informing me if I am to descend to *Orleans* or proceed to the federal city, and, if the latter, permitting me to pass by Louisiana, in order to visit and arrange the affairs of my family, to whom I beg the favor of my general to communicate the certainty of the existence of myself and Dr. Robinson, who begs to be sincerely remembered to you.

The general will pardon the requests I have made of him, knowing the confidence of my heart, in the paternal and soldierly esteem which he has manifested for him, who has the honor to be,

with every sentiment of esteem,

respect, and high consideration,

dear general,

your obedient humble servant,

(Signed)   Z. M. PIKE.

His excellency gen. Wilkinson.

N.B. Please to present my respectful compliments to your lady, and the doctor's; and mine to James, [Lieutenant Wilkinson], who, I hope, has long ere this arrived in safety.

(Signed)   P.

[PIKE TO WILKINSON][225]

Nachitoches, 5th July, 1807.

DEAR GENERAL,

Once more I address you from the land of freedom and under the banners of our country. Your esteemed favor of the 20th May now lies before me, in which I recognise the sentiments of my general and friend, and will endeavor, as far as my limited abilities permit, to do justice to the spirit of your instructions.

I must premise to your excellency that my letter of the 20th April, dated at Chihuahua, went through a perusal by general Salcedo, previous to his forwarding it.

That letter stated the mode of my being brought into Santa Fe, and

I will now state to your excellency the proceeding on the subject of my papers. I will omit the hauteur of the reception given me by governor Allencaster, for a more particular communication, which changed afterwards to extreme politeness. Being under no restrictions previous to arriving at Santa Fe, I had secreted all my papers which I conceived necessary to preserve, leaving my book of charts, my orders, and such others as to induce the governor to know me in my proper character, and to prevent his suspicions being excited to a stricter enquiry.

On examining my commission, orders, &c. he told me to remove my trunk to my own quarters, and that on the morrow he would converse with me on the subject. I had caused the men to secrete my papers about their bodies, conceiving it safer than in the baggage; but in the evening, finding the ladies of Santa Fe were treating them to wine, &c. I was apprehensive their intemperance might discover the secret, and took them from all but one (who had my journal in full) who could not be found, and put them in my trunk, conceiving that the inspection was over; but next morning an officer, with two men, waited on me and informed me he had come for me to visit the governor, and brought these two men to take up my trunk. I immediately perceived I was outgeneraled. On my arrival at the governor's house, his excellency demanded if I had the key. My reply was in the affirmative; when he observed "it is well"; my trunk would be a sacred deposit in the charge of the officer, who would escort me to Chihuahua, for which place, after dinner, I marched, under the escort of lieutenant *Don Facundo Malgares,* and 65 men, whose character I beg leave to introduce to the attention of your excellency as an European possessing all the high sense of honor which formerly so evidently distinguished his nation, as the commandant of the 600 troops who made the expedition to the *Pawnees,* as an officer of distinguished merit, who in his mode of living fully justified the pomp and style of his actions, outshines many of their governors of provinces, and whom in my future reports I shall have frequent occasion to quote. He observed to me, "The governor informs me, sir, your trunk is under restrictions, but your word of honor as a soldier that no papers shall be taken out, and you have free ingress, as usual." I gave it, and I presume it is scarcely necessary to add it was religiously adhered to.

On our arrival at Chihuahua the general demanded my trunk, and on its being opened and the papers laid on the table, he took them in hand one by one and demanded what was the purport of each, which *truth* obliged me to declare; and had I been disposed to have equivocated, ensign Walker, of his Catholic majesty's service, who stood present and assisted in the examination, could have immediately detected the fraud; also his excellency understands sufficient of the English language to discover the general purport of any paper.

After going throug them in this manner and separating them into two piles, he observed to me, "You will leave those papers for my inspection, and in the mean while, in concert with ensign Walker (who will give the Spanish translation) you will give me a detailed account of your route, views, destination, &c. and during that time I will examine the papers now before me." To this I complied, flattering myself that it was his intention to return me my papers, by his demanding a sketch; also, so great was my confidence in the all-protecting *name* of my *country*, I conceived it was a greater step than the general would venture to take, to seize on the papers. But when I had finished the proposed sketch and presented it, and found a still further delay, I addressed the general on the subject, when, after a few days, some were returned but I was officially informed that "the remaining papers were seized on, but would be kept in the secret cabinet of that captain-generalship, until the pleasure of his Catholic majesty was known,"—at the same time presenting me with a certificate specifying the number and contents of those detained, and added that they were assorted by my *own hand, and voluntarily.* This assertion was so contrary to truth, honor, or the line of conduct a general should have pursued with a young gentleman, that I took the liberty of telling one of the officers who signed said certificate that it was incorrect. But as serjeant Meek was still in the rear, with nearly all my baggage, I took care to give him orders that none of said baggage should be opened, except by force, which will evince that, although I preferred acting like a gentleman to obliging general Salcedo to resort to rough treatment, yet that it was not a volunteer surrender of my papers. But the general will please to recollect that my journals were saved at Santa Fe, which were continued and are entire to this post; a fortunate circumstance of the doctor's having copied my courses and distances through all the route (except an excursion we made to the source of the river La Platte) unto the Spanish territories, preserved them. These will enable me to exhibit a correct chart of the route, although not so minutely as the one seized on, which was plotted daily by the eye and angular observations. Thus the only essential papers lost were my astronomical observations, meteorological tables, and a book containing remarks on minerals, plants, &c. with the manners, population, customs, &c. of the savages; but the result of the former were in part communicated, and probably my journal may supply part of the balance, and our memories will make the loss of the latter of but little consequence. While in the Spanish territories

I was forbid the use of pen and paper, notwithstanding which I kept a journal, made meteorological observations, took courses and distances, from the time I entered their country until my arrival at this place, all of which I brought safe off in the men's guns (where I finally secreted my papers) without detection.

From our unremitting attention day and night, the immense territory they led us through, the long time we were in their country, I have been able to collect (I make bold to assert) a correct account of their military force, regular and irregular; also, important and interesting information on geographical situations, political sentiments, and dispositions of the people of every class, manners, arts, resources, riches, revenues, value and productions of their mines, situation, &c. &c. also, with the annual revenues paid Bonaparte, and had we possessed as great a knowledge of the Spanish language when we entered the territories as when we left them, our information would have been nearly as complete as I could have wished it, if sent expressly for the purpose of acquiring it, by the open authority of his majesty. But the French language was greatly beneficial, in which my communications were sometimes made. By the serjeant, who is still in the rear and never suffered to join me, as general Salcedo conceived he would probably procure some information from him, which he could not if immediately under my orders, I expect many other communications of importance from many individuals, who promised to forward them by him. But I presume the general has found himself in an error, as I perceive by a letter from him to governor Cordero, the serjeant killed one of his [Salcedo's] men, in consequence of some improper conduct, and the general accuses him of great intractibility, as he is pleased to term it. From the foregoing statement your excellency will observe that I yet possess immense matter, the result of one year's travel, in a country desert and populated, which have *both* been long the subject of curiosity to the philosopher, the anxious desires of the miser, and the waking thoughts and sleeping dreams of the man of *ambition* and the *aspiring* soul, and in our present critical situation, I do conceive, immensely important, and which opens a scene for the *generosity* and *aggrandisement* of our country, with a wide and splendid field for harvests of honor for individuals. But my papers are in a mutilated state, from the absolute necessity I was under to write on small pieces in the Spanish country; also, from being injured in the gun barrels, some of which I filed three times off to take out the papers. These circumstances make it necessary, in the first place, to take a rough copy as they stand; then it will be necessary to assort the matter, as military, political, moral, trade, clime, soil, &c. all now form an undigested mass: then, sir, the combining each, the plotting, &c. would take up a time of considerable extent for one man; and to make duplicates after they were in order could not be done in three months. The general may recollect it was nearly that period before my reports were completed last year, although assisted by Mr. [Antoine] Nau and the serjeant-major, sometimes by lieutenants [James B.] Wilkinson and [Henry Richard] Graham. Also, with respect to the Spanish country, I must know the extent of the objects in view, in order to embrace those points in my reports; and further, my dear sir, my health is by no means the most perfect, my eyes extremely weak; that it is almost impossible for me to continue for one hour with the pen in my hand, and by that time have a considerable pain in my breast. From those circumstances my general will perceive the almost *impracticability* of my complying with the contents of his letter as to duplicate reports from this place; but I shall immediately commence the business of arranging and digesting my papers, and will proceed with the labour with every perseverance my situation will permit of until the arrival of my serjeant and the balance of the party (should they not retard more than 20 days) when I shall proceed immediately to St. Louis, and from thence through Kentucky, Virginia, &c. to the federal city, making no unnecessary delay, and all the whole of the route prosecuting my business at every leisure moment. When at Washington I flatter myself with your assistance and advice. As I propose taking courses, distances, &c. from thence to St. Louis, it will be making the tour of the greatest part of Louisiana, crossing the main rivers at different points, when I am certain with the survey of the Missouri by captains Lewis and Clark, my own of the Mississippi, lieutenant Wilkinson's of the lower Arkansaw (which river I surveyed to its source), and Mr. Dunbar's of Red river, can be formed the completest survey of Louisiana ever yet taken.

The instruments I had with me I wish the general to inform me in what light they stood, as the most of them were ruined in the mountains by the falling of the horses from precipices, &c. and I left an order at Chihuahua for the serjeant to sell them at a certain price, as the addition of a land carriage of 500 leagues would not add to their benefit. Baroney, if alive, is with my serjeant, and has proved a noble fellow in his line, and I beg liberty to recommend him to some appointment near the Kans, should any offer. I must further add the following anecdote of my men, in whose breasts lay the whole secret of my papers, and whom I frequently, when in the Spanish territories, was obliged to punish severals [severely] for out-rages committed when in a state of intoxication, yet never did one offer, or show a disposition to discover it. It is certain they knew *instant death* would follow; but still their fidelity to their trust is remarkable. I have charged them as to communications, and shall dispose of them in such a manner as not to put it in their power to give things much publicity. Dr. Robinson has accompanied me to the whole route, is still with me, and of whom I take a pleasure in acknowledging I have received important services, as my companion in dangers and hardships, counsellor in difficulties, and to whose chymical, botanical, and mineralogical knowledge the expedition was greatly indebted: in short, sir, he is a young gentleman of talents, honor and perseverance, possessing, in my humble opinion, a military turn of mind, and would, I believe, in case of an augmentation of the army, enter, if he could obtain a rank above a subaltern. I hope the general will be pleased to have my copies *forwarded* by lieutenant Wilkinson, so that I can command the use of them at Washington; also, all my letters written him in the expedition, as they contain information I wish to refer to, and the copies were seized. Dr. [John] Sibley has informed me the expedition up the Arkansaw is suspended, which supercedes the necessity of my sending the express ordered.

I congratulate the general on the safe arrival of lieutenant Wilkinson, and am sorry to hear of the difficulties he encountered. I have been obliged to draw money of the Spanish government, which I have to pay to their ambassador at Washington. I supported those of my men with me all the time in the Spanish country, separated from my baggage, and never permitted to have it join me, presented to the commandant-general in a blanket cappot [capote]: I was under the necessity of going into very considerable expense to support what I not only considered my own honor, but the dignity of our army. This, where a captain's pay is 2400 dollars per annum, was a ruinous thing to my finances; but I hope it may be taken into due consideration.

After making myself pretty perfect in the French language, I have obtained such a knowledge of the Spanish as to make me confident in asserting, in three or four years I will with ease make myself master of the latter, Italian and Portuguese, sufficient to read all, and speak and write the Spanish. The doctor has even exceeded me in that point. I mention this to the general, as I know the interest he takes in the improvement of his military protege.

We had heard in the Spanish dominions of the convulsions of the western country, originating in Mr. Burr's plans, and that you were implicated; sometimes that you was arrested, sometimes superceded, &c. Those reports (although I never gave credit to them) gave me great unhappiness, as I conceived that the shafts of calumny were aiming at your fame and honor, in a foreign country, where they had hitherto stood high, and were revered and respected by every class. At St. Antonio colonel Cordero informed me of the truth of the statement [falsity of those reports], which took a load from my breast and made me comparatively happy, and I hope ere long will the villainy be unmasked and malignity and slander hide their heads. The before mentioned gentleman sent you by me a box of Spanish chocolate, which I shall forward to colonel Cushing. Governor Herrara said the *maliciousness* of the world was such as to forbid his writing, but begged to be sincerely remembered to you. A letter addressed to me Cincinnatti, Ohio, may possibly reach me on my route, when I hope to receive the approbation of my conduct. Many letters written to me, addressed to this place, have been secreted or destroyed; possibly the general can give me a hint on the subject.

Those ideas have made a deep impression on my mind, and did not an *all ruling passion* sway me irresistibly to the profession of *arms* and the *paths* of military *glory,* I would long since have resigned my sword for the rural cot, where peace, health and content would at least be our inmates, should not our *brows* be crowned with laurel.

I must now conclude, as this letter has far exceeded the bounds proposed when commenced; but the effusions of my heart are such on its contents, that I could not limit them to a more contracted space. Excuse my scrawl, as I am entirely out of practice, but believe me to be,

dear general,

with high respect and esteem,

your obedient, servant,

(Signed)   Z. M. PIKE, captain.

General Wilkinson.

[GOVERNOR ALENCASTER'S ORDERS TO PARTIES
SENT OUT TO INTERCEPT PIKE]

The contrast between Pike's forlorn and crippled handful of men and the formal and elaborate preparations for his reception by the Spaniards is illustrated by Governor Alencaster's orders to his scouts issued October 18 when Pike was just reaching the Arkansas River:

"Instructions which must govern 1st Lieutenant Don Nicholas de Almanza, and 2d Lieutenant Don Ignatius Sotelo, at the Posts they are to establish, the first at the Place called Las Conchas, four days march from the Plazas del Bado, and the second at the proper point to watch the known approaches by the Sangre de Christo and River Almagre [Arkansas], about five days' journey from Taos: both to have parties consisting of one captain and eight soldiers and a total of 32 men including Citizens and Indians in each.

1st— First they are to select the most advantageous ground and establish a Scout Service extending their survey as far as possible to see if they discover any tracks, or if they see any people approaching, so that at the first notice they may go out to inspect them.

2d— The expert or scouting explorers must be kept at work always within a reasonable distance, because as small parties have to march by night and on foot, taking precautions not to be seen and reconnoitre from distant and favorable points during the day, they must report whatever they see, but making sure their reports are faithful and exact, especially as to whether few or many people are discovered, since reports carelessly made always lead to trouble, and this must be understood by those sent out on these parties, and that on the accuracy of their reports their recommendation will depend.

3d— Just as soon as they are posted they are to send me a courier every third day, even when nothing has happened, letting me know that this is so and that they are at their Post, these couriers are to be called ordinary, and for any special news that may come up which admits of no delay, an extraordinary courier must be dispatched ordering the rapidity of his journey according to the requirements of the case.

❦

6th—The aforesaid Commanders, as soon as any party of troops or armed men presents itself, will send forward a man to deliver to the Commandant the letter in French which each is to carry by way of precaution, it being expected that the said Leader will advance in front of his troop to receive it, and on seeing that he has halted and read the letter, the Officer of the Post will advance as if implying that he is ready to talk with him; if the other Commander marches on, he will follow him at a distance with the same number of men that he sees the other has, taking in his Company the Interpreter of the Comanches or of the Pawnees.

7th—As the said letter is for the purpose of asking the object of their coming, (whether) to give notice of Pike and his party (or) is itself aimed at that end, and if the party does not go on, and if the Commander wishes to come and talk with me, with a squad of not more than ten men and as many of the scouting party as a sufficient escort, the officer of the post will in such terms as he can, insinuate that in this way harmonious relations may be confirmed, whether the party that appears before him be large or small, and in case the strangers relying on their superior force persist in going forward, either by using arms, or by trampling down the small scouting party, the said Commandant will retire to join the rear-guard; but it will be better to avoid such an encounter, by warning the Commander, or making him understand if possible that he will meet many troops stationed in advantageous positions who will not permit him to pass, and if every means fails, if he is determined, after holding him sufficiently long and letting him proceed, he (the Spanish commander) will leave a small party at the post and come back to join the Commandant of the rear-guard, either by a direct or circuitous route, at any opportune hour or time or by any means, and above all he will exert himself to the utmost to send him the proper advices.

8th—As soon as he sees or is notified that any large number of people are approaching his post, he will at once inform the Commandant of the rear-guard, that he may be warned by a special or cautionary report, for the information of the said Commandant only, but if he is sure of the numbers and that they are capable, if they attempt it, of overcoming the rear-guard detachment, even though the probability be remote, he will dispatch an extraordinary messenger for me.

9th—In the aforesaid event of having to join the Commandant of the rear-guard for a hostile movement, if he thinks our forces are sufficient to defend the way in favorable positions he must encourage his men so that he can confidently hope to conquer, and they must obey the orders of the Commandant, who in case of reunion will be Don Nicholas Almanza and Don Antonio de Vargas, and if the number of our men should be so inferior that offering resistance to the enemy is doubtful, all the Commanders are to encourage their men by assuring them that I will not be long in re-enforcing them with a considerable number of troops.

10th—The Commandants aforesaid on the first day that they make a halt outside a settlement, will hold a special review of their men, and of the preparations they think best while under arms, but the chief point will be to tell them my order that every man of those under their command, in case of alarm, whether being under orders to use their arms, or believing themselves about to be attacked, shall run away, fleeing or separating himself from the party, shall be pursued and shot down when caught, and likewise every one who while in action helps another (to flee) or lifts his voice for flight. Also every man of the advanced guard who deserts from it, escaping to the Mountains or a settlement, shall be judged by a court-martial to be shot, being proven in such cases a coward, unfaithful and a traitor to His Sovereign.

[Remainder concerns careful use of ammunition and other general orders.]
Santa Fe 18th of October, 1806"—*Howbert Transcripts from Spanish Archives* in Colorado College.

PART FIVE

Diary of a Tour, Made through the Interior Provinces of New Spain, in the Year 1807, by Captain Z.M. Pike, of the Army of the United States, When under an Escort of Spanish Dragoons

27th February, Friday.—In the morning I discovered the Spanish lieutenant [Salteol], was writing letters addressed to the governor and others; on
which I demanded if he was not going on with me to Santa Fe. He appeared
confused and said no: that his orders were so positive as to the safe conduct
and protection of my men, that he dare not go and leave any behind; that
his companion [Fernandez] would accompany me to Santa Fe with 50 men,
whilst he with the others would wait for the sergeant [Meek] and his party.
I replied that he had deceived me and had not acted with candor; but that
it was now too late for me to remedy the evil.

We marched about 11 o'clock, ascending the Rio del Norte [Conejos],
five miles more S. 60° W. when we went round through a chain of hills and
bore off to the south. We proceeded on nine miles further, when we crossed
the main branch of that stream, which was now bearing nearly west towards
the main chain of the third chain of [San Juan] mountains. We encamped
on the opposite side. Distance 15 miles. Intensely cold, obliged to stop frequently and make fires. Snow deep.

28th February, Saturday.—We marched late. One of the Frenchmen
informed me, that the expedition which had been at the Pawnees, had
descended the Red river 233 leagues and from thence crossed to the Pawnees
expressly in search of my party (this was afterwards confirmed by the gentleman who commanded the troops.) He then expressed great regret at my

misfortunes, as he termed them in being taken, and offered his services in secreting papers &c. I took him at his word, and for my amusement I thought I would try him and give him, a leaf or two of my journal (copies) which mentioned the time of my sailing from Belle Fontaine, and our force. This I charged him to guard very carefully and give to me after the investigation of my papers at Santa Fe. This day we saw a herd of wild horses. The Spaniards pursued them and caught two colts, one of which the indians killed and eat; the other was let go. We pursued our journey over some hills, where the snow was very deep, and encamped at last on the top of a pretty high hill, among some pines. Distance 36 miles. We left the river which in general ran about 6, 8, and 10 miles to the left or east of us. Saw great sign of elk.

1st March, Sunday.—We marched early and although we rode very hard we only got to the village of L'eau Chaud or Warm Spring [Ojo Caliente], sometime in the afternoon, which was about 45 miles. The difference of climate was astonishing, after we left the hills and deep snows, we found ourselves on plains where there was no snow, and where vegetation was sprouting.

The village of the Warm Springs or Aqua caliente (in their language) is situated on the eastern branch [bank] of a creek of that name, and at a distance, presents to the eye a square enclosure of mud walls, the houses forming the wall. They are flat on top, or with extremely little ascent on one side, where there are spouts to carry off the water of the melting snow and rain when it falls, which we were informed, had been but once in two years, previous to our entering the country.

Inside of the enclosure were the different streets of houses of the same fashion, all of one story; the doors were narrow, the windows small, and in one or two houses there were talc lights. This village had a mill near it, situated on the little creek, which made very good flour.

The population consisted of civilized Indians, but much mixed blood.

Here we had a dance which is called the *Fandango*, but there was one which was copied from the Mexicans, and is now danced in the first societies of New Spain, and has even been introduced at the court of Madrid.

This village may contain 500 souls. The greatest natural curiosity is the warm springs, which are two in number, about 10 yards apart, and each afford sufficient water for a mill seat. They appeared to be impregnated with copper, and were more than 33° above blood heat. From this village the Tetaus drove off 2000 horses at one time, when at war with the Spaniards.

2d March, Monday.—We marched late, and passed several little mud walled villages and settlements, all of which had round mud towers of the ancient shape and construction, to defend the inhabitants from the intrusions of the savages. I was this day shewn the ruins of several old villages, which had been taken and destroyed by the Tetaus. We were frequently stopped by the women, who invited us into their houses to eat; and in every place where we halted a moment, there was a contest who should be our hosts. My poor lads who had been frozen, were conducted home by old men, who would cause their daughters to dress their feet; provide their victuals and drink, and at night, gave them the best bed in the house. In short, all their conduct brought to my recollection the hospitality of the ancient patriarchs, and caused me to sigh with regret at the corruption of that noble principle, by the polish of modern ages.

We descended the creek of Aqua Caliente, about 12 miles, where it joined the river of Conejos [Chama] from the west. This river was about 30 yards wide, and was settled, above its junction with the Aqua Caliente, 12 miles, as the latter was its whole course from the village of that name. From where they form a junction, it was about 15 miles to the Rio del Norte, on the eastern branch of which was situated the village of St. John's [San Juan's], which was the residence of the president priest of the province, who had resided in it 40 years.

The house tops of the village of St. John's, were crowded, as well as the streets, when we entered, and at the door of the public quarters, we were met by the president priest. When my companion who commanded the escort, received him in a street and embraced him, all the poor creatures who stood round, strove to kiss the ring or hand of the holy father; for myself, I saluted him in the usual style. My men were conducted into the quarters, and I went to the house of the priest, where we were treated with politeness: he offered us coffee, chocolate, or whatever we thought proper, and desired me to consider myself at home in his house.

As I was going some time after, to the quarters of my men, I was addressed at the door by a man in broken English:—"My friend, I am very sorry to see you here: we are all prisoners in this country and never return: I have been a prisoner for nearly three years, and cannot get out." I replied, "that as for his being a prisoner, it must be for some crime, what with respect to myself, I felt no apprehension, and requested him to speak French, as I could hardly understand his English." When he began to demand of me so many different questions on the mode of my getting into the country, my intention, &c.; that by the time I arrived in the room of my men, I was perfectly satisfied of his having been ordered by some person to endeavor to obtain some confession or acknowledgment of sinister designs in my having appeared on the frontiers, and some confidential communications which might implicate me. As he had been rather insolent in his enquiries, I ordered my men to shut and fasten the door; I then told him that I believed him to be an emissary sent on purpose by the governor, or some person, to endeavour to betray me, that all men of that description were scoundrels, and never should escape punishment, whilst I possessed the power to chastise them, immediately ordering my men to seize him, and cautioning him at the same time, that if he cried out, or made the least resistance, I would be obliged to make use of the sabre, which I had in my hand; on which he was so much alarmed, that he begged me for God's sake not to injure him; that he had been ordered by the government to meet me, and endeavour to trace out, what, and who I was, and what were my designs, by endeavoring to produce a confidence in him, by his exclaiming against the Spaniards, and complaining of the tyranny which they had exercised towards him. After this confession, I ordered my men to release him, and told him, that I looked upon him as too contemptible for further notice, but that he might tell the governor, the next time he employed emissaries, to choose those of more abilities and sense, and that I questioned if his excellency would find the sifting of us an easy task.

This man's name was Baptiste Lalande,[226] he had come from the Illinois to the Pawnees, to trade with goods furnished him by William Morrison, a gentleman of the Illinois, and from thence to New Mexico with the goods, which he had procured and established himself, and was the same man on whom Robinson had a claim. He returned into the priest's house with me, and instead of making any complaint, he in reply to their inquiries of who I was, &c. informed them, that when he left Louisiana, I was governor of the Illinois. This I presume he took for granted from my having commanded for some time the post of Kaskaskias, the first military post the United States had established in that country since the peace; however the report served but to add to the respect with which my companion and host treated me. Having had at this place the first good meal, wine, &c. with the heat of the house, and perhaps rather an immoderate use of the refreshments allowed me, produced an attack of something like the cholera morbus, which alarmed me considerably, and made me determined to be more abstemious in future. This father was a great naturalist, or rather florist; he had large collections of flowers, plants, &c. and several works on his favorite studies, the margin and bottoms of which were filled with his notes in the Castilian language. As I had neither a natural turn for botany, sufficient to induce me to puzzle my head much with the Latin, and did not understand the Castilian, I enjoyed but little of his lectures, which he continued to give me nearly for two hours on those subjects, but by the exercise of a small degree of patience, I entirely acquired the esteem of this worthy father, he calling me his son, and lamenting extremely that my fate had not made me one of the holy catholic church.

St. John's was enclosed with a mud wall, and probably contained 1000 souls; its population consisted principally of civilized Indians, as indeed does all the villages of New Mexico, the whites not forming the one twentieth part of the inhabitants.

3d, March, Tuesday.—We marched after breakfast, B. Lalande accompanying us, and in about six miles came to a village [Santa Cruz], where I suppose there were more than 2000 souls. Here we halted at the house of the priest, who understanding that I would not kiss his hand, would not present it to me.

The conduct and behaviour of a young priest who came in, was such as in our country would have been amply sufficient forever to have banished him from the clerical association, strutting about with a dirk in his boot, a cane in his hand, whispering to one girl, chucking another under the chin, and going out with a third, &c. From this village to another small village of 500 inhabitants [Pojouque], is seven miles. At each of those villages is a small stream, sufficient for the purpose of watering their fields. At the father's house we took coffee. From this village, it was 17 miles to another [Tesuque] of 400 civilized Indians. Here we changed horses and prepared for entering the capital, which we came in sight of in the evening. It is situated along the banks of a small creek, which comes down from the mountains, and runs west to the Rio del Norte. The length of the capital on the creek may be estimated at one mile; it is but three streets in width.

Its appearance from a distance, struck my mind with the same effect as a fleet of the flat bottomed boats, which are seen in the spring and fall seasons, descending the Ohio river. There are two churches, the magnificence of whose steeples form a striking contrast to the miserable appearance of the houses. On the north side of the town is the square of soldiers homes, equal to 120 or 140 on each flank. The public square is in the centre of the town; on the north side of which is situated the *palace* (as they term it) or government house, with the quarters for guards, &c. The other side of the square is occupied by the clergy and public officers. In general the houses have a shed before the front, some of which have a flooring of brick; the consequence is, that the streets are very narrow, say in general 25 feet. The supposed population is 4,500 souls. On our entering the town, the crowd was great, and followed us to the government house. When we dismounted, we were ushered in through various rooms, the floors of which were covered with skins of buffalo, bear, or some other animal. We waited in a chamber for some time, until his excellency appeared, when we rose, and the following conversation took place in French.

Governor. Do you speak French?

Pike. Yes sir.

Governor. You come to reconnoitre our country, do you?

Pike. I marched to reconnoitre our own.

Governor. In what character are you?

Pike. In my proper character, an officer of the United States army.

Governor. And this Robinson, is he attached to your party?

Pike. No.

Governor. Do you know him?

Pike. Yes, he is from St. Louis. [I had understood the doctor was sent 45 leagues from Santa Fe, under a strong guard, and the haughty and unfriendly reception of the governor induced me to believe war must have been declared, and that if it was known Dr. Robinson accompanied me, he would be treated with great severity. I was correct in saying he was not attached to my party, for he was only a volunteer, he could not properly be said to be one of my command.]

Governor. How many men have you?

Pike. Fifteen.

Governor. And this Robinson makes sixteen.

Pike. I have already told your excellency that he does not belong to my party, and shall answer no more interrogatories on that subject.

Governor. When did you leave St. Louis?

Pike. 15th July.

Governor. I think you marched in June.

Pike. No, sir!

Governor. Well! return with Mr. Bartholemew to his house, and come here again at seven o'clock, and bring your papers; on which we returned to the house of my friend Bartholemew, who seemed much hurt at the interview.

At the door of the government house, I met the old Frenchman, to whom I had given the scrap of paper on the 27th February. He had left us in the morning, and as I suppose, hurried in to make his report and I presume had presented this paper to his excellency. I demanded with a look of contempt, if he had made his report? to which he made a reply in an humble tone, and began to excuse himself, but I did not wait to hear his excuses. At the hour appointed we returned, when the governor demanded my papers; I told him, I understood my trunk was taken possession of by his guard: he expressed surprise, and immediately ordered it in, and also sent for one Solomon Colly, formerly a serjeant in our army, and one of the unfortunate company of Nolan.[227] We were seated, when he ordered Colly to demand my name, to which I replied; he then demanded in what province I was born; I answered in English, and then addressed his excellency in French, and told him that I did not think it necessary to enter into such a catechising; that if he would be at the pain of reading my commission from the United States, and my orders from my general, it would be all that I presumed would be necessary to convince his excellency that I came with no hostile intentions towards the Spanish government, on the contrary, that I had express instructions to guard against giving them offence or alarm, and that his excellency would be convinced that myself and party were rather to be considered objects, on which the so-much-celebrated generosity of the Spanish nation might be exercised, than proper subjects to occasion the opposite sentiments.

He then requested to see my commission and orders, which I read to him in French; on which he got up and gave me his hand, for the first time, and said he was happy to be acquainted with me as a man of honor and a gentleman; that I could retire this evening, and take my trunk with me; that on the morrow he would make further arrangements.

4th March, Wednesday.—Was desired by the governor to bring up my trunk, in order that he might make some observations on my route, &c. When he ordered me to take my trunk over night, I had conceived the examination of papers was over, and as many of my documents were entrusted to the care of my men, and I found that the inhabitants were treating the men with liquor; I was fearful they would become intoxicated, (and through inadvertancy) betray or discover the papers; I had therefore obtained several of them and had put them in the trunk, when an officer arrived for myself and it, and I had no opportunity of taking them out again before I was taken up to the palace. I discovered instantly that I was deceived, but it was too late to remedy the evil.

After examining the contents of my trunk, he informed me, I must (with my troops) go to Chihuahua, province of Biscay, to appear before the commandant-general; he added, you have the key of your trunk in your own possession; the trunk will be put under charge of the officer who commands your escort. The following conversation then took place.

Pike. If we go to Chihuahua we must be considered as prisoners of war?

Governor. By no means.

Pike. You have already disarmed my men without my knowledge, are there arms to be returned or not?

Governor. They can receive them any moment.

Pike. But sir, I cannot consent to be led three or four hundred leagues out of my route, without its being by force of arms.

Governor. I know you do not go voluntarily, but I will give you a certificate from under my hand of my having obliged you to march.[228]

Pike. I will address you a letter on the subject.[229]

Governor. You will dine with me today, and march afterwards to a village about six miles distant escorted by captain Anthony D'Almansa, with a detachment of dragoons, who will accompany you to where the remainder of your escort is now waiting for you, under the command of the officer [Malgares] who commanded the expedition to the Pawnees.

Pike. I would not wish to be impertinent in my observations to your excellency, but pray sir! do you not think in was a greater infringement of our territory to send 600 miles in the Pawnees, than for me with our small party to come on the frontiers of yours with an intent to descend Red river?

Governor. I do not understand you.

Pike. No sir! any further explanation is unnecessary. I then returned to the house of my friend Bartholemew and wrote my letter to his excellency, which I had not finished before we were hurried to dinner.

In the morning I had received from the governor by the hands of his private secretary twenty one dollars, notifying to me that it was the amount of the king's allowance for my party to Chihuahua and that it would be charged to me on account of my subsistence; from this I clearly understood that it was calculated that the expenses of the party to Chihuahua would be defrayed by the United States. I also received by the same hands from his excellency a shirt and neck cloth, with his compliments, wishing me "to accept of them as they were made in Spain by his sister and never had been worn by any person;" for which I returned him my sincere acknowledgments, and it may not be deemed irrelevant if I explain at this period the miserable appearance we made and situation we were in; with the causes of it. When we left our interpreter and one man on the Arkansaw, we were obliged to carry all our baggage on our backs, consequently that which was the most *useful* was preferred to the few ornamental parts of dress we possessed. The ammunition claimed our first care, tools secondary, leather, leggins, boots and mockinsons were the next in consideration; consequently, I left all my uniform, clothing, trunks, &c. as did the men, except what they had on their backs; conceiving that which would secure the feet and legs from the cold, as preferable to any less indispensable portion of our dress. Thus, when we presented ourselves at Santa Fe; I was dressed in a pair of blue trousers, mockinsons, blanket coat and a cap made of scarlet cloth, lined with fox skins and my poor fellows in leggings, breech cloths and leather coats and not a hat in the whole party. This appearance was extremely mortifying to us all, especially as soldiers, and although some of the officers used frequently to observe to me, that "worth made the man," &c. with a variety of adages to the same amount. Yet the first impression made on the ignorant is hard to eradicate; and a greater proof cannot be given of the ignorance of the common people, than their asking if we lived in houses or camps like the indians, or if we wore hats in our country; those observations are sufficient to shew the impression our uncouth appearance made amongst them.

The dinner at the governor's was rather splendid, having a variety of dishes and wines of the southern provinces, and when his excellency was a little warmed with the influence of cheering liquor, he became very sociable. He informed me that there existed a serious difficulty between the commandant general of the internal provinces and the marquis Caso Calvo, who had given permission to Mr. Dunbar, to explore the Ouchata [Washita] contrary to the general principles of their government; and in consequence of which, the former had made representations against the latter to the court of Madrid. After dinner his excellency ordered his coach; captain D'Almansa, Batholemew and myself entered with him, and he drove out 3 miles. He was drawn by six mules and attended by a guard of cavalry. When we parted his adieu was "remember Allencaster, in peace or war."

Left a note for my sergeant, with instructions to keep up good discipline and not be alarmed or discouraged. As I was about leaving the public square, poor Colly (the American prisoner,) came up with tears in his eyes and hoped I would not forget him, when I arrived in the United States.

After we left the governor we rode on about three miles to a defile where we halted for the troops and I soon found that the old soldier who accompanied us and commanded our escort was fond of a drop of the cheering liquor, as his boy carried a bottle in his cochmelies [Cojinillos] (a small leather case attached to the saddle for the purpose of carrying small articles.) We were accompanied by my friend Bartholemew. We ascended a hill and galloped on until about ten o'clock; snowing hard all the time, when we came to a precipice [La Bajada] which we descended, meeting with great difficulty (from the obscurity of the night) to the small village where we put up in the quarters of the priest, he being absent.

After supper, captain D'Almansa related to me that he had served his catholic majesty, 40 years to arrive at the rank he then held, which was a first lieutenant in the line, and a captain by brevet, whilst he had seen various young Europeans promoted over his head; after the old man had taken his *quantum sufficit* and gone to sleep, my friend and myself sat up for some hours, he explaining to me their situation, the great desire they felt for a change of affairs, and an open trade with the United States. I pointed out to him with chalk on the floor the geographical connection and route, from North Mexico and Louisiana, and finally gave him a certificate addressed to the citizens of the United States, stating his friendly disposition and his being a man of influence. This paper he seemed to estimate as a very valuable acquisition, as he was decidedly of opinion we would invade that country the ensuing spring and not all my assurances to the contrary, could eradicate that idea.

5th March, Friday.—It snowing very bad in the morning we did not march until 11 o'clock. In the mean time Bartholemew and myself paid a visit to an old invalid Spaniard, who received us in the most hospitable manner, giving us chocolate &c. He made many enquiries as to our government and religion, and of [Bartholemew] . . . who did not fail to give them the brightest colouring; he being enthusiastic in their favor from his many conversations with me, and drawing comparisons with his own country. What appeared to the old veteran, most extraordinary, was, that we ever changed our president; I was obliged to draw his powers on a nearer affinity with those of a monarch, than they really are, in order that they might comprehend his station and that there was a perfect freedom of conscience permitted in our country. He however expressed his warm approbation of the measure. In the priests house in which we put up, were two orphan girls, who were adopted by him in their infancy and at this time constituted his whole family.

I bid adieu to my friend Bartholemew and could not avoid shedding tears; he embraced me, and all my men.

We arrived at the village of St. Domingo at two o'clock. It is as I supposed, nine miles on the east side of the Rio del Norte, and is a large village, the population being about 1000 natives, generally governed by its own chief. The chiefs of the villages were distinguished by a cane with a silver head and black tassell and on our arrival at the public house; captain D'Almansa was waited on by the governor, cap in hand, to receive his orders as to the furnishing of our quarters and ourselves with wood, water, provisions &c. for the house itself contained nothing but bare walls and small grated windows, and brought to my recollection the representation of the Spanish inhabitants, as given by Dr. [John] Moore in his travels through Spain, Italy, &c. This village as well as that of St. Philip's and St. Bartholemew, are of the nation of Keres [Queres], many of whom do not yet speak good Spanish.

After we had refreshed ourselves a little, the captain sent for the keys of the church: when we entered it, and I was much astonished to find enclosed in mudbrick walls, many rich paintings, and the Saint (Domingo) as large as life, elegantly ornamented with gold and silver: the captain made a slight inclination of the head, and intimated to me, that this was the patron of the village. We then ascended into the gallery, where the choir are generally placed. In an outside hall was placed another image of the saint, less richly ornamented, where the populace repaired daily, and knelt to return thanks for benefactions received, or to ask new favors. Many young girls, indeed, chose the time of our visit to be on their knees before the holy patron. From the flat roof of the church we had a delightful view of the village; the Rio del Norte on our west; the mountains of St. Dies [Sandia] to the south, and the valley round the town, on which were numerous herds of goats, sheep, and asses; and upon the whole, this was one of the handsomest views in New Mexico.

6th March, Friday.—Marched down the Rio del Norte on the east side. Snow one foot deep. Passed large flocks of goats. At the village of St. Philip's [San Felipe], crossed [The Rio Grande] a bridge of eight arches, constructed as follows, viz. the pillars made of neat wood work, something similar to a crate, and in the form of a keel boat, the sharp end, or bow, to the current; this crate or butment was filled with stone, in which the river lodged sand, clay, &c. until it had become of a tolerable firm consistency. On the top of the pillars were laid pine logs, length ways, squared on two sides, and being joined pretty close, made a tolerable bridge for horses, but would not have been very safe for carriages, as there were no hand rails.

On our arrival at the house of the father, we were received in a very polite and friendly manner, and before my departure, we seemed to have been friends for years past.

During our dinner, at which we had a variety of wines, and were entertained with music, composed of bass drums, French horns, violins and cymbals; we likewise entered into a long and candid conversation as to the creoles, wherein he neither spared the government nor its administrators. As to government and religion, Father Rubi displayed a liberality of opinion and a fund of knowledge, which astonished me. He shewed me a statistical table, on which he had in a regular manner, taken the whole province of New Mexico, by villages, beginning at Tous, on the northwest, and ending with Valencia on the south, and giving their latitude, longitude, and population, whether natives or Spaniard, civilized or barbarous, Christians or Pagans, numbers, name of the nation, when converted, how governed, military force, clergy, salary, &c. &c. ; in short, a complete geographical, statistical and historical sketch of the province. Of this I wished to obtain a copy, but perceived that the captain was somewhat surprised at its having been shewn to me. When we parted, we promised to write to each other, which I performed from Chihuahua.

Here was an old Indian who was extremely inquisitive to know if we were Spaniards, to which an old gentleman, called Don Francisco, who appeared to be an inmate of father Rubi, replied in the affirmative; but says the Indian, "they do not speak Castilian," true replied the other, but you are an Indian of the nation of Keres, are you not? Yes. Well the Utahs are Indians also? Yes. But still you do not understand them, they speaking a different language. True replied the Indian; well, said the old gentleman, those strangers are likewise Spaniards, but do not speak the same language with us. This reasoning seemed to satisfy the poor savage, and I could not but smile at the ingenuity displayed to make him believe there was no other nation of whites but the Spaniards.

Whilst at dinner, father Rubi was informed one of his parishioners was at the point of death, and wished his attendance to receive his confession.

We took our departure, but were shortly after overtaken by our friend, who after giving me another hearty shake of the hand, left us. Crossed the river and passed two small hamlets and houses on the road to the village of St. Dies, opposite the mountain of the same name, where we were received in a house of father Rubi, this making part of his domains.

7th March, Saturday.—Marched at nine o'clock through a country better cultivated and inhabited than any I had yet seen. Arrived at Albuquerque, a village on the east side of the Rio del Norte. We were received by father Ambrosio Guerra in a very flattering manner, and led into his hall. From thence, after taking some refreshment, into an inner appartment, where he ordered his adopted children of the female sex to appear, when they came in by turns, Indians of various nations, Spanish, French, and finally, two young girls, who from their complexion I conceived to be English; on perceiving I noticed them, he ordered the rest to retire, many of whom were beautiful, and directed those to sit down on the sofa beside me; thus situated, he told me that they had been taken to the east by the Tetaus; passed from one nation to another, until he purchased them, at that time infants, but they could recollect neither their names nor language, but concluding they were my country-women, he ordered them to embrace me as a mark of their friendship, to which they appeared nothing loth; we then sat down to dinner, which consisted of various dishes, excellent wines, and to crown all, we were waited on by half a dozen of those beautiful girls, who like Hebe at the feast of the gods, converted our wine to nectar, and with their ambrosial breath shed incense on our cups. After the cloth was removed some time, the priest beckoned me to follow him, and led me into his "sanctum sanctorum," where he had the rich and majestic images of various saints, and in the midst the crucified Jesus, crowned with thorns, with rich rays of golden glory surrounding his head; in short, the room being hung with black silk curtains, served but to augment the gloom and majesty of the scene. When he conceived my imagination sufficiently wrought up, he put on a black gown and mitre, kneeled before the cross, and took hold of my hand and endeavoured gently to pull me down beside him; on my refusal, he prayed fervently for a few minutes and then rose, laid his hands on my shoulders, and as I conceived, blessed me. He then said to me, "You will not be a Christian; Oh! what a pity! oh! what a pity!" He then threw off his robes, took me by the hand and led me out of the company smiling; but the scene I had gone through had made too serious an impression on my mind to be eradicated, until we took our departure, which was in an hour after, having received great marks of friendship from the father.

Both above and below Albuquerque, the citizens were beginning to open the canals, to let in the water of the river to fertilize the plains and fields which border its banks on both sides; where we saw men, women and children of all ages and sexes at the joyful labor which was to crown with rich abundance their future harvest and ensure them plenty for the ensuing year. Those scenes brought to my recollection the bright descriptions given by Savary of the opening of the canals of Egypt. The cultivation of the fields was now commencing and every thing appeared to give life and gaiety to the surrounding scenery. We crossed the Rio del Norte, a little below the village of Albuquerque where it was 400 yards wide, but not more than three feet deep and excellent fording. At father Ambrosio's, was the only chart we saw in the province, that gave the near connection of the sources of the Rio del Norte and the Rio Coloredo of California, with their ramifications. On our arriving at the next village a dependency of father Ambrosio, we were invited into the house of the commandant; when I entered, I saw a man sitting by the fire reading a book, with blooming cheeks, fine complexion and a genius speaking eye, he arose from his seat. It was Robinson! not that Robinson who left my camp, on the head waters of the Rio del Norte, pale, emaciated, with uncombed locks and beard of eight months growth, but with fire, unsubdued enterprise and fortitude. The change was indeed surprising. I started back and exclaimed "Robinson!" "Yes;" "but I do not know you;" I replied; "but I know you," he exclaimed "I would not be unknown to you here, in this land of tyranny and oppression; to avoid all the pains they dare to inflict. Yet, my friend I grieve to see you here and thus, for I presume you are a prisoner." "I replied no? I wear my sword you see, and all my men have their arms, and the moment they dare to ill treat us we will surprise their guards in the night, carry off some horses and make our way to Appaches and then set them at defiance." At this moment captain D'Almansa entered and I introduced Robinson to him, as *Companion de Voyage* and friend, he having before seen him at Santa Fe. He did not appear much surprised and received him with a significant smile, as much as to say, I knew this. We then marched out to the place where the soldiers were encamped, not one of whom would recognize him (agreeably to orders,) until I gave them the sign. Then it was a joyful meeting, as the whole party was enthusiastically fond of him. He gave me the following relation of his adventures after he left me.

"I marched the first day up the branch [Conejos] on which we were situated, as you know we had concluded it would be the most proper to follow it to its source, and then cross the mountains west, where we had conceived we should find the Spanish settlements, and at night encamped on its banks; the second day I left it a little and bore more south, and was getting up the side of the mountain, when I discovered two indians, for whom I made; they were armed with bows and arrows, and were extremely shy of my approach, but after some time, confidence being somewhat restored; I signified a wish to go to Santa Fe, when they pointed due south, down the river I left you on. As I could not believe them I reiterated the enquiry and received the same reply. I then concluded that we had been deceived, and that you were on the Rio del Norte, instead of Red river, and was embarrassed whether I should not immediately return to apprise you of it, but concluded it to be too late, as I was discovered by the indians, whom if I had not met or some others I should have continued on and crossed the mountain on the waters of the Coloredo, and descended them, until from their course I should have discovered my mistake. I therefore offered them some presents to conduct me in; they agreed, conducted me to their camp where their women were, and in about five minutes we were on our march. That night we encamped in the woods, and I slept very little, owing to my distrust of my companions. The next day at three o'clock, P. M. We arrived at the village of Aqua Caliente, where I was immediately taken into the house of the commandant, and expresses dispatched to Santa Fe. That night I was put to sleep on a matrass on the floor. The next day we departed early, leaving my arms and baggage at the commandants, he promising to have them forwarded to me at the city. On our arrival at Santa Fe, the governor received me with great austerity at first, and entered into an examination of my business and took possession of all my papers. After all this was explained, he ordered me to a room where the officers were confined when under an arrest and a non-commissioned officer to attend me, when I walked out into the city, which I had free permission to do. I was supplied with provisions from the governor's table, who had promised he would write to Babtiste Lalande to come down and answer to the claim I had against him; whose circumstance I had apprized myself of. The second day the governor sent for me, and informed me, that he had made enquiry as to the abilities of Lalande, to discharge the debt, and found that he possessed no property, but that at some future period, he would secure the money for me. To this I made a spirited remonstrance, as an infringement of our treaties and a protection of a refugee citizen of the United States against his creditors, which had no other effect than to obtain me an invitation to dinner, and rather more respectful treatment than I had hitherto received from his excellency, who being slightly afflicted with the dropsy, requested my advice as to his case; on which I prescribed a regimen and mode of treatment which happened to differ from the one adopted by a monk and practising physician of the place, brought on me his enmity and ill offices. The ensuing day I was ordered by the governor to hold myself in readiness to Proceed to the internal parts of the country, to which I agreed; determining not to leave the country in a clandestine manner, unless they attempted to treat me with indignity or hardship; and conceiving it in my power to join you on your retreat, or find Red river and descend it; should you not be brought in, but in that case to share your destiny: added to this I feel a desire to see more of the country for which purpose I was willing to run the risk of future consequence. We marched the ensuing day, I having been equipped by my friend, with some small articles of which I stood in need of, such as I would receive out of the numerous offers of his country. The fourth day I arrived at the village of St. Fernandez, where I was received, and taken charge of by Lt. Don Faciendo Malgares who commanded the expedition to the Pawnees, and whom you find a gentleman, a soldier and one of the most gallant men you ever knew; with him I could no longer keep the disguise and when he informed me, (two days since) that you were on the way in, I confessed to him my belonging to your party, and we have ever since been anticipating the pleasure we three will enjoy in our journey to Chihuahua; for he is to command the escort, his dragoons being now encamped in the field, waiting your arrival. Since I have been with him I have practiced physic in the country in order to have an opportunity of examining the manners, customs, &c. of the people, and to endeavor to ascertain the political and religious feelings and to gain every other species of information which would be necessary to our country or ourselves. I am now here, on a visit to this man's wife; attended by a corporal of dragoons as a guard, who answers very well as a waiter guide, &c in my excursions through the country; but I will immediately return with you to Malgares." Thus ended Robinson's relation, and I in return related what had occurred to the party and myself. We agreed upon our future line of conduct and then joined my old captain in the house; who had been persuaded to tarry all night, provided it was agreeable to me, as our host wished Robinson to remain until the next day; with this proposition, I complied in order that Robinson and myself might have a further discussion before we joined Malgares, who I suspected would watch us close. The troops proceeded on to the village of Tousac, that evening.

8th March, Sunday.—Marched after taking breakfast and halted at a little village, three miles distance, called Tousac, situated on the west side of the Rio del Norte. The men informed me that on their arrival over night, they had all been furnished with an excellent supper, and after supper, wine, and a violin, with a collection of the young people to a dance. When we left this village the priest sent a cart down to carry us over, as the river was nearly four feet deep. When we approached the village of St. Fernandez, we were met by lieutenant Malgares, accompanied by two or three other officers; he received me with the most manly frankness and the politeness of a man of the world. Yet my feelings were such as almost overpowered me and obliged me to ride by myself for a short period in order to recover myself: those sensations arose from my knowledge, that he had now been absent from Chihuahua ten months, and it had cost the king of Spain more than 10,000 dollars, to effect that which a mere accident and the deception of the governor had effected.

Malgares finding I did not feel myself at ease took every means in his power to banish my reserve, which made it impossible on my part not to endeavor to appear chearful; we conversed as *well as we could* and in two hours were as well acquainted as some people would be in the same number of months. Malgares possessing none of the haughty Castillian pride, but much of the urbanity of a Frenchman; and I will add my feeble testimony to his loyalty, by declaring that he was one of the few officers or citizens whom I found, who was loyal to their king, felt indignant at the degraded state of the Spanish monarchy; who deprecated a revolution or separation of Spanish America, from the mother country; unless France should usurp the government of Spain. These are the men who possess the heads to plan, the hearts to feel and the hands to carry this great and important work into execution. In the afternoon our friend wrote the following notification to the Alcaldes of several small villages around us. "Send this evening six or eight of your handsomest young girls, to the village of St. Fernandez, where I propose giving a fandango, for the entertainment of the American officers arrived this day."

(Signed)   DON FACIENDO.

This order was punctually obeyed, and pourtrays more clearly than a chapter of observations, the degraded state of the common people. In the evening when the company arrived, the ball began after their usual manner, and there was really a handsome display of beauty.

It will be proper to mention here, that when my small paper trunk was brought in, Lt. Malgares struck his foot against it, and said: "the governor informs me this is a prisoner of war, or that I have charge of it, but, sir, only assure me, that you will hold the papers therein contained sacred, I will have nothing to do with it." I bowed assent, and I will only add, that the condition was scrupulously adhered to; as I was bound by every tie of military and national honor; and let me add gratitude not to abuse his high confidence in the honor of a soldier. He further added that "Robinson being now acknowledged as one of your party, I shall withdraw his guard and consider him, as under your parole of honor." Those various marks of politeness and friendship, caused me to endeavor to evince to my brother soldier, that we were capable of appreciating his honorable conduct towards us.

9th March, Monday.—The troops marched about ten o'clock. Lt. Malgares and myself accompanied captain D'Almansa, about three miles back on his rout to Santa Fe, to the house of a citizen, where we dined; after which we separated. I wrote by the captain to the governor, in French and to father Rubi in English, D'Almansa presented me with his cap and whip, and gave me a letter of recommendation to an officer at Chihuahua. We returned to our old quarters and being joined by our waiters, commenced our route. Passed a village called St. Thomas [Tomé] one mile distant from the camp. The camp was formed in an ellipsis, the two long sides presenting a breast work formed of the saddles and heads of the mules, each end of the ellipsis having a small opening to pass and repass at; in the centre was the commandant's tent. Thus in case of an attack on the camp there were ready formed works to fight from. Malgares' mode of living, was superior to any thing we have an idea of in our army; having eight mules loaded with his common camp equipage, wines, confectionary, &c. But this only served to evince the corruption of the Spanish discipline, for if a subaltern indulged himself with such a quantity of baggage, what would be the cavalcade attending on an army? Doctor Robinson had been called over the river to a small village to see a sick woman and did not return that night. Distance 12 miles.

10th March, Tuesday.—Marched at eight o'clock and arrived at the village of Sibiletta [Old La Joya], passed on the way the village of Sabinez on the west side, and Xaxales, on the same side. Sibilleta is situated on the east side and is a regular square, appearing like a large mud wall on the outside, the doors, windows, &c. facing the square, and is the neatest and most regular village I have yet seen; it is governed by a sergeant at whose quarters I put up.

11th March, Wednesday.—Marched at eleven o'clock came 12 miles and encamped, the troops having preceeded us. Lieutenant Malgares not being well, took medicine. The village we staid at last night, being the last, we now entered the wilderness and the road became rough, small hills running into the river, making vallies; but the bottoms appear richer than those more to the north.

12th March, Thursday.—Marched at seven o'clock, and passed on the west side of the river, the mountains of Magdalen, the black mountains on the east. Passed the encampment of the caravan, going out with about 15,000 sheep for the other provinces from which they bring back merchandize. This expedition consisted of about 300 men, chiefly citizens escorted by an officer and 35 or 40 troops; they are collected at Sibilleta and separate there on their return. They go out in February and return in March; a similar expedition goes out in the autumn, during the other parts of the year no citizen travels the road, the couriers excepted. At the pass [Juarez, Mexico] of the Rio del Norte, they meet and exchange packets, when each return to their own province. Met a caravan of 50 men and probably 200 horses, loaded with goods for New Mexico. Halted at twelve o'clock and marched at three. Lt. Malgares shewed me the place where he had been in two affairs with the Appaches; one he commanded himself, and the other was commanded by captain D'Almansa; in the former there was one Spaniard killed and eight wounded and ten Appaches were made prisoners, in the latter 52 Appaches were wounded and 17 killed; they being surprised in the night. Malgares killed two himself, and had two horses killed under him.

13*th, March, Friday.*—Marched at seven o'clock, saw many deer. Halted at eleven o'clock and marched at four o'clock. This day one of our horses threw a young woman and ran off, (as was the habit of all the Spanish horses, if by chance they throw their rider) when many of the dragoons and Malgares pursued him. I being mounted on an elegant horse of Malgares, joined in the chase, and notwithstanding their superior horsemanship overtook the horse, caught his bridle and stopped him, when both of the horses were nearly at full speed. This act procured me the applause of the Spanish dragoons, and it is astonishing how much it operated on their good will.

14*th March, Saturday.*—Marched at ten o'clock, and halted at a mountain, distance ten miles, this is the point from which the road leaves the river [Fra Cristobal] for two days journey bearing due south, the river taking a turn south west, by the river, five days to where the roads meet.[230] We marched at four o'clock and eight miles below, crossed the river to the west side, two mules fell in the water, and unfortunately they carried the stores of lieutenant Malgares, by which means we lost all our bread, an elegant assortment of buiscuit, &c. Distance 18 miles.

15*th March, Sunday.*—Marched at half past ten o'clock. Made 28 miles, the route rough and stony; course S. 20° W.

16*th March, Monday.*—Marched at 7 o'clock, and halted at twelve. Passed on the east side the horse mountain [Caballo Cone], and the mountain of the dead. Came on a trail of appearance of 200 horses, supposed to be the trail of an expedition from the province of Biscay, against the indians.

17*th March, Tuesday.*—Marched at ten o'clock, and at four in the afternoon, crossed the river to the east side; saw several fresh indian tracks, also the trail of a large party of horses, supposed to be Spanish troops in pursuit of the indians. Marched down the river 26 miles, fresh signs of indians, also of a party of horses; country mountainous on both sides of the river.

18*th March, Wednesday.*—Marched down the river 26 miles; fresh sign of indians, also a party of horses; country mountainous on both sides of the river.

19*th March Thursday.*—Struck out east about three miles and fell in with the main road, (or a large flat prairie) which we left at the mountain of the friar Christopher.

20th March, Friday.—Halted at ten o'clock, at a salt lake. Marched until two o'clock, halted for the day; vegetation began to be discoverable on the 17th and this day the weeds and grass were quite high.

21st March, Saturday.—Marched in the morning and arrived at the passo del Norte at 11 o'clock, the road leading through a hilly and mountainous country. We put up at the house of Don Francisco Garcia who was a merchant and a planter; he possessed in the vicinity of the town 20,000 sheep and 1000 cows; we were received in a most hospitable manner, by Don Pedro Roderique Rey, the lieutenant governor, and father Joseph Prado, the vicar of the place.

22d March, Sunday.—Remained at the *Passo.*

23d March, Monday.—Mass performed, leave the Passo at three o'clock, to fort Elisiaira [Elizario], accompanied by the lieutenant governor, the Vicar and Allencaster a brother of the governor. Malgares, myself and the doctor took up our quarters at the house of cap.————————, who was then at Chihuahua; but his lady and sister entertained us in a very elegant and hospitable manner. They began playing cards and continued until late the third day. Malgares who won considerably, would send frequently 15 or 20 dollars from the table to the lady of the house, her sister and others; and beg their acceptance, in order that the goddess of fortune, might still continue propitious, in this manner he distributed 500 dollars; around this fort were a great number of Appaches, who were on a treaty with the Spaniards. These people appeared to be perfectly independent in their manners, and were the only savages I saw in the Spanish dominions, whose spirit was not humbled, whose necks were not bowed to the yoke of their invaders. With those people Malgares was extremely popular and I believe he sought popularity with them, and all the common people, for there was no man so poor or so humble, under whose roof he would not enter and when he walked out, I have seen him put a handful of dollars in his pocket give them all to the old men, women and children before he returned to his quarters; but to equals he was haughty and overbearing. This conduct he pursued through the whole province of New Mexico and Biscay, when at a distance from the seat of government, but I could plainly perceive that he was cautious of his conduct, as he approached the capital [Chihuahua]. I here left a letter for my sergeant.

24th March, Tuesday.—Very bad weather.

25th March, Wednesday.—The troops marched, but Lt. Malgares and my men remained.

26th March, Thursday.—Divine service was performed in the morning, in the garrison, at which all the troops attended under arms; at one part of their mass, they present arms, at another, sink on one knee and rest the muzzle of the gun on the ground, in signification of their submission to their divine master. At one o'clock, we bid adieu to our friendly hostess, who was one of the finest women I had seen in New Spain. At dusk arrived at a small pond made by a spring, which arose in the centre, called the *Ogo mall a Ukap*, and seemed formed by providence to enable the human race, to pass that route as it was the only water within 60 miles, on the route; here we overtook sergeant Belardie with the part of dragoons from Senora and Biscay, who had left us at fort Elisiaira, where we had received a new escort. Distance 20 miles.

27th March, Friday.—Arrived at Carracal [Carizal], at twelve o'clock. Distance 28 miles; the road well watered and the situation pleasant. The father-in-law of our friend, commanded six or seven years here; when we arrived at the fort, the commandant, Don Pedro Rues Saramende received Robinson and myself, with a cold bow and informed Malgares, that we could repair to the public quarters. To this Malgares indignantly replied, that he should accompany us and turned to go when the commandant took him by the arm, made many apologies to him and us, and we at length reluctantly entered his quarters; here for the first time, I saw the Gazettes of Mexico, which gave rumors of colonel Burr's conspiracies, the movements of our troops, &c. &c. but which were stated in so vague and undefined a manner, as only to create our anxiety without throwing any light on the subject.

28th March, Saturday.—Marched at half past three o'clock and arrived at the Warm Springs [Alamo de Peña] at sun down; crossed one little fosse on the route.

29th March, Sunday.—Marched at ten o'clock and continued our route, with but a short halt, until sun down; when we encamped without water. Distance 30 miles.

30th March, Monday.—Marched before seven o'clock, the front arrived at water, at eleven o'clock; the mules at twelve. The spring on the side of the mountain to the east of the road, a beautiful situation, I here saw the first ash timber, I observed in the country. This water is 52 miles from the Warm Springs. Yesterday and today, saw Cabrie [antelope], marched fifteen miles further and encamped, without wood or water; passed two other small springs to the east of the road.

31st March, Tuesday.—Marched early and arrived at an excellent spring at ten o'clock. The roads from Senora, Tanos and Buenaventura, &c. joins about 400 yards, before you arrive at the spring.

Arrived at the village of [El Peñol]————at night, a large and elegant house, for the country; here were various labors carried on by criminals in irons.

We here met with a Catalonian, who was but a short time from Spain, and whose dialect was such that he could scarcely be understood by Malgares, and whose manners were much more like those of a citizen of our western frontiers, than of a subject of a despotic prince.

1st April, Wednesday.—In the morning Malgares dispatched a courier, with a letter to the commandant general Salcedo to inform him of our approach and also one to his father in law.

2d April, Thursday.—When we arrived at Chihuahua, we pursued our course through the town to the house of the general. I was much astonished to see with what anxiety Malgares anticipated the meeting with his military chief; after having been on the most arduous and enterprizing expedition, ever undertaken by any of his majesty's officers from these provinces and having executed it with equal spirit and judgment, yet was he fearful of his meeting him, with an eye of displeasure; and appeared to be much more agitated than ourselves, although we may be supposed to have also had our sensations, as on the will of this man depended our future destiny, at least until our country could interfere in our behalf. On our arrival at the general's we were halted in the hall of the guard, until word was sent to the general of our arrival, when Malgares was first introduced, who remained some time, during which a Frenchman came up and endeavored to enter into conversation with us, but was soon frowned into silence as we conceived he was only some authorised spy. Malgares at last came out and asked me to walk in. I found the general sitting at his desk; he was a middle sized man, apparently about fifty-five years of age, with a stern countenance, but he received me graciously and beckoned to a seat: he then observed "you have given us and yourself a great deal of trouble."

Captain Pike. "On my part entirely unsought, and on that of the Spanish voluntary."

General. "Where are your papers?"

Captain Pike. "Under charge of lieutenant Malgares," who was then ordered to have my small trunk brought in; which being done, a lieutenant

Walker came in, who is a native of New Orleans, his father an Englishman, his mother a French woman, and spoke both those languages equally well, also the Spanish. He was a lieutenant of dragoons in the Spanish service, and master of the military school at Chihuahua. This same young gentleman was employed by Mr. Andres Ellicott, as a deputy surveyor on the Florida line between the United States and Spain, in the years '97 and '98.[231] General Salcedo then desired him to assist me in taking out my papers, and requested me to explain the nature of each, and such as he conceived was relevant to the expedition, he caused to be laid on one side, and those which were not of a public nature on the other; the whole either passing through the hands of the general or Walker, except a few letters from my lady, which on my taking up and saying they were letters from a lady, the general gave a proof, that if the ancient Spanish bravery had degenerated in the nation generally, their gallantry still existed, by bowing, and I put them in my pocket. He then informed me that he would examine the papers, but that in the mean while he wished me to make out and present to him a short sketch of my voyage,[232] which might probably be satisfactory. This I would have positively refused, had I had an idea that it was his determination to keep the papers, which I could not at that time conceive, from the urbanity and satisfaction which he appeared to exhibit on the event of our interview. He then told me that I would take up my quarters with Walker, in order (as he said) to be better accommodated by having a person with me who spoke the English language; but the object as I suspected, was for him to be a spy on our actions, and on those who visited us. Robinson all this time had been standing in the guard room, boiling with indignation at being so long detained *there*, subject to the observations of the soldierly and gaping curiosity of the vulgar. He was now introduced by some mistake of one of the aid-de-camps. He appeared and made a slight bow to the general, who demanded of Malgares who he was? He replied a doctor who accompanied the expedition. "Let him retire," said the governor, and he went out. The general then invited me to return and dine with him, and we went to the quarters of Walker, where we received several different invitations to take quarters at houses where we might be better accommodated, but understanding that the general had designated our quarters we were silent.

We returned to dine at the palace, where we met Malgares, who, with ourselves, was the only guest. He had at the table the treasurer *Truxillio*, and a priest called father Rocus.

3d April, Friday.—Employed in giving a sketch of our voyage for the general and commandant of those provinces. Introduced to Don Bernardo Villamil, Don Alberto Mayner, lieutenant colonel and father-in-law to Malgares, and Don Manuel Zuloaga, a member of the secretary's office, to whom I am under obligations of gratitude and shall remember with esteem. Visited his house in the evening.

4th April, Saturday.—Visited the hospital where were two officers, who were fine looking men, and I was informed had been the gayest young men of the province, who were mouldering away by disease, and there was not a physician in his majesty's hospital who was able to cure them; but after repeated attempts had given them up to perish. This shews the deplorable state of the medical science in the provinces. I endeavored to get Robinson to undertake the cure of these poor fellows, but the jealousy and envy of the Spanish doctors made it impracticable.

5th April, Sunday.—Visited by lieutenant Malgares, with a very polite message from his excellency, and delivered in the most impressive terms, with offers of assistance, money, &c. for which I returned my respectful thanks to the general. Accompanied Malgares to the public walk, where we found the secretary, captain Villamil, Zuloaga and other officers of distinction. We here likewise met the wife of my friend Malgares, to whom he introduced us. She was like all the other *ladies* of New Spain, a little *en bon point*, but possessed the national beauty of eye in a superior degree. There were a large collection of ladies, amongst whom were two of the most celebrated in the Capital—Senora Maria Con. Caberairi, and Senora Marguerite Vallois, the only two ladies who had spirit sufficient, and their husbands generosity enough to allow them to think themselves rational beings, to be treated on an equality, to receive the visits of their friends, and give way to the hospitality of their dispositions without constraint: they were consequently the envy of the ladies, and the subject of scandal to prudes; their houses were the rendezvous of all the fashionable male society; and every man who was conspicuous for science, arts or arms, was sure to meet a welcome. We, as unfortunate strangers, were consequently not forgotten. I returned with Malgares to the house of his father-in-law, lieutenant colonel Mayner, who was originally from Cadiz, a man of good information.

6th April, Monday.—Dined with the general. writing, &c. In the evening visited Malgares and the secretary.

After dinner wine was set on the table, and we were entertained with songs in the French, Italian, Spanish and English languages. Accustomed as I was to sitting some time after dinner I forgot their *siesta*, (or repose after dinner) until Walker suggested the thing to me, when we retired.

7th April, Tuesday.—Dined at Don Antonio Caberairi's, in company with Villamil, Zuloaga, Walker, &c. . . . . Sent in a sketch of my voyage to the general. Spent the evening at colonel Mayner's with Malgares.

8th April, Wednesday.—Visited the treasurer, who showed me the double-barrel gun given by governor Claiborne, and another formerly the property of Nolan.

9th April, Thursday.—In the evening was informed that David Fero was in town and wished to speak to me. This man had formerly been my father's ensign, and was taken with Nolan's party at the time the latter was killed. He possessed a brave soul, and had withstood every oppression since his being made prisoner, with astonishing fortitude. Although his leaving the place of his confinement (the village of St. Jeronimie [San Jeronimo]) without the knowledge of the general, was in some measure clandestine, yet, a countryman, an acquaintance, and formerly a brother soldier, in a strange land, in distress, had ventured much to see me—could I deny him the interview from any motives of delicacy? No; forbid it humanity! forbid it every sentiment of my soul!

Our meeting was affecting, tears standing in his eyes. He informed me the particulars of their being taken, and many other circumstances since their being in the country. I promised to do all I could for him consistent with my character and honor, and their having entered the country without the authority of the United States. As he was obliged to leave the town before day, he called on me at my quarters, when I bid him adieu, and gave him what my *purse* afforded, not what my *heart* dictated.

10th April, Friday.—In the evening at colonel Maynor's. Captain Rodiriques [Rodriguez] arrived from the province of Texas, who had been under arrest one year, for going to Natchitoches with the marquis Cassa Calvo.

11th April, Saturday.—Rode out in the coach with Malgares; was hospitably entertained at the house of one of the Vallois; here we drank London Porter. Visited the secretary Villamil.

12th April, Sunday.—Dined (with the doctor) at Don Antonio Caberarie's with our usual guests. In the evening at the public walks.

13*th April, Monday.*—Nothing extraordinary.

14*th April, Tuesday.*—Spent the forenoon in writing; the afternoon at Don Antonio Caberarie's.

15*th April, Wednesday.*—Spent the evening at colonel Maynor's with our friend Malgares. Wrote a letter to governor Salcedo on the subject of my papers.

16*th April, Thursday.*—Spent the evening at the secretary's Don Villamil's.

17*th April, Friday.*—Sent my letter to his excellency. Spent the evening with my friend Malgares.

18*th April, Saturday.*—Spent the evening at Caberarie's, &c. Wrote to governor Allencaster.

19*th April, Sunday.*—In the evening at a Fandango.

20*th April, Monday.*—We this day learned that an American officer had gone on to the city of Mexico. This was an enigma to us inexplicable, as we conceived that the jealousy of the Spanish government would have prevented any foreign officer from penetrating the country; and what the United States could send an authorised agent to the vice royalty, when the Spanish government had at the seat of our government a charge des affairs, served but to darken the conjectures. The person alluded to was Mr. Burling, a citizen of Mississippi Territory, whose mission is now well known to the government. We likewise received an account of a commercial treaty having been entered into between Great Britain and the United States, which by the Dons was only considered as the preliminary step to an alliance offensive and defensive between the two nations.

21*st, April, Tuesday.*—Presented the commanding general with a letter for general Wilkinson, which he promised to have forwarded to the governor of Texas.

22*d April, Wednesday.*—Spent the day in reading and studying Spanish; the evening at captain Villamil's.

23*d April, Thursday.*—Dined at Don Pedro Vallois; the evening with colonel Maynor; bid him adieu as he was to march the next day. In the evening received a letter from the commandant general, informing me my papers were to be detained, giving a certificate of their numbers, contents, &c. &c.[233]

24*th April, Friday.*—Spent the evening at Zuloaga's with his relations. About sun down an officer of the government called upon me, and "told me that the government had been informed, that in conversations in all societies, Robinson and myself had held forth political maxims and principles, which if *just*, I must be conscious if generally disseminated, would in a very few years be the occasion of a revolt of *those* kingdoms; that those impressions had taken such effect as that it was no uncommon thing (in the circles in which we associated) to hear the comparative principles of a republican and monarchical government discussed; and even the allegiance due (*in case of certain events*) to the court called in question; that various characters of consideration had indulged themselves in those conversations, *all of whom were noted and would be taken care of,* but, that, as it respected myself and companion, it was the desire of his excellency, that whilst in the dominions of Spain we would not hold forth any conversations whatsoever, either on the subject of religion or politics," I replied, that "it was true I have held various and free conversations on the subjects complained of, but only with men high in office, who might be supposed to be firmly attached to the king, and partial to the government of their country. That I had never gone amongt the poor and illiterate, preaching up republicanism or a free government. That as to the catholic religion, I had only combatted some of what I conceived to be its illiberal dogmas; but that I had spoken of it in all instances as a respectable branch of the Christian religion, which as well as all others, was tolerated in the United States; but that, had I came to that kingdom in a diplomatic characters, delicacy towards the government would have sealed my lips. Had I been a prisoner of war, personal safety might have had the same effect; but being there in the capacity which I was; not voluntarily, but by coercion of the Spanish government, but, who at the same time had officially notified me that they did not consider me under *any restraint whatever*—therefore, when called on, should always give my opinions freely, either as to politics or religion; but at the same time with urbanity, and a proper respect to the legitimate authorities of the country where I was."

He replied, "Well you may then rest assured your conduct will be represented in no very favorable point of view to your government."

I replied, "To my government I am certainly responsible, and to no other." He then left me, and I immediately waited on some of my *friends* and notified them of the threat, at which they appeared much *alarmed,* and we went immediately to consult [Melgares]————who, to great attachment to his friends, joined the most incorruptible loyalty and the confidence of the government. Our consultation ended in a determination only to be silent and watch events.

We suspected [Walker]————to be the informant, but whether just in our suspicion or not, I will not pretend to determine, for Robinson and myself frequently used to hold conversations in his presence purposely to have them communicated; but he at last discovered our intentions, and told us, that if we calculated on making him a carrier of news, we were mistaken; that he despised it.

25th April, Saturday.—At eleven o'clock called on his excellency, but was informed he was engaged; about three o'clock received a message from him by lieutenant Walker, informing me that he was surprized I had not returned, and to call without ceremony in the evening, which I did, and presented him with a letter. He then also candidly informed me my party would not join me in the territory of the king of Spain, but that they should be attended to punctually, and forwarded on immediately after me; but requested that I should give orders to my sergeant to deliver up all his ammunition, and dispose in some manner of the horses of which he had charge. I stated in reply, "that with respect to the ammunition, I would give orders to my sergeant to deliver (if demanded) all they possessed, more than was necessary to fill their horns; but that as to the horses, I considered their loss was a charge which must be adjusted between the two governments, therefore should not give any directions respecting them, except as to bringing them on as far and as long as they were able to travel." He then gave me an invitation to dine with him on the morrow.

26th April, Sunday.—Dined at the general's. In the evening went to Malgares, Zuloaga's and others. Wrote to my sergeant and Fero; to the latter of whom I sent ten dollars, and to the other 161 dollars 84 cents, to purchase clothes for the party. We had been for some time suspicious that the doctor was to be detained, but this evening he likewise obtained permission to pursue his journey with me, which diffused general joy through all the party.

27 April, Monday.—Spent the day in making arrangements for our departure; writing to the sergeant, &c. I will here mention some few anecdotes relative to [Walker]————, with whom we boarded during our stay in Chihuahua. When we came to the city, we went to his quarters, (by order of the general) and considered ourselves as guests, having not the least idea that we should be charged with board, knowing with what pleasure any American officer would receive and entertain a foreign brother soldier situated as we were, and that we should conceive it a great insult to be offered pay under similar circumstances. But one day after we had been there about a week, he presented to me an account for Robinson's and my board, *receipted*, and begged if the general enquired of me, that I would say I had paid it. This naturally led me to demand how the thing originated; he with considerable embarrassment observed, that he had taken the liberty to remark to the general, that he thought he should be allowed an extra allowance, in order to be enabled to treat us with some little distinction. The general flew into a most violent passion, and demanded if I had not paid him for our board? to which the other replied no, he did not expect pay of us. He ordered him immediately to demand pay, to receive it, sign a receipt and lodge it in his hands; and added, he would consult me if the thing was done, but which he never did, yet I took care every Sunday after that, to deposit in the hands of Walker, a sum which was considered the proportion for Robinson and myself. Malgares and several other of the Spanish officers having heard of the thing, waited on us much mortified—saying, with what pleasure they would have entertained us had not the designation of the general pointed out his will on the subject [Walker]————had living with him an old negro, (the only one I saw on that side of St. Antonio) who was the property of some person who resided near Natchez, who had been taken with Nolan. Having been acquainted with him in the Mississippi country, solicited and obtained permission for old Caesar to live with him. I found him very communicative and extremely useful. The day I arrived, when we were left alone he came in, and looked around at the walls of the room and exclaimed, "What! all gone." I demanded an explanation, and he informed me that the maps of the different provinces as taken by [Walker]———— —and other surveyors, had been hung up against the walls, but the day we arrived they had all been taken down and deposited in a closet which he designated. W———gave various reasons for his having left the United States and joined the Spanish service; one of which was, his father having been ill-treated as he conceived by G. at Natchez. At Chihuahua he had charge of the military school, which consisted of about 15 young men of the first families of the provinces; also of the public waterworks of the city, on a plan devised by the royal engineer of Mexico; of the building of a new church; of the casting of small artillery, fabrication of arms, &c. &c. Thus, though he had tendered his resignation, they knew his value too well to part with him, and would not accept of it, but still kept him in a subordinate station, in order that he might be the more *dependent* and the more *useful*. And although he candidly confessed his disgust to their service, manners, morals, and political establishments, yet, he never made a communication to us which he was bound in honor to conceal; but on the contrary fulfilled the station of informer, which in that country is considered no disgrace, with great punctuality and fidelity. In this city the proverb was literally true, that "the walls had ears," for there was scarcely any thing could pass that his excellency did not know in a few hours after. In the evening I was notified to be ready to march the next day at three o'clock.

28th April, Tuesday.—In the morning Malgares waited on us, and informed us he was to accompany us some distance on the route. After bidding adieu to all our friends, marched at a quarter pass three o'clock, and encamped at nine o'clock at night at a spring—stony—passed near Chihuahua a small ridge of mountains, and there encamped in a hollow.

This day as we were riding along, Malgares rode up to me and informed me that the general had given orders that I should not be permitted to make any astronomical observations. To this I replied, that he well knew I never had attempted making any since I was conducted into the Spanish dominions.

29th April, Wednesday.—Arrived at a settlement at eight o'clock—plenty of milk, &c. When about to make my journal, Malgares changed color, and informed me it was his orders I should not take notes, but added, you have a good memory, and when you get to Cogguilla [Coahuila] you can bring it all up. At first I felt considerably indignant, and was on the point of refusing to comply; but thinking for a moment of the many politenesses I had received from his hands, induced me merely to bow assent with a smile, and we proceeded on our route, but had not proceeded far before I made a pretext to halt—established my boy as a vedet, and sat down peaceably under a bush and made my notes, &c. this course I pursued ever after, not without some very considerable degree of trouble to separate myself from the party.

Arrived at the fort of St. Paul at eleven o'clock, situated on a small river of the same name, the course of which is north-east by south-west. At the time we were there the river was not wider than a mill stream, but sometimes it is three hundred yards wide and impassable. Distance 30 miles.

30th April, Thursday.—Marched at six o'clock, and at eleven arrived at the river Conchos [Saucillo] 24 miles—beautiful green trees on its banks. I was taken very sick at half past ten o'clock.

Arrived at night at a small station [Las Garzas] on the river Conchos, garrisoned by a sergeant and ten men from the fort Conchos, fifteen leagues up said river. Distance 43 miles.

1st May, Friday.—Marched up the Conchos to its confluence with the river Florada, 15 leagues from where we left the former river, and took up the latter, which bears from the Conchos S. 80° and 50° E. On its banks, are some very flourishing settlements, and they are well timbered. A poor miserable village [Santa Rosalia] at the confluence. . . . . Came ten miles up the Florada to dinner, and at night stopt at a private house. This property or plantation was valued formerly at 300,000 dollars, extending on the Florada from the small place we slept at on the last of April, 30 leagues up said river. Distance 45 miles.

Finding that a new species of discipline had taken place, and that the suspicions of my friend Malgares were much more acute than ever, I conceived it necessary to take some steps to secure the notes I had taken, which were clandestinely acquired. In the night I arose, and after making my men charge all their pieces well, I took my small books and rolled them up in small rolls, and tore a fine shirt to pieces, and wrapt it round the papers and put them down in the barrels of the guns, until we just left room for the tompoins [tampons], which were then carefully put in; the remainder we secured about our bodies under our shirts. This occupied about two hours, but was effected without discovery, and without suspicions.

2d May, Saturday.—Marched early, and in four and a quarter hours arrived at Guaxequillo; situated on the river Florada, where we were to exchange our friend Malgares for captain Barelo, who was a Mexican by birth, born near the capital, and entered as a cadet at Guaxequillo near twenty years past, and by his extraordinary merits (being a Creolian) had been promoted to a captain, which was even by himself considered as his ultimate promotion. He was a gentleman in his manners—generous and frank; and I believe a good soldier.

3d May, Sunday.—At Guaxequillo the captain gave up his command to Malgares. At night the officers gave a ball, at which appeared at least sixty women, ten or a dozen of whom were very handsome.

4th May, Monday.—Don Hymen Guloo arrived from Chihuahua, accompanied by a citizen and the friar, who had been arrested by order of the commandant general, and was on his way to Mexico for trial.

5th May, Tuesday.—The party marched with all the spare horses and baggage.

6*th May, Wednesday.*—Marched at five o'clock; ascended the river four miles, when we left it to our right and took off south 60°, east eight miles. Our friend Malgares accompanied us a few miles, to whom we bad an eternal adieu, if war does not bring us together in the field of battle opposed as the most deadly enemies, when our hearts acknowledge the greatest friendship. . . . . Halted at ten o'clock, and marched again at four. No water on the road; detached a Spanish soldier in search of some, who did not join us until 12 o'clock at night. Encamped in the open prairie; no wood or water except what the soldier brought us in gourds. The mules came up at eleven o'clock at night. Distance 30 miles.

7*th May, Thursday.*—Marched very early, wind fresh from the south. The punctuality of captain Barelo as to hours was remarkable. Arrived at half past nine o'clock at a spring, the first water from Guaxequillo. The mules did not unload, but continued on 9 miles to another spring at the foot of a mountain—good pasturage round it—mountains on each side all day. Distance 28 miles.

8*th, May, Friday.*—Marched at five miles due west, through a gap in the mountain, then turned S. 20° E. and more south to a river [Cerro Gordo] about twenty feet wide—high steep banks; now dry except in holes, but sometimes full and impassable. Halted at seven o'clock and sent on the loaded mules. Marched at five o'clock, came 10 miles and encamped without water. Distance 18 miles.

9*th May, Saturday.*—Marched between four and five o'clock and arrived at Pelia [Pelayo] at eight. This is only a station for a few soldiers, but is surrounded by [copper] mines. At this place are two large warm springs, strongly impregnated with sulphur, and this is the water obliged to be used by the party who are stationed there. Here we remained all day. Captain Barelo had two beeves killed for his and my men and charged nothing to either. Here he received orders from the general to lead us through the wilderness to Montelovez [Monclova], in order that we should not approximate to the frontiers of Mexico, which we should have done by the usual route of Patos, Paras, &c.

10*th May, Sunday.*—Marched past one copper mine [oruilla] new diligently worked. At this place the proprietor had 100,000 sheep, cattle, horses, &c. Arrived at the Cadena, a house built and occupied by a priest. It is situated on a small stream at the pass of the mountains called by the Spaniards the Door of the Prison [Puerta de Cadena] from its being surrounded with [Mimbres] mountains. The proprietor was at Sumbraretto, distant six days march. This hacienda was obliged to furnish accommodations to all travellers.

Marched at five o'clock and passed the chain of mountains due east 12 miles, and encamped without water. Distance 31 miles.

11*th May, Monday.*—Marched and arrived at Maupemie [Mapimi] at eight o'clock, a village situated at the foot of mountains of minerals, where they worked eight or nine mines. The mass of the people were naked and starved wretches. The proprietor of the mines gave us an elegant repast. Here the orders of Salcedo were explained to me by the captain. I replied, that they excited my laughter, as there were disaffected persons sufficient to serve as guides should an army every come into the country.

Came on three miles further, where were fig-trees and a fruit called by the French La Grain, situated on a little stream which flowed through the gardens, and formed a terrestrial paradise. Here we remained all day sleeping in the shade of the fig-trees, and at night continued our residence in the garden. We obliged the inhabitants with a ball, who expressed great anxiety for a relief from their present distressed state and a change of government.

12*th May, Tuesday.*—Was awoke in the morning by the singing of the birds and the perfumes of the trees around. I attempted to send two of my soldiers to town, when they were overtaken by a dragoon and ordered back—they returned, when I again ordered them to go, and if a soldier attempted to stop them to take him off his horse and flog him. This I did, as I conceived it was the duty of the captain to explain his orders relative to me, which he had not done, and I conceived that this would bring on an explanation. They were pursued by a dragoon through the town, who rode after them making use of ill language. They attempted to catch him but could not. As I had mentioned my intentions of sending my men to town after some stores to captain Barelo, and he had not made any objections, I conceived it was acting with duplicity to send men to watch the movements of my messengers; I therefore determined they should punish the dragoons unless their captain had candor sufficient to explain the reasons for his not wishing the men to go to the town, in which wish I should undoubtedly have acquiesced; but as he never mentioned the circumstance, I was guardedly silent, and the affair never interrupted our harmony.

We marched at five o'clock and came on 15 miles and encamped without water. One mile on this side of the little village the road branches out into three, the right hand one by Pattos, Paras, Saltelo, &c. being the main road to Mexico and St. Antonio. The road which we took, leaves all the villages a little to the right, passing only some plantations; the left hand one goes immediately through the mountains to Montelovez, but is dangerous for small parties on account of the savages. This road is called the route by the Bolson of Maupene, and was first travelled by Monsieur De Croix, (afterwards viceroy of Peru.) In passing from Chihuahua to Texas, by this route, you make in seven days what it takes you 15 or 20 by the ordinary one, but it is very scarce of water, and your guards must either be so strong as to defy the Appaches, or calculate to escape them by swiftness, for they fill those mountains, whence they continually carry on a predatory war against the Spanish settlements and caravans.

We this day passed on to the territories of the marquis De San Miquel [Miguel], who owns from the mountains of the Rio del Norte to some distance into the kingdom of Old Mexico.

13th May, Wednesday,—Came on to the river [Nasas] Brasses Ranche de St. Antonio, part of the marquis' estate. My boy and self halted at the river Brasses to water our horses, having rode on ahead, and took the bridles from their mouths, in order that they might drink free, which they could not do with the Spanish bridles. The horse I rode had been accustomed to being held by his master in a peculiar manner when bridled, and would not let me put it on again for a long time, when in the mean time my boy's horse ran away, and it was out of our power to catch him again, but when we arrived at the Ranche, we soon had out a number of boys, who brought in the horse and all his different equipments which were scattered on the route. This certainly was a strong proof of their honesty, and did not go unrewarded. In the evening we gave them a ball on the green according to custom. We here learnt that one peck of corn, with three pounds of meat per week, was the allowance given a grown person.

14th May, Thursday.—Did not march until half past four o'clock [A. M.], and about 9 o'clock an officer arrived from St. Rosa with 24 men and two Appaches in irons. They were noble looking fellows, of large stature, and appeared by no means cast down by their misfortunes, although they knew their fate was transportation beyond the sea, never more to see their friends and relations. . . . .Knowing as I did the intension of the Spaniards towards those people, I would have liberated them if in my power. I went near them and gave them to understand we were friends, and conveyed to them some articles which would be of service if chance offered.

This day the thermometer stood at 30° Raumauer, 99° 1-2 Farenheit and the dust and drought of the road obliged us to march in the night, when we came 15 miles and encamped without water—indeed this road which the general obliged us to take, is almost impassable at this season for want of water, whilst the other is plentifully supplied.

15*th May, Friday.*—Marched early and came on five miles, when we arrived at a pit dug in a hollow, which afforded a small quantity of muddy water for ourselves and beasts. Here we were obliged to remain all day in order to travel in the night, as our beasts could enjoy the benefit of water. Left this at half past five o'clock and came on 15 miles by eleven o'clock, when we encamped without water or food for our beasts. Passed a miserable burnt up soil. Distance 20 miles.

16*th May, Saturday.*—Marched two hours and arrived at a wretched habitation, where we drew water from a well for all the beasts. Marched in the evening and made 15 miles further. The right hand road we left on this side of Maupeme, and joined it about four miles further. Distance 15 miles.

17*th May, Sunday.*—Marched and about seven o'clock came in sight of *Paras,* which we left on the right and halted at the Hacienda of St. Lorenzo, a short league to the north of said village. At the Hacienda of St. Lorenzo was a young priest, who was extremely anxious for a change of government, and came to our beds and conversed for hours on the subject.

18*th May, Monday.*—Marched early and came through a mountainous tract of country but well watered, and houses situated here and there amongst the rocks. . . . . Joined the main road at a Hacienda of [Crenega Grande]————belonging to the marquis De San Miquel—good gardens and fruit—also a fine stream. The mules did not arrive until late at night, when it had commenced raining.

19*th May, Tuesday.*—Did not march until three o'clock, the captain not being very well. He here determined to take the main road notwithstanding the orders of general Salcedo. Came on ten miles. Met a deserter from captain Johnston's company [2d Infantry?]. He returned and came to the camp, and begged of me to take him back to his company, but I would not give any encouragement to the scoundrel, only a little change, as he was without a farthing.

20*th May, Wednesday.*—Came to the Hacienda of Pattos by nine o'clock. This is a handsome place, where the marquis De San Miquel frequently spends his summers, the distance enabling him to come from [City of] Mexico in his coach in ten days. Here we met the Mexican post-rider going to Chewawa. Don Hymie who had left us at Paras, joined in a coach and six, in which we came out to a little settlement called the Florida, one league from Pattos, due north. Distance 18 miles.

The Hacienda of Pattos was a square enclosure of about three hundred feet, the building being one story high, but some of the apartments very elegantly furnished. In the centre of the square was a Jet d'eau, which cast forth water from eight spouts, extended from a colosean female form. From this fountain all the neighboring inhabitants got their supply of water. The marquis had likewise a very handsome church, which, with its ornaments cost him at least 20,000 dollars; to officiate in which, he maintained a little stiff superstitious priest. In the rear of the palace (for so it might be called) was a fish-pond, in which were immense numbers of fine fish. The population of Florida as about 2,000 souls. This was our nearest point to the city of Mexico.

21st May, Thursday.—Marched down the [San Antonio] water course over a rough and stony road about ten miles, when we left it on the right, and came on eight miles further to a horse range of the marquis's, where he had four of his soldiers as a guarda caballo. Halted at half past nine o'clock. At this place we had a spring of bad water.

22d May, Friday.—Marched at three o'clock and came on 16 miles to a small shed, and in the afternoon to la Rancho, eight miles to the left of the main road near the foot of the mountain, where was a pond of water but no houses. Some Spanish soldiers were here. We left Pattos mountain on our left and right, but here there was a cross mountain [El Monte del los Tres Rios] over which we were to pass in the morning.

The marquis maintains 1500 troops to protect his vassals and property from the savages. They are all cavalry, and as well dressed and armed as the king's, but are treated by the king's troops as if vastly inferior.

23d May, Saturday.—Marched early and came to a spring in the mountain.

24th May, Sunday.—Marched at an early hour and passed through the mountain, (scarcely any road,) called the mountain of the Three Rivers. At the 13th mile joined the main road which we had left to our right on the 22d instant, and in one hour after, came to the main Mexican road from the eastern provinces; from thence north-west to the Rancho, nine miles from Montelovez, whence the captain sent in an express to give notice of our approach.

25th May, Monday.—In the afternoon lieutenant Adams, commandant of the company of Montelovez arrived in a coach and six to escort us to town, where we arrived about five o'clock, P. M. In the evening visited captain De Ferara, the commandant of the troops of Cogquilla, and inspector of the five provinces.

Lieutenant Adams who commanded this place, was the son of an Irish engineer in the service of *Spain*. He had married a rich girl of the Passo Del Norte, and they lived here in elegance and style for the country. We put up at his quarters and were very hospitably entertained.

26th May, Tuesday.—Made preparations for marching the next day. I arose early before any of our people were up and walked nearly round the town; and from the hill took a small survey, with my pencil and a pocket compass which I always carried with me—returned and found them at breakfast, they having sent three or four of my men to search for me. The Spanish troops at this place were remarkably polite, always fronting and saluting when I passed. This I attributed to their commandant, lieutenant Adams.

27th May, Wednesday.—Marched at seven o'clock, after taking an affectionate leave of Don Hymen, and at half past twelve arrived at the Haciendo of Don Melcher [Michon], situated on the same stream of Montelovez.

Don Melcher was a man of very large fortune, polite, generous and friendly. He had in his service a man who had deserted from captain Lockwood's company, first regiment of infantry, by the name of Pratt. From this man he had acquired a considerable quantity of crude indigested information relative to the United States, and when he met with us his thirst after knowledge or our laws and institutions appeared to be insatiable. He caused a fine large sheep to be killed and presented to my men.

28th May, thursdy.—Marched early and arrived at Encina Haciendo at ten o'clock. This place was owned by Don Barego.

When we arrived at the Haciendo of Encina, I found a youth of 18 sitting in the house quite genteely dressed, whom I immediately recognized from his physiognomy to be an American, and entered into conversation with him. He expressed great satisfaction at meeting a countryman, and we had a great deal of conversation. He sat at a table with us and partook of a cold collation of fruits and confectionary, but I was much surprised to learn shortly after we quit the table, that he was a deserter from our army, on which I questioned him, and he replied, that his name was Griffith, he had enlisted in Philadelphia; arrived at New Orleans and deserted as soon as possible; that the Spaniards had treated him much better than his own countrymen, and that he should never return. I was extremely astonished at his insolence, and mortified that I should have been betrayed into any polite conduct towards the scoundrel. I told him "that it was astonishing he should have had the impertinence to address himself to me, knowing that I was an American officer." He muttered something about being in a country where he was protected, &c. on which I told him, "If he again opened his mouth to me, I would instantly chastize him, notwithstanding his supposed protection." He was silent, and I called up one of my soldiers and told him in his hearing, that if he attempted to mix with them to turn him out of company, which they executed by leading him to the door of their room a short time after, when he entered it. When dinner was nearly ready, I sent a message to the proprietor, that "we assumed no right to say whom he should introduce to his table, but, that we should think it a great indignity offered to a Spanish officer to attempt to set him down at the same board with a deserter from their army; and that, if the man who as at the table in the morning, was to make his appearance again, we should decline eating at it." He replied, "that it was accident which produced the event of the morning; that he was sorry our feelings had been injured, and that he would take care he [Griffith] did not appear again whilst we were there."

Our good friend Don Melcher here overtook us, and passed the evening with us.

This day we passed the last mountains, and again entered the great Mississippi valley, it being six months and thirteen days since we first came in sight of them. Distance 20 miles.

29th May, Friday.—Marched at seven o'clock and came to the river Millada and Rancho.

30th May, Saturday.—Marched at five o'clock and arrived at the river Sabine at eight—forded it. Marched in the evening at four o'clock, at ten encamped at the Second Ridge without water. Distance 27 miles.

31st May, Sunday.—Marched early and at nine o'clock arrived at a Rancho, a fine running water—course east and west. Marched eight miles further to a point of woods and encamped. No water. Distance 23 miles.

1st June, Monday.—Arrived at the Presidio Rio Grande at eight o'clock. This place was the position to which our friend Barelo was ordered, and which had been very highly spoke of to him, but he found himself miserably mistaken, for it was with the greatest difficulty we obtained any thing to eat, which mortified him extremely. When at Chihuahua, general Salcedo had asked me if I had not lost a man by desertion, to which I replied in the negative. He then informed me that an American had arrived at the Presidio Rio Grande in the last year; that he had at first confined him, but that he was now released and practicing physic, and that he wished me to examine him on my arrival: I therefore had him sent for; the moment he entered the room I discovered he never had received a liberal education, or been accustomed to polished society. I told him the reason that I had requested to see him, and that I had it in my power to serve him if I found him a character worthy of interference.

He then related the following story; "That his name was Martin Henderson, that he was born in Rock Bridge county, state of Virginia; that he had been brought up a farmer, but, that cominig early to the state of Kentucky and Tennessee, he had acquired a taste for a frontier life, and that in the spring of 1806, himself and four companions, had left the Saline in the District of Saint Genevieve, Upper Louisiana, in order to penetrate through the woods to the province of Texas; that his companions had left him on the White [Arkansas] River, and that he had continued on: that in swimming some western branch his horse sunk under him, and it was with difficulty that he had made the shore with his gun. Here he waited two or three days until his horse rose, and he then got his saddle bags, but that all his notes on the country, courses, &c. were destroyed. He then proceeded on foot for a few days, when he was met by 30 or 40 Osage warriors, who on his telling them he was going to the Spaniards were about to kill him, but on his saying he would go to the Americans, they held a consultation over him, and finally seized on his clothes, and divided them between them; then his pistols, compass, dirk and watch, which they took to pieces and hung in their noses and ears; then stripped him naked, and round his body they found a belt with gold pieces sewed in it; this they also took, and finally seized on his gun and ammunition, and were marching off to leave him in that situation, but he followed them, thinking it better to be killed than left in that state to die by hunger and cold. The savages after some time halted, and one pulled off an old pair of leggins and gave him, another mockinsons, and a third a buffalo robe, and the one who had carried his heavy rifle had by this time became tired of his prize, (they never using rifles) and they counted him out 25 charges of powder and ball, then sent two Indians who put him on a war trace, which they said led to American establishments;

and as soon as the Indians left him he directed his course as he supposed for Saint Antonio. He then killed deer and made himself some clothes. He proceeded on and expended all his ammunition three days before he struck the Grand Road, nearly at the Rio Grande. He further added, that he had discovered two mines, one of silver and the other of gold, the situation of which he particularly described; but, that the general had taken the samples from him. That he would not attempt to pass himself on us for a physician, and hoped as he only used simples and was careful to do no harm we would not betray him. He further added, that since his being in the country, he had made (from information) maps of all the adjacent country, but that they had been taken from him."

I had early concluded that he was an agent of Burr's, and was revolving in my mind whether I should denounce him as such to the commandant, but felt reluctant from an apprehension that he might be innocent, when one of my men came in and informed me that it was Trainer, who had killed major Bashier in the wilderness, between Natchez and Tennessee, when he was his hireling. He shot him (when taking a nap at noon through the head) with his own pistols. The governor of the state and the major's friends offered a very considerable reward for his apprehension, which obliged him to quit the state; and with an Amazonian woman, who handled arms and hunted like a savage, he retreated to the source of the White River, but being routed from that retreat by captain Maney [James B. Many], of the United States army, and a party of Cherokees, he and his female companion bore west (and she proving to be pregnant, was left by him in the desert, and (I was informed) arrived on the settlements of Red river, but by what means is to me unknown. The articles and money taken from him by the Osage's were the property of the deceased major. I then reported the circumstances to captain Barelo, who had him immediately confined, until the will of governor Cordero was known, who informed me (when at Saint Antonio) he would have him sent to some place of perpetual confinement in the interior. Thus vengeance has overtaken the ingrate and murderer when he least expected it.

In the evening we went to see some performers on the slack rope, who were no wise extraordinary in their performances, except in language which would almost bring a blush on the cheek of the most abandoned of the female sex in the United States.

2d June, Tuesday.—In the day time were endeavoring to regulate our watches by my compass, and in an instant that my back was turned some person stole it; I could by no means recover it, and I had strong suspicions that the theft was approved, as the instrument had occasioned great dissatisfaction.

This day the captain went out to dine with some monks, who would have thought it profanation to have had us their guests, notwithstanding the priest of the place had escorted us round the town and to all the missions; and we found him a very communicative, liberal and intelligent man. We saw no resource for a dinner, but in the inventive genius of a little Frenchman who had accompanied us from Chihuahua, where he had been officiating one year as cook to the general, of whom he gave us many interesting anecdotes, and in fact he was of infinite service to us; we supported him and he served us as cook, interpreter, &c. It was astonishing with what zeal he strove to acquire news and information for us; and as he had been four times through the provinces, he had acquired considerable knowledge of the country, people, &c. He went off and in a very short time returned with table-cloth, plates, and a dinner of three or four courses, a bottle of wine with a pretty girl to attend on the table. We enquired by what magic he had brought it about, and found he had been to one of the officers and notified, that it was the wish of the commandant that he should supply the two Americans with a decent dinner, (this we explained to Barelo in the evening, and he laughed heartily) which was done, but we took care to compensate them for their trouble.

We parted from the captain with regret, and assurances of remembrance. Departed at five o'clock, escorted by ensign————and———— men, and came on to the Rio Grande, which we passed and encamped at a Rancho on the other side. Distance 7 miles.

3d June, Wednesday,—The musquetoes which had commenced the first night on this side Montelovez, now had become very troublesome. This day saw the first horse-flies—saw some wild horses—came on in the open plain, and in a dry time, where there was no water. Distance 30 miles.

4th June, Thursday.—Came 16 miles to a pond and dined—great sign of wild horses—in the afternoon to the river Noissour [Nueces] swiming, where we arrived, although not more than ten steps wide. Distance 36 miles.

5th June, Friday.—After loosing two horses in passing the river (the water having fallen so that we forded) crossed and continued our route. Passed two herd of wild horses, who left the road for us. Halted at a pond on the left of the road, 15 miles, where we saw the first oak since we entered

New Mexico, and this was scrub oak. Passed many deer yesterday and to day. Came on to a small creek at night, where we met a party of the company of Saint Fernandez returning from the line. Distance 31 miles.

6th June, Saturday.—Marched early and met several parties of troops returning from Texas, where they had been sent to reinforce, when our troops were near the line. Immense numbers of cross roads made by the wild horses. Killed a wild hog [peccary], which on examination I found to be very different from the tame breed, smaller, brown, long hair and short legs: they are to be found in all parts between Red river and the Spanish settlements.

Passed an encampment made by the *Lee Panes* [Lipans]—met one of said nation with his wife. In the afternoon struck the wood land, which was the first we had been in from the time we left the Osage nation. Distance 39 miles.

7th June, Sunday.—Came on 15 miles to the river [Medina] Mariano, the line between Texas and Cogquilla—a pretty little stream, Rancho. From thence in the afternoon to Saint Antonio. We halted at the mission of Saint Joseph [San José]—received in a friendly manner by the priest of the mission and others.

We were met out of Saint Antonio about three miles by governors Cordero and Herrara, in a coach. We repaired to their quarters, where we were received like their children. Cordero informed me that he had discretionary orders as to the mode of my going out of the country: that he therefore wished me to choose my time, mode, &c. and, that any sum of money I might want was at my service: that in the mean time Robinson and myself would make his quarters our home; and that he had caused to be vacated and prepared a house immediately opposite for the reception of my men. In the evening his levee was attended by a croud of officers and priests, at which was father M'Guire and Dr. Zerbin. After supper we went to the public square, where might be seen the two governors joined in a dance with people, who in the day time would approach them with reverence and awe.

We were here introduced to the sister of lieutenant Malgares's wife, who was one of the finest women we saw—she was married to a captain Ugarte, to whom we had letters of introduction.

8th June, Monday.—Remained at Saint Antonio.

9th June, Tuesday.—A large party dined at governor Cordero's, who gave as his first toast, "The President of the United States."—Vive la—I returned the compliment by toasting "His Catholic Majesty." These toasts were followed by "General Wilkinson," and one of the company then gave, "Those gentleman; their safe and happy arrival in their own country—their honorable reception, and the continuation of the good understanding which exists between the two countries."

10*th June, Wednesday.*—A large party at the governor's to dinner. He gave as a toast, "His companion, Herrara."

11*th June, Thursday.*—Preparing to march tomorrow. We this evening had a conversation with the two governors, wherein they exhibited an astonishing knowledge of the political character of our executive, and the local interests of the different parts of the union.

12*th June, Friday.*—One of the captains from the kingdom of [Nuevo] Leon having died, we were invited to attend the burial, and accompanied the two governors in their coach, where we had an opportunity of viewing the solemnity of the interment, agreeably to the ritual of the Spanish church, attended by the military honors, which was conferred on the deceased by his late brethren in arms. Governor Cordero gave the information of my intended expedition to the commandant general as early as July [1806]. The same month I took my departure. His information was received via Natchez.

13*th June, Saturday.*—This morning there was marched 200 dragoons for the sea coast to look out for the English, and that evening colonel Cordero was to have marched to join them.

We marched at seven o'clock; governor Cordero taking us out in his coach about two leagues, accompanied by father M'Guire, Dr. Zerbin, &c.

It may not be improper to mention here, something of father M'Guire and doctor Zerbin, who certainly treated us with all imaginable attention while at Saint Antonio. The former was an Irish priest, who formerly resided on the coast above [New] Orleans, and was noted for his hospitable and social qualities. On the cession of Louisiana, he followed the standard of the "king, his master," who never suffers an old servant to be neglected. He received at Cuba an establishment as chaplain to the mint of Mexico, whence the instability of human affairs carried him to Saint Antonio. He was a man of chaste classical taste, observation and research.

Doctor Zerbin formerly resided at Natchez, but in consequence of pecuniary embarrassments emigrated to the Spanish territories. Being a young man of a handsome person and insinuating address, he had obtained the good will of governor Cordero, who had conferred on him an appointment in the king's hospital, and many other advantages by which he might have made a fortune; but he had recently committed some very great indiscretions, by which he had nearly lost the favor of colonel Cordero; but whilst we were there he was treated with attention.

We took a friendly adieu of governor Herrara and our other friends at Saint Antonio.

I will here attempt to pourtray a faint resemblance of the characters of the two governors whom we found at Saint Antonio; but whose super-excellent qualities it would require the pen of a master to do justice.

Don Antonio Cordero, is about five feet ten inches in height, fifty years of age, fair complexion, and blue eyes: he wore his hair turned back, and in every part of his deportment was legibly written "The Soldier." He yet possessed an excellent constitution, and a body which appeared to be neither impaired by the fatigues of the various campaigns he had made, nor disfigured by the numerous wounds received from the enemies of his king. He was one of the select officers who had been chosen by the court of Madrid to be sent to America about 35 years since, to discipline and organize the Spanish provincials, and had been employed in all the various kingdoms and provinces of New Spain. Through the parts which we explored, he was universally beloved and respected; and when I pronounce him by far the most *popular man* in the *internal provinces,* I risk nothing by the assertion. He spoke the Latin and French languages well—was generous, gallant, brave, and sincerely attached to his king and country. Those numerous qualifications have advanced him to the rank of colonel of cavalry, and governor of the provinces of Cogquilla and Texas. His usual residence was Montelovez, which he had embellished a great deal, but since our taking possession of Louisiana, he had removed to Saint Antonio, in order to be nearer the frontier, to be able to apply the remedy to any evil which might arise from the collision of our lines.

Don Simon de Herrara, is about five feet eleven inches high, has a sparkling black eye, dark complexion and hair. He was born in the Canary Islands, served in the infantry in France, Spain and Flanders, and speaks the French language well, and a little of the English. He is engaging in his conversation with his equals; polite and obliging to his inferiors, and in all his actions one of the most gallant and accomplished men I ever knew.

He possesses a great knowledge of mankind from his experience in various countries and societies, and knows how to employ the genius of each of his subordinates to advantage. He had been in the United States during the presidency of general Washington, and had been introduced to that hero, of whom he spoke in terms of exalted veneration. He is now lieutenant-colonel of infantry, and governor of the kingdom of New Leon. His seat of government is Mont Elrey [Monterey]; and probably, if ever a chief was adored by his people it is Herrara. When his time expired last, he immediately repaired to Mexico, attended by 300 of the most respectable people of his government, who carried with them the sighs, tears and prayers of thousands that he might be continued in that government. The viceroy thought proper to accord to their wishes *pro tempore*, and the king has since confirmed his nomination.

When I saw him he had been about one year absent, during which time the citizens of Rank in Mont Elrey had not suffered a marriage or baptism to take place in any of their families, until their common father could be there, to consent and give joy to the occasion by his presence. . . . .What greater proof could be given of their esteem and love?

In drawing a parallel between the two friends, I should say that Cordero was the man of greatest reading, and that Herrara possessed the greatest knowledge of the world. Cordero has lived all his life a batchelor. Herrara married an English Lady in early youth, at Cadiz, who by her suavity of manners makes herself as much beloved and esteemed by the ladies as her noble husband does by the men. By her he has several children, one now an officer in the service of his royal master.

The two friends agree perfectly in one point, their hatred to tyranny of every kind; and in a secret determination never to see that flourishing part of the New World, subject to any other European lord, except *him*, whom they think their honor and loyalty bound to defend with their lives and fortunes. But should Bonaparte seize on European Spain, I risque nothing in asserting, those two gentlemen would be the first to throw off the yoke, draw their swords, and assert the independence of their country.

Before I close this subject, it may not be improper to state, that we owe to governor Herrara's prudence, that we are not now engaged in a war with Spain. This will be explained by the following anecdote which he related in the presence of his friend Cordero, and which was confirmed by him. When the difficulties commenced on the Sabine, the commandant general and the viceroy consulted each other, and they mutually determined to maintain (what they deemed) the dominions of their master, inviolate. The viceroy therefore ordered Herrara to join Cordero with 1300 men, and both the viceroy and general Salcedo, ordered Cordero to cause our troops to be attacked, should they pass the Rio Oude. Those orders were positively reiterated to Herrara, the actual commanding officer of the Spanish army on the frontiers, and gave rise to the many messages which he sent to general Wilkinson when he was advancing with our troops; but finding they were not attended to, he called a council of war on the question to attack or not; when it was given as their opinion, that they should immediately commence a predatory warfare, but avoid a general engagement; yet, notwithstanding the orders of the viceroy, the commandant general, governor Cordero's and the opinion of his officers, he had the firmness (or temerity) to enter into the agreement with general Wilkinson, which at present exists relative to our boundaries on that frontier. On his return he was received with coolness by Cordero, and they both made their communication to their superiors. Until an answer was received, said Herrara, "I experienced the most unhappy period of my life, conscious I had served my country faithfully, at the same time I had violated every principle of military duty." At length the answer arrived, and what was it, but the thanks of the viceroy and the commandant general, for having pointedly disobeyed their orders, with assurances that they would represent his services in exalted terms to the king. What could have produced this change of sentiment is to me unknown, but the letter was published to the army, and confidence again restored between the two chiefs and the troops.

Our company consisted of lieutenant Jn. Echararria, who commanded the escort. Captain Eugene Marchon, of New Orleans, and father Jose Angel Cabaso, who was bound to the camp at or near the Trinity, with a suitable proportion of soldiers. We came on 16 miles to a place called the Beson, where we halted until the mules came up. Marched again at four o'clock, and arrived at the river of Guadalupe at eight o'clock at night. Distance 30 miles.

14th June, Sunday.—When we left Saint Antonio, every thing appeared to be in a flourishing and improving state, owing to the examples and encouragement given to industry, politeness and civilization by their excellent governor Cordero and his colleague Herrara; also the large body of troops maintained at that place in consequence of the difference existing between the United States and Spain.

Came on to the Saint Mark [Rio San Marco] in the morning—in the afternoon came on 15 miles further, but was late, owing to our having taken the wrong road. Distance 30 miles.

15th June, Monday.—Marched 20 miles in the morning to a small pond, which is dry in a dry season, where we halted. Here commenced the oak timber, it having been musqueet [mesquite] in general from Saint Antonio. Prairie like the Indiana territory. In the afternoon came on six miles further to a creek, where we encamped early. Distance 26 miles.

16th June, Tuesday.—Marched early, and at eight o'clock arrived at Red river.[234] Here was a small Spanish station and several lodges of Tancards, tall, handsome men, but the most naked savages I ever yet saw without exception. They complained much of their situation. In the afternoon passed over hilly, stony land; occasionally saw pine timber. Encamped on a small run. Distance 26 miles. Killed one deer.

17th June, Wednesday.—Came on by nine o'clock to a large encampment of Tancards, more than 40 lodges. Their poverty was as remarkable as their independence. Immense herds of horses, &c. I gave a Camanche and Tancard, each a silk handkerchief, and a recommendation to the commandant at Natchitoches. In the afternoon came on three hours and encamped on a hill, at a creek on the right hand side of the road. Met a large herd of mules escorted by four soldiers; the lieutenant took some money from them which they had in charge. Distance 30 miles.

18th June, Thursday.—Rode on until half past ten o'clock, when we arrived at the river Brassos. Here is a stockade guard of one corporal, six men, and a ferry boat. Swam our horses over—one was drowned and several others near it, owing to their striking each other with their feet. We then came on about two miles on this side of a bayou called the Little Brassos, which is only a branch of the other, and which makes an impassable swamp at certain seasons between them. Distance 31 miles.

19th June, Friday.—Came on through prairies and woods alternately 20 miles to a small creek, *Corpus Christi* well wooded rich land. In the afternoon came on ten miles, and passed a creek which in high water is nearly impassable four miles. Overflows swamps, ponds, &c. Encamped about one mile on this side on high land to the right of the road. Met the mail, Indians and others. Distance 30 miles.

20th June, Saturday.—Came on 16 miles in the morning—passed several herds of mustangs or wild horses, good land, ponds and small dry creeks, prairie and woods alternately. It rained considerably. We halted to dry our baggage long before night. Distance 20 miles.

21st June, Sunday.—Came on to the river Trinity by eight o'clock. Here was stationed two captains, two lieutenants and three ensigns, with nearly 100 men, all sick, one scarcely able to assist the other. Met a number of runaway negroes, some French and Irishmen. Received information of lieutenant Wilkinson's safe arrival. Crossed with all our horses and baggage with much difficulty. Distance 20 miles.

22d June, Monday.—Marched the mules and horses in the forenoon, but did not depart ourselves until three o'clock P. M. Father Jose Angel Cabaso, separated from us at this place for the post of————where he was destined. Passed thick woods and a few small prairies with high rich grass. Sent a dispatch to Nacogdoches. Distance 22 miles.

23d June, Tuesday.—Came on 20 miles in the forenoon to a small creek of standing water; good land and well timbered. Met a sergeant from Nacogdoches. In the afternoon made 20 miles and crossed the river Natchez, running N. W. & S. E. 20 yards wide; belly deep to horses at that time, but sometimes impassable. Two miles on this side encamped on a hill in a little prairie—mules and loads arrived at twelve o'clock. The sandy soil and pine timber began again this afternoon, but good land near the river. Distance 20 miles.

24th June, Wednesday.—The horses came up this morning; lost six over night. We marched early and in 15 miles came to the river Angeline [Rio Angelina], about the width of the Natchez, running N. & S. Good land on its borders—two miles further was a settlement of Barr and Davenport's, where were three of our lost horses—one mile further found two more of our horses where we halted for dinner. Marched at four o'clock, and at half past eight arrived at Nacogdoches—were politely received by the adjutant and inspector [Don Francisco Viana], and captain Herrara, Davenport, &c. This part of the country is well watered, but sandy; hilly soil—pine, scrub oak, &c. Distance 37 miles.

25th June, Thursday.—Spent in reading a gazette from the United States, &c. A large party at the adjutant and inspector's to dinner. 1st toast, "The President of the United States." 2nd. "The King of Spain." 3d. "Governors Herrara and Cordero."

26th June, Friday.—Made preparations to march the next day. Saw an old acquaintance, also Lorrimier's son-in-law from the district of cape

Jerardeau [Girardeau]. Dined with the commandant, and spent the evening at Davenport's.

27th June, Saturday.—Marched after dinner and came only 12 miles. Was escorted by lieutenant Guodiana and a military party. Mr. Davenport's brother-in-law who was taking in some money also accompanied us.

Don Francis Viana, adjutant and inspector of the Internal provinces, who commanded at Nacogdoches, is an old and veteran officer, and was one of those who came to America at the same time with colonel Cordero; but possessing a mind of frankness, he unfortunately spoke his opinions too freely in some instance, which finding their way to court, prevented his promotion. But he is highly respected by his superiors, and looked up to as a model of military conduct by his inferiors. He unfortunately does not possess flexibility sufficient to be useful in the present state of the Spanish kingdoms. He is the officer who caused major Sparks and Mr. Freeman to return from their expedition on the Red River.

28th June, Sunday.—Marched early and at nine o'clock crossed the little river called [Toyac]———, from whence we pushed on in order to arrive at the house of———, a Frenchman,———miles distant from the Sabine. We stopped at a house on the road, where the lieutenant informed me an American by the name of Johnson lived, but was surprized to find he had crossed the line with his family, and a French family in his place. When we began conversing with them they were much alarmed thinking we had come to examine them, and expressed great attachment to the Spanish government, but was somewhat astonished to find I was an American officer, and on my companions stepping out, expressed themselves in strong terms of hatred to the Spanish nation. I excused them for their weakness, and gave them a caution. Fine land, well watered and timbered, hickory, oak, sugar-tree, &c. Distance 40 miles.

29th June, Monday.—Our baggage and horses came up about ten o'clock, when we dispatched them on. . . . . Marched ourselves at two o'clock, and arrived at the river Sabine by five. Here we saw the cantonment of the Spanish troops, when commanded by colonel Herrara, on the late affair between the two governments. Crossed the Sabine river and came about one league on this side to a little prairie, where we encamped. Parted with lieutenant Guodiana and our Spanish escort. And here I think proper to bear testimony to the politeness, civility and attention of all the officers, who at different periods and in different provinces commanded my escort, (but in a particular manner, to Malgares and Barelo, who appeared studious to please and accommodate, all that lay in their power) also the obliging, mild dispositions evinced in all instances by their rank and file. On this side of the Sabine I went up to a house where I found 10 or 15 Americans hovering near the line, in order to embrace an opportunity of carrying on some illicet commerce with the Spaniards, who on their side were equally eager. Here we found Tharp and Sea, who had been old sergeants in general Wayne's army. Distance 15 miles.

30th June, Tuesday.—Marched early and came on to a house at a small creek 15 miles, where lived a Dutch family named Faulk, where we left a small roan horse which had given out. Marched twelve miles further to a large bayou, where had been an encampment of our troops, which I recognized by its form, and took pleasure in imagining the position of the general's marquee and the tents of my different friends and acquaintances. Distance 28 miles.

1st July, Wednesday.—Finding that a horse of doctor Robinson's which had come all the way from Chihuahua, could not proceed, was obliged to leave him here. Yesterday and to day passed many Choctaws, whose clothing, furniture, &c. evidently marked the superiority of situation of those who bordered on our frontiers, to those of the naked, half starved wretches whom we found hanging round the Spanish settlements. Came on and passed a string of huts, supposed to be built by our troops, and at a small run a fortified camp but a half mile from the hill, where anciently stood the village Adyes.

We proceeded on to a spring where we halted for our loads, and finding the horses much fatigued, and not able to proceed, left them and baggage and proceeded on, when we arrived at Natchitoches about four o'clock P. M.

Language cannot express the gaiety of my heart, when I once more beheld the standard of my country waved aloft!—"All hail cried I, the ever sacred name of country, in which is embraced that of kindred, friends, and every other tie which is dear to the soul of man!!" Was affectionately received by colonel Freeman, captains Strong and Woolstoncraft, lieutenant Smith, and all the officers of the post.

Z. M. Pike.[235]

Notes

1. All Pike's private papers were destroyed by fire when his grandson's house burned; all the regimental records touching him were likewise destroyed when the British burned Washington.
2. Another biography of Pike, somewhat inaccurate, is that of General A. W. Greeley in his *Explorers & Travellers*, a volume of *Men of Achievement Series*.
3. "The great objects in view by this expedition (as I conceived) in addition to my instructions, were to attach the Indians to our government, and to acquire such geographical knowledge of the south-western boundary of Louisiana as to enable government to enter into a definitive arrangement for a line of demarkation between that territory and North Mexico." Pike's preface to *An Account of Expeditions*, 4.

   It is true that some of this region was shown on the map of New Spain which Alexander von Humboldt had prepared in 1804. He had never surveyed the country this far north, however, and had no accurate idea of it. His map is consequently most vague and shows definitely only the sources of the Rio Grande.

   The head waters of another river were indicated, it is true, but it was doubtful to Humboldt whether this were the river known in Louisiana as the Arkansas. A confused mass to the north intended to represent Pike's Peak was shown, too, and labeled "Sierra de Allmagre." This, however, is the extent of the information shown on the northern part of Humboldt's elaborate map. It cannot be considered as a representation of the Arkansas and Platte regions.
4. See pp. 57–60.
5. *American Historical Review*, "Papers of Zebulon M. Pike, 1806–7." XIII, 798–800.
6. *An Account of Expeditions*, App. to Pt. III, 57–59.

7. *An Account of Expeditions*, App. to Pt. III, 80–83.
8. *American Historical Review*, XIII, No. 4 (July 1908), 798.
9. *Id.*, 798–799.
10. Cf. *An Account of Expeditions*, App. to Pt. III, 59.
11. April 20, 1925.
12. May 12, 1927.
13. Translation from the Spanish of Cover of File
of
Documents Relating to
Zebulon Pike
In the Department of Foreign Affairs
of the Republic of Mexico
Mexico City, Mexico
United States of Mexico
Secretariat of Foreign Relations
Boundaries
Number 30
Year of 1910
Department of Boundaries
Miscellaneous
Documents taken from the Traveler Palke

Estados Unidos Mexicanos.

SECRETARIA DE RELACIONES EXTERIORES

Limites.
Numero 30
Ano de 1910.
Mlsa d Limites.
Varios.
Documentos recojidos al viaJero.
Paike.
14. Letter, S. W. Boggs, Acting Chief, Division of Publication, to R. H. Hart, Nov. 15. 1927.
15. Letter the Adjutant General to R. H. Hart, Nov. 25, 1927.
16. For complete critical bibliography see Isaac J. Cox, *Early Explorations of Louisiana*, pp. 153 to 160.
17. E. Coues, *The Expeditions of Zebulon Pike*, LXI. Our many references to Mr. Coues' monumental edition of Pike will hereafter be by name only.
18. *Id.* xii.
19. *An Account of Expeditions*, App. Pt. III, 60.
20. *Id.* iv.
21. *Id.* 592. Pike used another source, however, for the map of his Mexican tour. I refer to a map of New Spain by Alexander von Humboldt, which Pike incorporated in his volume without appropriate credit to the author.

That this was the result of an error by the map-maker, as well as poor proof-reading, is evident from Pike's statement regarding the fashioning of his map: "I have carefully markd on said Chart all the parts by actual survey and the Gentlemen by whom surveyed, in order that each, may lay claim to his proper proportion of fame." This formal statement is as singular (in a day when borrowing was the rule and giving credit the exception) as the error which permitted the map to appear without credit to Humboldt who, very naturally, resented it in *Le Moniteur* in the following words: "Mais les cartes du Mexique, publié sons son nom, ne sont que des réductions d' une grande carte de la Nouvelle-Espagne, sur laquelle le voyageur a tracé sa route de Santa-Fé par Colahuila á Nacodeollés [Nacodoches or Natchitoches]." Pike's character was so honorable that one is inclined to believe that his instructions to Nau to acknowledge the borrowing were neglected and that poor proof-reading, or lack of any, led to the unfortunate mistake. Pike's critics have, however, blamed him both for pilfering from Humboldt and for Humboldt's grave mistakes as that the Canadian was Red River! Cf. Note 3.

22. For complete description of early editions see Coues, xxxiii–xlv.

23. K. S. Crichton, "Zeb. Pike," *Scribner's Magazine*, LXXXII, 462–467.

24. I. J. Cox, *The Early Exploration of Louisiana*. 113, 115. Our critical comments on Pike's detractors do not involve this author except insofar as he is inconsistent in his own findings. Dr. Quaife's edition of Pike's *Journal* in no way whatever classes him as a critic of Pike's, as is made plain later.

25. *American Historical Review*, XIII, 822–3, 827.

26. Dearborn to Pike, Feb. 24, 1808. *An Account of Expeditions*, App. To Pt. III, 67.

27. See pp. 130–134. A misunderstanding, if not disagreement, occurred on Oct. 15th, when Wilkinson was ordered to march to and encamp in a designated point of wood. Instead he proceeded to the nearby Arkansas River—giving Pike the scare recounted in his *Journal*, Oct. 16th–18th.

28. "The local name among the Kiowas for the Red River was 'Rio Palo Duro,' for the Washita, 'Rio Negro,' and for the Canadian, 'Rio Colorado' . . . This confusion of names was doubtless one cause of the mistakes of Baron von Humboldt and Colonel Long in taking the headwaters of the Canadian for the source of the Red River"—G. L. Albright, *Official Explorations for Pacific Railroads*, 107.

29. See pp. 127–129.

30. See pp. 118–121.

31. Item 18, *An Account of Expeditions* App. to Pt. III, 81. This slight sketch in the space of some nine inches purports to show the trail line from the lower Platte across the Kansas River to the Arkansas. Crossing that stream at one of the noted crossing places (See Note 129) the "Cimarron Desert" route of the later "Santa Fe Trail" was followed to Wagon Mound and Taos or Santa Fé. Cf. No. 18 p. 21.

32. K. S. Crichton in *Scribner's Magazine*, op. cit. The editor has inquired of Mr. Crichton the basis for his statement, but no answer was received.

33. F. S. Dellenbaugh, *The Romance of the Colorado River*, 118.

34. Z. Pike, *Exploratory Travels* (London, 1811), 236, n. The latitude is given by Editor Rees as 41° 42." "It is remarkable," says this editor, "that no mention is made in the proper place in the [Pike's] journal of the discovery of this stream." Looking at this connection from the north Perrin du Lac's "Carte du Missouri (1802)" states that the Platte takes its source (38° Lat.) opposite that of "la riviere de Santa Fe"—*South Dakota Historical Collections*, VII.
35. *Jefferson Papers*, Ser. I. Vol. 12, No. 250.
36. From: AN ACCOUNT OF EXPEDITIONS / TO THE / SOURCES OF THE MISSISSIPPI / AND THROUGH THE / WESTERN PARTS OF LOUISIANA, / TO THE SOURCES OF THE/ ARKANSAW, KANS, LA PLATTE, AND PIERRE / JAUN, RIVERS; / PERFORMED BY ORDER OF THE / GOVERNMENT OF THE UNITED STATES / DURING THE YEARS 1805, 1806, AND 1807. / AND A TOUR THROUGH / THE / INTERIOR PARTS OF NEW SPAIN, / WHEN CONDUCTED THROUGH THESE PROVINCES, / BY ORDER OF / THE CAPTAIN-GENERAL, / IN THE YEAR 1807. / BY MAJOR Z. M. PIKE. / ILLUSTRATED BY MAPS AND CHARTS. / PHILADELPHIA: / PUBLISHED BY C. & A. CONRAD, & CO. NO. 30, CHESTNUT STREET. SOMER- / VELL & CONRAD, PETERSBURGH. BONSAL, CONRAD, & CO. NORFOLK, / AND FIELDING LUCAS, JR. BALTIMORE. / JOHN BINNS, PRINTER . . 1810 /, 107–109. Our copy of the letter following is Dr. Bolton's in *American Historical Review*, XIII, 812–814.
37. James Biddle Wilkinson was General Wilkinson's son, aged twenty-four; he entered the army as second lieutenant in 1801 and became first lieutenant in 1803. He was made captain in 1808. He died in 1813.
38. The role of Lieutenant Pike's Arkansas party "consisted of the following persons: to wit,

Captain Z. M. PIKE,
Lieut. JAMES B. WILKINSON*
Doctor JOHN H. ROBINSON,
Serj'ts { JOSEPH BALLENGER,*
{ WILLIAM E. MEEK†
Corporal JEREMIAH JACKSON†

PRIVATES.

John Boley, *   Jacob Carter,†   Theodore Miller,†
Henry Kennerman, [deserted] Thomas Dougherty,†   Hugh Menaugh,
Samuel Bradley,*   William Gorden,   John Mountjoy,†
John Brown,   Solomon Huddleston,*   Alexander Roy,
John Sparks,†   Patrick Smith,†   Freegift Stoute,
                                          John Wilson,*
Interpreter, BARONEY VASQUEZ.†

*Those thus marked descended the Arkansaw river [with Lieutenant Wilkinson], and arrived at New Orleans sometime about the—of February, 1807.

†Those thus marked are still detained in New Spain.
The balance arrived at the Nachitoches on or about the 1st of July, 1807."
An Account of Expeditions, App. to Pt. III, 68.

39. *An Account of Expeditions*, 109–110.
40. John Hamilton Robinson, M.D., was born in Augusta Co., Virginia, January 24, 1782. He studied medicine and came West to St. Louis in 1804, marrying in that city the sister-in-law of Dr. Antoine Saugrain, prominent physician. Instantly he and Pike now formed that intimate friendship which only suffering, danger and eminent prospect of death can hallow and cement. Pike's high tribute to his friend's credit did not secure for Robinson on their return a position as surgeon in the army. Instead, Dr. Robinson went to Mexico in 1815 and fought four years for Mexican independence, winning the stripes of a brigadier-general. In 1819 he settled near Natchez, Miss., and died there shortly after. Robinson's purpose in accompanying Pike is nowhere explained (Cf. Index references); his presence lends color to the "spy" theory of Pike's mission, although (see Note 220) an opposite view can be taken—that he was already interested in the Mexican revolutionist's cause.
41. From *An Account of Expeditions*, 111–204.
42. Z. M. Pike, *Manuscript Maps*, U. S. War Department. For detailed account of Belle Fontaine, as of most points mentioned by Pike, see E. Coues, *Expeditions of Zebulon Montgomery Pike*, 357, n. Hereafter our many references to Coues will be by page only to avoid repetition.
43. R. I. Holcomb *History of Vernon Co., Mo.* 1887, 24.
44. *An Account of Expeditions*, App. to Pt. II, 32–33.
45. *American Historical Review*, XIII, 814–5. George Henry (mentioned by Pike July 17th) who figures as a sort of mysterious attaché to the party (joining it the 17th, steering a boat the 19th, getting lost Aug. 5th and returning to St. Louis Sept. 3rd) is now promptly consigned by General Wilkinson to perdition, but he remains with Pike forty-seven days longer.
46. Manual Lisa or de Liza the noted St. Louis trapper and trader was born in New Orleans in 1771 and came to the Upper Mississippi emporium in his nineteenth year. His unbounded energy in promoting the fur trade is a part of the history of the West and he is well described as "the most remarkable man among the pioneer merchants of St. Louis." One chapter of his wide activities, his relations with the Osages, is hinted at in several of Pike's diary entries, which imply that the de Lisa interests were hostile to, or tended to counteract, the purposes of Pike's mission to the Osages, Pawnees and Comanches since they visioned a three-cornered trade including the Spaniards in New Mexico. For these entries, see Index.
47. *An Account of Expeditions*, App. to Pt. II, 33.
48. *American Historical Review*, 815–816.
49. Coues placed this camp correctly at New Haven, Franklin Co., formerly known as Miller's Landing. The Shepherd River enters a mile above Griswold or a mile below the railway station, Etlah. Lewis and Clark assigned it that name (Shepherd); it is better known, however, as Berger River or Creek.

50. This camp was located a mile or so above the present town of Hermann, Gasconade Co.
51. Camp on the night of July 25 is not marked on the original chart. It is given in the Nau map, however, and is described by Pike as at the mouth of the Gasconade River. Coues describes this site as follows:

> This is much the largest tributary of the Missouri thus far reached; Pike elsewhere allows it 200 yards' width at the mouth, and navigability at times of 100 m. Gasconade City is a place on the tongue of land that makes into the Missouri on the upper side of the Gasconade; being a mere village or hamlet, is as appropriately named as the river itself, which got its name from the way some persons bragged about their exploits when they returned to St. Louis. (Page 367, n. 18.)

52. This is one of Pike's few references to the grounds for the "spy" interpretation of his expedition. Once again, the truth doubtless lies fairly on the surface. Surely, if Pike had had "secret instructions" (of any except casual import) there could have been no call for any remarks like these. If he had been given secret advices they would have, above all else, covered his actions in case of interception or capture. Anything else is unthinkable. Mr. Coues tried to define his own suspicions by restating Pike's idea in the following words, supposedly Pike's: " . . . should I meet a Spanish party from the villages near Santa Fé, I think it would be good policy to give them to understand (1) that my party was going to join our troops near Natchitoches, but had mistaken the Rio Grande for Red River; (2) that if it would be agreeable to the Spanish commandant, some or all of us would pay him a polite visit; and (3) that if he did not wish us to do this, we would go direct to Natchitoches. In any event I flatter myself that I shall get out of the scrape somehow. But if Spanish jealousy of Americans, and the Aaron Burr conspiracy, cause us to be made prisoners of war (in time of peace), I trust that you will see that we are released, and they are punished for the insult. Moreover, if I do not feel assured they will treat us well in Mexico, I will fight them, no matter how many there are, before I will let them take us there"—Coues, II, 571, n. 6. Nothing could have been more unscholarly than this interpretation of Pike's words. It changes the real meaning of the words "domestic traitors" and both Pike's and Wilkinson's references to the de Lisa party. It repudiates the secret instructions theory outright; for on what topic would such instructions deal if not on Pike's behavior if intercepted or captured? With what disgust would General Wilkinson have viewed this outburst of "enthusiasm," not born of any "dictates of prudence," if he had secretly bidden Pike what to do and how to do it? Even the effusive young officer would, under such circumstances, have known that such words were inexcusably purile. Yet other writers, anxious to make capital out of the "spy" theory, actually quote Coues' words as Pike's!

What Pike meant is as plain as a hurried, impulsive letter could be expected to define. Countless instances of intrusions, similar to what the

Spaniards might think Pike's was, on shadowy borderlands of every country of earth had been a commonplace of history. Pike was merely stating, in as bellicose language as the subject would bear, what he would do if challenged on the border; and using phraseology that would make his general believe that his deportment would not be pusillanimous.

53. *An Account of Expeditions*, App. to Pt. II 33–35.

54. To a camp just above Humphrey Creek.

55. The site of this poorly-chosen camp is not indicated on the Nau map. On Pike's chart No. 32 it is indicated just above the sharp northward bend between the towns of Tuscumbia and Bagnell, both in Miller Co.

56. This camp, mention of which was omitted on the Nau map and by Coues, was about seven miles from Rockdale, Camden Co. Gravois Creek, the mouth of which Pike passed today, is called Gravel Creek on his chart.

57. Camp tonight was three miles above Hogles Creek, where it can be definitely placed by the islands above and below and by the bluff on the south bank. This is now in Hickory County, and the nearest town is Fairfield, Benton Co., five miles southeast. The stream charted is Upper Potatoe River, and is known also as Pomme de Terre River. The trace above it is Hogles Creek.

58. *An Account of Expeditions*, App. to Pt. II, 37.

59. In the bight of the loop which the Osage makes near present Iconium, St. Clair Co. "East River," "Light Creek," and "Straight Creek," shown here on Pike's Charts, are creatures of the imagination. As yet it has proved impossible to explain why Pike delineated them. None corresponding to them are, or were, found on the actual topography. Only two streams of any description empty from the west here, Muddy Creek and a little brook four miles above, and they are too small to deserve such thick tracings. The same three streams had been marked on the published map and had troubled Coues (page 382 N. 39). He decided that East River was Muddy Creak, a reasonable guess, and that Light Creek was Galliniper Creek, a poor hypothesis, for Galliniper Creek is far below instead of far above the loop of Camp 27.

60. *An Account of Expeditions*, App. to Pt. II, 38–40.

61. This remark has been taken advantage of by critics of Pike who infer that the Lieutenant was encouraged to write candidly to Wilkinson but vaguely or deceptively to the Secretary of War, thus furthering the "intrigue" theory. The more simple interpretation seems to be the just one. The General is advising his protégé to make his official reports to the Secretary of War on matters of fact only—excluding therefrom all forecasting as to probabilities. Whereas, to Wilkinson, he need not refrain from reporting more intimately his doubts, fears, hopes and expectations; just as Wilkinson himself wrote to Pike (as July 18th) with a candid familiarity he would not have displayed in any formal letter to the Secretary of War. Those who might have reached to this straw to strengthen their "spy" theory may note and reflect on the point that, on Pike's tour of the preceding year to the Upper Mississippi, he was not in communication at all with the War Department, but only with General Wilkinson. If the theory advanced by them is tenable, how much more now, than before, would Wilkinson desire that all communications

should be made to him alone? Why an innovation now, if Pike is acting in a deceptive role? The answer must be that now, if not before, Wilkinson's desire is to regularize the affair, make it a national undertaking—as, in effect, it was, being done at the order of the Commander-in-Chief—for which the government must assume responsibility, as it eventually did. This interpretation makes the sentence quoted harmonize perfectly with the further suggestion of honor to be won and elevation in rank, i.e. "make your future life comfortable." Pike was advanced to the rank of Captain six days after this letter was written, August 12th.

62. Francisco Miranda (1754–1816), famous solider-of-fortune, equipped the *Leander* in 1806 at the expense of himself and two other Americans, backed by the English admiral, Sir A. Cochrane, and landed at Carácas and proclaimed the Columbian republic. The episode failed April 28th.

63. *History of Vernon Co.* 131–3. Cf. Grant Foreman's admirable treatment of the Osages and their country in both his *Pioneer Days* and *Indians and Pioneers*.

64. *History of Vernon Co.*: 115.

65. Joseph Brown of New York, whom President Jefferson had recently appointed Secretary of Louisiana Territory, which had been created by Congress in 1805. Brown was the brother-in-law of Aaron Burr. It is to be noted that Pike, of his own motion, and not according to any instructions issued to him, here put himself at once in touch with the civil authorities and, to that further degree, tended to regularize his actions and his expedition in the eyes of all men.

66. Pike's address was found among his papers in Mexico by Dr. Bolton. The Ms. was signed by him but was not in his handwriting. It read:

My brothers,
    Before speaking to you myself I will give you a word from your father who is in St. Louis, which is addressed to the white haired men, but which concerns many in all the Osage nation.
    here is the word from the General. * * *
My brothers,
    You see by the word of your father that I am giving you at present, that he does not desire that you remain inactive, when your enemies come to kill you, but that you be prepared to destroy those who wish to do harm to you.
My brothers,
    For this reason I am of the opinion that you ought to send some spies to the Missouri, and if you find that your enemies are approaching, be brave, make an ambuscade and destroy them.
My brothers,
    It is only to defend yourselves, it is not to go to the villages of your enemies in order to kill their women and their children, who are innocent [Cf. p. 117–118].
My brothers,
    You see by this last word, as well as by the delivrance of your women

and your children from captivity [from Pottawattomies], how sincere is the friendship of your american father.
My brothers,
    You see us here, we have been sent in order to protect your children, that we have redeemed, to your nation. We have done it. Besides this I have orders to make peace between your nation and the Kans who have sent word to your father in St. Louis that they desire and that they are ready to make peace with the Osages.
My brothers,
    Wise men must know that peace is better than war and if you are at peace with all nations we shall not hear the voice of sorrow among you but that of Joy.
My brothers,
    In order to succeed in this affair your Great father at Washington has commanded your father at St. Louis, to do as it seemed best for him to do.
My brothers,
    Thus he has commanded me to make the osages meet with the Kans, in order to smoke the peace pipe, to bury the tomahawk in the ground, and to be as the same nation.
My brothers,
    For this reason I ask that some of your chiefs and of your warriors accompany me to the republic of the Panis, from where I will send for the Kans.
My brothers,
    When you will be among the panis, you and the Kans will be on the ground of a foreign nation [neutral, inserted between lines], and the one will not fear the other, and as a consequence the peace that you will make will be strong and Sincere.
My brothers,
    You will be able to meet also some of the Maitons or Comanches, and I hope to make peace between them and you.
My brothers,
    I desire also that two or three of your warriors descend the Arkansas river, with a party of my warriors, to the village of the grand Peste [Great Plague], for which I have a word from your father in St. Louis.
My brothers,
    They have said to your father in St. Louis that the tribes of the Grand peste killed some Frenchmen, and that they stole their horses.
My brothers,
    The grand Peste and his people are not Osage, if they are, why do they make war against the children of your great father.
My brothers,
    If the word that your great father in St. Louis sent by me for the grand peste, and for which I desire to be accompanied by some of your warriors, does not open his eyes, your great father will abandon him, and

will no longer wish that he and his nation be his subjects, but will suffer that his white and red warriors raise the tomahawk against him.
My brothers,

You who have been in the united states, know well what hospitality you have experienced, and that everything was granted you that you wished. We have come now to ask you to accompany us in return, and I ask for horses from you in order to go from here among the panis, from where some of your warriors can bring them back to your land again.
My brothers,

I desire that some of you accompany me during all my trip, and you will become acquainted with the red nations who are to the west, and you will see on the lower Mississippi your great father in St. Louis who will recompense you for your faithfulness.
My brothers,

I address myself to both villages as if they were the same, as it is the will of your great father. he sees you as the same nation, take council together and be strong.

I have spoken.
My brothers,

We are going to make a long trip. when we are with the osages, we consider ourselves at home, and vous etes practie de la parte de votre père. [Untranslatable.]

I have not brought gifts for you, but as proof of our esteem, I give you even to the last drop of our whiskey, a little tobacco, and some things to keep in remembrance of this day.—*American Historical Review*, XIII, 824–6.

67. On the 24th of August, the son, son-in-law and interpreter of the Cheveux Blanche, came to camp, when the son-in-law spoke as follows:—vis: "I am come to give you the news of our village, which is unfortunate for us, our chief having assembled his young men and warriors and proposed to them to furnish horses, &c. they having generally refused him; but I, who am the principal man after Cheveux Blanche, will accompany you."

The son.—"Our young men and warriors will not take pity on my father, nor on me, nor on you, and have refused to comply with your request; but I will accompany you with two horses to carry provisions for your voyage."

The interpreter.—"The Cheveux Blanche was ashamed to bring you this answer, but will again assemble his village and to-morrow come and give you the answer."

I replied—"That I had made the demand without explanation, merely to let the Osage act agreeably to their inclination, in order that we might see what disposition they would exhibit towards us: but why do I ask of their chiefs to follow me to the Pawnees? Is it for our good, or their own? Is it not to make peace with the Kans? To put the wives and children out of danger! As to their horses which they may furnish us with, I will pay them for their hire; but it is uncertain whether I can pay them here, or give them an order on the superintendent of Indian affairs at St. Louis; but this I do not now wish them to be made acquainted with."—Pike, *An Account of Expeditions*, 130–131.

68. This remark substantiates our explanation (Note 61) of General Wilkinson's invitation to Pike to write confidentially to him in a way that would appear unseemly in a formal report of the Secretary of War—a fact which Pike's critics have cited as indicative of intrigue. The gossip of the camp here related would not be appropriate in a report to the War Department; whereas, to Wilkinson, it might be exceedingly valuable.

Mr. Coues inserted "and Wilkinson" in brackets before the words "down the Arkansaw" in Pike's third paragraph (p. 97). The thing of greatest interest in Pike's remark is the slur on the Osages for having no one "brave" enough to accompany Pike into the Comanche country at the head of the Arkansas River. Even now it was apparent that the exciting, if not dangerous, portion of the expedition lay to the westward, beyond Osages and Pawnees, at the head of the Arkansas and Red rivers. Pike's remark shows that it required bravery to advance into that No-Man's Land where the boundaries of the United States and Spain met and where the fierce Comanches held sway. Doubly singular, then, must it appear to any unbiased person that General Wilkinson should suggest, if not order, the return of his son when the Arkansas River was reached (as noted in our Introduction) if Pike possessed "secret instructions" to do more by way of spying than his formal orders called for. If the romance of the adventure was to begin where the Osages were accused of not being brave enough to follow, how strange that the General's own son should also be ordered to stop there!

69. *An Account of Expeditions*, App. to Pt. II, 43.

70. *Id.* 43–44.

71. About on the Kansas-Missouri boundary in the vicinity of Hoover and Stotesburg, Bourbon Co., Kansas.

72. Deer Creek Camp was on the west branch, near Carlyle, Allen Co.

73. "Grand fork" was the Neosho River. Pike forded it just above its confluence with Martin Creek. This is proved not only by the courses of the streams but by the bluff due east of Martin Creek. This bluff is recorded on Pike's Chart 29 and is crossed by the line representing his track. Coues was in doubt about this ford. Once across the Neosho, Pike left it and cut north-west. He crossed three creeks far above their mouths. These he considered separate streams and recorded them as such but actually they are three branches of the same tributary—Turkey Creek and South and North Big Creeks, which unite before they meet the Neosho. He spent the night on North Big Creek, five or six miles south-west of Burlington, the seat of Coffey Co.

74. Eagle Creek.

75. Three or four miles southwest of Hartford, Lyons Co. The plan seemed to have been to ascend Eagle Creek to its head and descend into the valley of the Vermillion or Verdegris River.

76. Near the Atchison, Topeka and Santa Fé station, Olpe, Lyons Co.

77. These were probably two forks of the Moon branch, Rock Creek and Faun Creek.
78. The Neosho. Camp was pitched on the upper waters of the south fork of Cottonwood Creek.
79. Pike's Chart No. 29 shows his course clearly across two tributaries of the south fork of Cottonwood River and then across the main stream near present-day Matfield Green, Chase Co. Camp was pitched on the east bank of the Cottonwood, three or four miles below Florence, Marion Co., and a mile above Cedar Grove and Cedar Point—quite as Coues traces him, except for placing his camp on the west bank of the stream.
80. Near Marion, Marion Co.
81. This camp was near Durham, Marion Co. During today's march Pike's Chart shows that the "Road of the Kansas to the Arkansas" was crossed. This was the main track of the far-famed Santa Fé Trail which, coming westward from noted Council Grove in Morris Co., followed closely the Rock Island Railway tracks from Tampa to Durham in Marion County, where it crossed the Cottonwood.—A. B. Hulbert, *American Transcontinental Trails*, V. Map Nos. 16, 17 and 18.
82. To the headwaters of Smoky Hill River, a tributary of the Kansas. Camp tonight was made near the corner of Saline, McPherson and Marion counties, at the source of Hobbs Creek, a branch of Gypsum. Coues interpreted incorrectly Pike's trail for this day, trying to explain an excessive mileage by making Pike take a very complicated roundabout track and setting his encampment far to the east, near Canton, McPherson Co.; whereas he took the direct trail shown on his Chart No. 29. Pike often recorded excessive mileages which can be explained easily by error or fatigue.
83. The streams here spanned were the sources of Gypsum, North Gypsum and Stag creek, and camp was made in the hills east of Lindsborg, McPherson Co.
84. Smoky Hill River at Bridgeport, Saline Co. Breakfast was eaten on Dry Creek six miles beyond, as is delineated clearly on Chart No. 28.
85. Mulberry Creek, above its junction with Spring Creek, near Salina.
86. Saline River, which was forded near the present Culver, Ottawa Co.
87. Branch of Salt or Covert Creek, between Minneapolis and Ada, Ottawa Co., and called "Little Saline" on the Nau map. Pike was now travelling nearly north instead of northwest as his Chart No. 28 shows.
88. On a branch of Salt Creek, north of Ada.
89. A discrepancy in the record for Sept. 21 and 22 is avoided by reading "two" for "twelve" in this passage, thus putting the party on one of the small creeks that fall into the right bank of Solomon River near Glasco, Simpson and Asherville, Cloud Co.
90. Pike's crossing place was southwest of Beloit, Mitchell Co. He continued across Buffalo Creek, pitching camp near Randall, Jewell Co., on a dry branch. Pike drew this stream as a tributary of the Solomon instead of the Republican. Coues set this day's camp too far east (on Buffalo Cr. near Jamestown, Republic Co., page 408 N. 68) and as a result mislocated most of the following camps to the Arkansas River.

91. Pike now closely paralleled the highland route of the Missouri Pacific Railway through Jewell Co. and crossed Buffalo Creek near Jamestown.

92. This camp was on White Rock Creek, west of Burr Oak; it is identified by means of Pike's Chart by two features, namely, the pronounced bend in the creek above Burr Oak and the fork a few miles above camp, at Salem. Coues located this camp on the same stream but almost twenty miles further east (page 410 n. 70).

93. Sarecherish, "Angry Chief."

94. [Upon Pike's return to Washington in 1807 the following footnote was prepared as an explanation of the reference to Malagres "late visit," of which mention has been made heretofore, p. 41. The critics of Pike's reconnoissance, intent upon emphasizing culpability on his part, have kept very silent on the topic of this contemporaneous Spanish expedition which came many miles beyond the known American-Spanish borderline—though much concerned over Pike's stepping across the Rio Grande!] I will here attempt to give some memoranda of this expedition, which was the most important ever carried on from the province of New Mexico, and in fact the only one directed northeast, except that mentioned by the abbe Raynal (in his history of the Indies) [*Histoire . . les Deux Indes*, 1770] to the Pawnees—of which see a more particular account hereafter. In the year 1806, our affairs with Spain began to wear a very serious aspect, and the troops of the two governments almost came to actual hostilities on the frontiers of Texas and the Orleans territory. At this time, when matters bore every appearance of coming to a crisis, I was fitting out for my expedition from St. Louis, where some of the Spanish emissaries in that country transmitted the information to Majar. Merior and the Spanish council at that place, who immediately forwarded on the information to the then commandant of Nacogdoches (captain Sebastian Rodreriques), who forwarded it to colonel Cordero, by whom it was transmitted to the seat of government [Chihuahua]. This information was personally communicated to me, as an instance of the rapid means they possessed of transmitting the information relative to the occurrences transacting on our frontiers. The expedition was then determined on, and had three objects in view: viz.—

1st. To descend the Red river, in order, if he met our expedition, to intercept and turn us back, or should major [Richard] Sparks and Mr. [Thomas] Freeman have missed the party from Nacogdoches, under the command of captain Viana, to oblige them to return and not penetrate further into the country, or make them prisoners of war.

2d. To explore and examine all the internal parts of the country from the frontiers of the province of New Mexico to the Missouri, between the La Platte [to the North Platte].

3d. To visit the Tetaus, Pawnees republic, Grand Pawnees; Pawnee Mahaws and Kans. To the head chief of each of those nations: the commanding officer bore flags, a commission; grand medal, and four mules; and with all of whom he had to renew the chains of ancient amity, which was said to have existed between their father, his most Catholic majesty, and his children the red people.

The commanding officers also bore positive orders to oblige all parties or persons in the above specified countries, either to retire from them into the acknowledged territories of the United States, or make prisoners of them and conduct them into the province of N. Mexico. Lieut. Don Facundo Malgares, the officer selected from the five internal provinces, to command this expedition, was an European, (his uncle was one of the royal judges of the kingdom of New Spain) and had distinguished himself in several long expeditions against the Apaches and other Indian nations, with whom Spaniards were at war: added to these circumstances, he was a man of immense fortune, and generous in its disposal, almost to profusion: possessed a liberal education, high sense of honor, and a disposition formed for military enterprize. This officer marched from the province of Biscay with 100 dragoons of the regular service, and at Santa Fé, (the place where the expedition was fitted out from) he was joined by 500 of the mounted militia of that province, armed after the manner described by my notes on that subject, and compleatly equipt with ammunition, &c. for six months; each man leading with them (by order) two horses and one mule, the whole number of their beasts were two thousand and seventy five. They descended the Red river 233 leagues, met the grand bands of the Tetaus; held councils with them, then struck off N. E. and crossed the country to the Arkansaw, where lieut. Malgares left 240 of his men, with the lame and tired horses, whilst he proceeded on with the rest to the Pawnee republic; here he was met by the chiefs and warriors of the Grand Pawnees; held councils with the two nations, and presented them the flags, medals, &c. which were destined for them. He did not proceed on to the execution of his mission with the Pawnee Mahaws and Kans, as he represented to me, from the poverty of their horses, and the discontent of his own men, but as I conceive, from the suspicion and discontent which began to arise between the Spaniards and the Indians. The former wishing to avenge the death of *Villineuve* and party, whilst the latter possessed all the suspicions of conscious villany deserving punishment. Malgares took with him all the traders he found there from our country, some of whom having been sent to Natchitoches, were in abject poverty at that place, on my arrival, and applied to me for means to return to St. Louis. Lieut. Malgares returned to Santa Fe the—of October, when his militia was disbanded, but he remained in the vicinity of that place, until we were brought in, when he, with dragoons, became our escort to the seat of government.—Pike, *An Account of Expeditions*, 142–3.

95. This "beautiful eminence," whereon the State of Kansas erected a monument in 1901 to commemorate Pike's historic visit, lies two miles from Republic City. Public interest in preserving the historic spot, awakened and fostered by Mrs. Elizabeth A. Johnson, culminated in the erection of the monument and the elaborate centennial celebration held here in 1906.—*Kansas Historical Society Coll.* X, 15–159.

96. Characterish's commission from the governor of New Mexico was dated Santa Fé, 15th June, 1806.—Pike.

97. Kiwiktaka, "White Bull," formerly a chief of note and still sufficiently venerated to "break the spell" in favor of Pike.

98. *An Account of Expeditions,* App. to Pt. II, 45–46.
99. *An Account of Expeditions,* App. to Pt. II, 47–50.
100. This was erroneous, but it was my impression at the time.—Pike.
101. This camp was on White Rock Creek, not on Rock Creek as stated by Coues (page 419 n. 3).
102. Site of Salem.
103. Fifteen miles south of Smith Center, Smith Co., on Oak Creek, Pike charted this stream correctly as to size and position but made it run east into Buffalo Creek instead of southeast.
104. Pike's camp was on the southern bank of the north fork of Solomon's Creek above Cawker City, Mitchell Co., twenty-five miles from his crossing place of September 23rd. Distinct features on Pike's Chart prove the site: a main fork just below camp, a ridge above camp, between two branches. The fork is easily recognized as that at Cawker City. Such a ridge as Pike shows is found between the forks and near Downs and Osborne, Osborne Co. The accuracy of this location reinforces the correctness of our previous identification of the Pawnee Republican Village. Coues placed Pike tonight in the vicinity of Beloit twenty-five miles southeast, or forty-five by the meandering course of the river.
105. Pike ascended Twin Creek, crossing the height of land at its head, near Potterville, Osborne Co.
106. Pike was now between Wolf Creek and its east fork, near Lucas, Russell Co., on the Union Pacific Railway. The Nau map hereabouts is quite incorrect, Pike's camp being placed where Pike's Chart shows a mark for a Spanish Camp and Wolf Creek being made to join Salt Creek to form the "Little Saline."
107. Camp was made on the north bank of Saline River, southwest of Sylvan Grove, Lincoln Co. So salt was the water that Pike commented on his Chart: "in boiling corn it sufficiently salted it and if boiled down twice, too salt to eat."
108. Crossing the Smoky Hill River, camp was made south of Wilson, Ellsworth Co., and opposite Coal Creek. The name given the Smoky Hill possibly means *La Fourche de la Cote du Kansas,* i.e. that fork of the Kansas which runs along the dividing ridge or coteau" which is perfectly true of the stream in question.
109. On the upper reaches of Coal Creek on the border of Russell and Barton counties in the vicinity of Forest Hill and Dubuque.
110. Reaching the head of Cow Creek, Pike crossed it near Claflin, Barton Co. As to his prairie camp near here we are in agreement with Mr. Coues—for the first time since the camp of September 21.
111. Cheyenne Bottoms.
112. Little Walnut Creek.
113. Proponents of the theory that Pike's essential purpose was the furtherance of some illegal filibustering by Wilkinson naturally overlook all such references as this, the more significant because so wholly incidental. The observation shows that the exploratory phase of the expedition, of the Arkansas by

young Wilkinson and of the Red by Pike, was its "national" object, and that the destruction of any of the party would mean the abandonment of one or both objectives.

114. In the matter of correct mapping of the Arkansas here at its famous Great Bend, Kansas, later site of the Fort Zarah Military Reservation (1853) and fort, the Nau map is more accurate than Pike's original chart; to make the former, Pike had the benefit of Lieut. Wilkinson's map made in the descent of the river. All trails focused on the Arkansas at this point; the Saline fields of Kansas impregnated the Arkansas below this point; above the Great Bend its waters were quite palatable.

115. The Wishtonwish of the Indians, prairie dogs of some travellers; or squirrels as I should be inclined to denominate them; reside on the prairies of Louisiana in towns or villages having an evident police established in their communities. The sites of their towns are generally on the brow of a hill, near some creek or pond, in order to be convenient to water, and that the high ground which they inhabit, may not be subject to inundation. Their residence, being under ground, is burrowed out, and the earth which answers the double purpose of keeping out the water, and affording an elevated place in wet seasons to repose on, and to give them a further and more distinct view of the country. Their holes descend in a spiral form, therefore I could never ascertain their depth; but I once had 140 kettles of water poured into one of them in order to drive out the occupant, but without effect. In the circuit of the villages, they clear off all the grass, and leave the earth bare of vegetation; but whether it is from an instinct they possess inducing them to keep the ground thus cleared, or whether they make use of the herbage, as food, I cannot pretend to determine. The latter opinion, I think entitled to a preference, as their teeth designates them to be of the granivorous species, and I know of no other substance which is produced in the vicinity of their positions, on which they could subsist; and they never extend their excursions more than half a mile from the burrows. They are of a dark brown color, except their bellies, which are white. Their tails are not so long as those of our grey squirrels, but are shaped precisely like theirs; their teeth, head, nails and body, are the perfect squirrel, except that they are generally fatter than that animal. Their villages sometimes extend over two and three miles square, in which there must be innumerable hosts of them, as there is generally a burrow every ten steps, in which there are two or more, and you see new ones partly excavated on all the borders of the town. We killed great numbers of them with our rifles and found them excellent meat, after they were exposed a night or two to the frost, by which means the rankness acquired by their subteraneous dwelling is corrected. As you approach their towns, you are saluted on all sides by the cry of Wishtonwish, from which they derive their names with the Indians, uttered in a shrill and piercing manner. You then observe them all retreating to the entrance of their burrows, where they post themselves, and regard every, even the slightest, movement you make. It requires a very nice shot with a rifle, to kill them, as they must be killed dead, for as long as life exists, they continue to work into their cells. It is

extremely dangerous to pass through their towns, as they abound with rattle snakes, both of the yellow and black species; and strange as it may appear, I have seen the Wishtonwish, the rattle snake, the horn frog, of which the prairie abounds, (termed by the Spaniards the cammellion, from their taking no visible sustenance) and a land tortoise all take refuge in the same hole, I do not pretend to assert, that it was their common place of resort, but I have witnessed the above facts more than in one instance.—Pike, *An Account of Expeditions*, 156.

116. *An Account of Expeditions*, App. to Pt. II, 50–52. The unreliability of Pike's instruments, or his inexperience in using them, or both, made him place the site of this camp at least thirty-five miles too far south.

117. Most editors have placed the formal "sic" after Red River here, to indicate a probable error of Pike's. It is singular that no one has read the sentence as Pike wrote it. Such reading adds a significant tang to the episode. The two spirited young men had had a falling out, unquestionably. Wilkinson had not proceeded according to directions when he separated from Pike Oct. 15th. Instead, he had proceeded to the Arkansas River. What Pike actually wrote was that the nettled, headstrong young man intended to ignore directions to descend the Arkansas, on account of lack of water, and strike south "on the most direct route" for Red River! Thus he would have launched a Red River expedition of his own and anticipated Pike's cherished dream of the summer! Additional ground for reading Pike's words as they stand is found in the acidity of young Wilkinson's attack on him (by letter to his father) for alleged niggerly treatment of him regarding equipment for his trip down the Arkansas. That vindictive letter may imply bitterness due to being baulked in a favorite design; cf. 130–131.

118. It will probably never be possible to trace and explain the confusion which made the men of Pike's era believe that the Canadian, the long Arkansas tributary, was the head of Red River. What became the Santa Fé Trail crossed the heads of both Arkansas tributaries, the Cimarron and Canadian. The former was approximately as long as the Red, a Mississippi tributary. But the much longer Canadian headed just about where Pike expected to look for the Red. All who romanced about ascending the Red to the Rockies must be held responsible for Pike's misconceptions. Mapmakers put the error in black and white as "Rio Colorado de Natchitoches" on the "Map of the Internal Provinces" in Pike's *An Account of Expeditions*; but the head springs of the Red River on which Natchidoches lay are east of Amarillo, Texas.

119. Compared with the modest appropriation of $2500 for the Lewis and Clark expedition, that of $600.00 for Pike's present Arkansas trip was exceedingly liberal. But, in view of the $8000 spent on the more or less inconsequential Red River expeditions of 1804–6, Pike might well have complained of his allowance—had he known all the facts. His observation, however, is of chief interest because it illustrates that lively sense of healthy jealousy which was Pike's chief incentive on the present expedition, namely, to make a name as an explorer. Cf. pp. 157–158, 183.

120. *American Historical Review*, XIII, 816.

121. *Id.* 817.
122. This camp was on the Santa Fé Trail about on the line between Range 15 and 16 W. Township 21 S.—Cf. A. B. Hulbert, *Transcontinental Trails,* V. No. 23.
123. The branch of the Santa Fé Trail pursued here by Pike crossed the later site of the Fort Larned Military Reservation (R. 14 W. T. 21 S.) and dropped straight south from there to the mouth of Coon Creek, three miles below Garfield, Kan.—*Id.* No. 24. Mr. Coues mentions three routes branching at Coon Creek (p. 433, n. 18); there were five forks debouching from the main trail, when railway surveyors first surveyed this region half a century later. See *Transcontinental Trails,* V. No. 25. Coon Creek marked the approximate boundary of the neutral ground between the Kansas-Osage-Pawnee nations to the east and the Comanche-Kiowa tribes of the west.—*Pacific Railroad Reports,* II, Pt. I, 25.
124. *Id.* 817–819.
125. Strands of the "Santa Fé Trail," so-called, covered the plains on each side of the Arkansas to the number of three or four or more on both sides. Here, at Coon Creek, the pathway taken by the Spanish company was again encountered.
126. "Left an up-river trail."—Coues.
127. Opposite Kingsley, Edwards Co.
128. Pike now enters one of the most interesting sections of the famed Santa Fé Trail, namely, that part of the old route which sent branches southward on the short cut through Cimarron Desert straight-away toward Wagon Mound, Taos and Santa Fé. He now camped on or near what became known as "Lower Crossing" at the mouth of Mulberry Creek near Ford, Ford Co., a stream which Pike's Chart calls "Swampe Creek." Neither here nor elsewhere—although Pike remains on the south side of the river, where any debouching trails would be most plainly visible—is there a single mention of the "Cimarron Desert" route of the Santa Fé Trail. This leads to the question, Was that route a white man's innovation? We treat it elaborately in Volume 2 of this series.
129. Pike's supply of lead will become an item of interest to the reader. If his guns were the regulation U. S. flint lock, model of 1795, 70 calibre, forty pounds of lead would produce about 600 balls. When we realize that those balls must provide practically all the food his party of sixteen would have, while searching in winter for a river that did not exist, the episode at once takes on the sinister suggestion of tragedy. It is a phase of the expedition that Pike's critics have not examined while exploiting their version of his "hostile advance on New Mexico"!
130. *An Account of Expeditions,* App. to Pt. III, 31–32.
131. About eighteen miles of Dodge City, Kansas, which lay four miles west of famous Fort Dodge.
132. "Middle Crossing" at Cimarron, Kansas, was passed today. From this point perhaps the most important "Desert Route" struck southward.
133. Today's camp was opposite Garden City, Finney Co. While the "official" Santa Fé Trail of later days followed the north shore of the Arkansas it is a

matter of note that near here (at Holcomb) the original Brown survey of the trail lay on the south side of the river for some twenty miles—to Chouteau's Island near present Hartland, "Upper Crossing." Cf. *Transcontinental Trails*, V, No. 31.

134. Pike's Chart No. 25 shows the bends of the Arkansas and allows us to place this camp near the Kearny-Finney county line, a little below Lakin, six miles beyond Coues' location of it, namely, opposite Deerfield.

135. Pike was now below and opposite Kendall, about six miles east of later Fort Aubrey and its well-known spring five miles east of present-day Syracuse. Coues misplaces the fort-site, locating it too far west. Tree growths are noticeable south of the river in the region east and west of Syracuse.

136. Camp tonight was just beyond the Kansas-Colorado state line near Holly. Pike's Chart shows a tracing of a stream from the north which was Wild Horse Creek. *Id.* No. 36. Pike was now beyond the "neutral ground" mentioned in Note 124.

137. The Nau map embellishes the scenery with traces of numerous streams flowing northward into the Arkansas. Pike's Chart (No. 25) shows but one, Two Butte, Grenada or Wolf Creek. The Nau map is inaccurate for the whole course of the Arkansas hereabouts.

138. Pike represented Big Sandy Creek, which enters the Arkansas from the north in R. 45 W. T. 22 S., by a double trace on his chart, which locates us definitely here in the famous "Big Timbers" section of the route. He also shows Willow Creek, which he crossed perhaps on the exact site of Lamar, Colo. He made camp two miles west of that point, four miles west of Coues' location. Coues, however, gave Pike a mileage of twelve miles for the 13th— and Pike's Chart confirms that figure.

139. Mud Creek, described on Pike's Chart No. 25 "Clear Creek Water & Deep." The red rocks mentioned refer to a rocky butte between Mud Creek and the Santa Fé Railway station Prowers, confused by Coues (page 443 N. 34) with the headland at the mouth of Clay Creek.

140. Caddoa Creek, which Pike named "Buffalo Creek" and Rule Creek which he named "Lookout Creek."

141. Such as those opposite the site of old Fort Lyon, near Las Animas, where the rocky front surmounts the plain by 400 feet.

142. Local atmospheric and weather conditions determine where and when the Rockies are first sighted by emigrants. Pike's Peak may come into vision first; or it may be that the Spanish Peaks, south of the Arkansas, can be first sighted.

143. The Purgatory River enters the Arkansas in Sec. 6 R. 51 W. T. 23 S. The story of this stream which drains the country southward to the Ratons (of the Sangre de Cristo range) is suggested by its international nomenclature: Rio Purgatorio, Rio Las Animas, Rivière Purgatoire, Purgatory and Picketwire.

144. Crossing the Purgatory a mile from its mouth on the old Van Horn Ranch, the Santa Fé Trail of 1806 led across the present site of Las Animas. Passing opposite the mouth of Adobe Creek (omitted on the Nau map) Pike camped on the Arkansas opposite the mouth of Horse Creek (likewise omitted).

145. Pike today passed opposite the future site of famous Bent's Fort, on the north bank of the Arkansas, close to dividing line between R. 53 and 54 W. T. 23 S., the story of which Grinnell has told in full. Reaching the La Timpas River, often called in the old days "the forks of the Arkansas," merely because the Santa Fé Trail forked here, camp was made on a tongue or island of land formed by an ancient curve of the Timpas which took its water east as the Arkansas was neared, paralleling that stream for a mile or more before joining it.

146. By the present site of Rocky Ford to about five miles below the Apishapa River near Catlin, Bent Co. Misled by the Nau map, Coues placed this camp above the Apishapa.

147. By the present site of Fowler, camping two miles below Nepesta where the Santa Fé Railway crosses the Arkansas.

148. The reader cannot, perhaps, but wonder at the underlying meaning of the word "pity"—practically the only direct quotation employed by Pike's interpreter from the Indian's lips, as quoted in his letter to General Wilkinson of Oct. 2 and now again here. In reading the words one feels the nearest approach to that impassable gulf between the two races and the clearest sense of the futility of ever hoping to understand things from the Indians' viewpoint. At this point, probably, the American flag first flew on Colorado soil. Cf. Note 218.

149. The turmoil of the day led to omissions of interesting geographical facts from the diary, such as the crossing of the important Huerfano River. Describing this, however, on his Chart Pike said: "[It rises] To the left of all the mountains." The stream comes from the Sierra Blanca basin. Camp tonight was pitched near Avondale, near the mouth of Chico and Six Mile Creeks.

149A. St. Charles River, rising in the Greenhorn Mountains.

150. Mouth of Fountain Creek, site of Pueblo, Colo.

151. London ed. "22½ miles."

152. London ed. "a pair."

153. In whatever way local antiquarians may diagnose Pike's actual pathways on Turkey Creek, and the actual point of his highest ascent on the "summit" of his "chain," the general position of that objective is fairly established by the leader's unequivocally describing his descent therefrom as "straight down the creek to avoid the hills." This description precludes all of the common sites from which Pike is popularly supposed to have viewed the Peak which lie to the north of Turkey Creek, as Cheyenne Mountain, Mount Manitou, Cameron's Cone, etc., etc. Pike's map shows his returning route to have been straight down Turkey Creek to the point where that stream veered southwest near Fountain reservoir; at that place Pike's trace mounts the "cedar cliffs" (like the modern highway) and proceeds directly southeast to the junction with the northward route near the point where the latter turned from the valley of Fountain Creek.

154. In inner bark of the cottonwood was the chief forage depended upon on the plains in winter season. This Comanche camp was on the north side of the river.

155. At the mouth of Dry Creek.
156. Pike's Chart (p. 145) shows this camp distinctly. The day's march was but ten miles; if Pike covered the fifteen mentioned, he did it by outriding or scouting. Mr. Coues located this camp too near Turkey Creek. The vagaries of Pike's route from Pueblo to Canon City (to use modern terms) would set any modern surveyor's nerves on edge. He tacked up and down the river's tributaries for miles at a stretch, whether only to find safe crossing-places or to acquaint himself with the vagaries of the terrain will probably never be known. The point of great interest is that Pike gave not the slightest thought to turning south on what was at least the fairly well-known and important route up the Huerfano River toward New Mexico and Santa Fé—even though winter was upon him, for which no one in the party was properly dressed. It was here at the junction of Sangre de Cristo range and the Arkansas that Spanish spies had expected Pike. Cf. p. 185.
157. This remark is inexplicable to those who know the Arkansas today. At below zero weather it seems strange that so much water was flowing as to necessitate swimming horses anywhere.
158. Two miles above the mouth of Turkey Creek.
159. Referring to the Mississippi tour of the year previous.
160. Pike in a footnote gives the altitude of the Peak noted previously, 18,581. Most interestingly he continues: "Indeed it was so remarkable as to be known to all the savage nation for hundreds of miles around, and to be spoken of with admiration by the Spaniards of N. Mexico, and was the bounds of their travels N. W. Indeed in our wandering in the mountains, it was never out of sight, (except when in a valley) from the 14th November to the 27th January."—*An Account of Expeditions*, 171. This, of course, was written at the end of the journey when Pike's Ms. was being prepared for publication. The reason for Pike's Peak's prominence over nearly thirty Colorado Peaks which exceed it in altitude is the fact that it springs right out of the plains and was, therefore, a landmark for as many as 150 miles away on a clear day. As to altitude-finding, Pike gives no evidence of knowing the simple test of taking the temperature of boiling water.
161. Pike's Chart (p. 145) shows that Beaver Creek from the north and Hardscrabble Creek from the south were passed today; camp was pitched two miles above the latter—somewhat east of the location fixed by Coues.
162. Oak Creek and the site of present-day Florence, Colo., was passed today, also Four Mile or Oil Creek which enters the Arkansas from the north at the Fremont County Farm seven miles above Florence. These Pike well charted (p. 145), likewise the "rocky carrying place" three miles below the mouth of Four Mile; he camped a mile above the carrying place.
163. So called in distinction from North Mountain, Pike's Peak. Camp was pitched just below present Canon City, Colo., at the entrance to the noted "Royal Gorge," through which the Arkansas descends.
164. What seems strange about Pike's losing the Malgares trace is that three scouting parties failed to find it now whereas it is found and followed without comment on the return of the party (p. 163). Turning south, perhaps at

Hardscrabble Creek, the Malgares column took that branch of the Santa Fé Trail which had ascended the Arkansas this high and went up the "Third Fork" (St. Charles River) on the general alignment of the present Greenhorn Mountain route, followed in part by the Pueblo-Trinidad highway today. Of course the country was filled with ancient trails, aborigine and Spanish, on which hunters had coursed for unknown generations. It is such that Pike now follows into South Park. If he had heard of a specific Spanish Trace in or beyond that Park another explanation is required—and is given later.

165. If a zero is not omitted from the figures here given (200) Pike's men certainly did not get very far into the Royal Gorge—or even get a good look at its mouth. In that case it is conceivable that the mouth of Grape Creek was not examined; for the trail from Canon City followed by Pike a month later ascended that stream (p. 163).

166. Pike's map shows that camp was moved two miles upstream today, a new fact not mentioned in the *Journal* or shown on the Nau map. This new site, within the limits of present-day Canon City, Colo., is important. Local tradition places this camp at a favorite picnic ground on the south side of the Arkansas near Grape Creek. Pike's map, however, shows that the site was on the north bank of the Arkansas. This site is clearly defined in its connection with a prominent ridge by which it can be fixed with some precision. This is the sandstone ridge which runs north and south just east of Sand Creek. This the chart shows unmistakably—the ridge, the valley on the other side and the two heights, Fremont's and Noonan's peaks. The blockhouse erected here on the return journey from South Park stood on the east tip of the ridge, where it abuts on the north bank of the river just south of the State Penitentiary. As the first house built by Americans in Colorado, no doubt, this blockhouse at Canon City will always have an historic interest. Cf. p. 162.

167. The Indian trail followed by Pike ascended Sand Creek and passed over into the Four Mile (Oil) Creek drainage. Camp was pitched about a mile from the latter creek.

168. Probably at the junction of Four Mile Creek and South Oil Creek. Pike's Chart (No. 22, the poorest made by the explorer) shows a tributary from the west and a group of high hills to the east.

169. Camping on West Oil Creek, just beyond its confluence with Pisgah and Martin's creeks.

170. The pass between Saddle Mountain and Thirty-Nine Mile Mountain, separating the drainage areas of the Missouri and Arkansas, in the broad sense.

171. The South Platte, near the head of Eleven Mile Canon in South Park.

172. Without question Pike had mentioned the "Rio Colorado" (see Index) to Indians he had met on his route. If he had been given any ground for finding a "Red" river north of the Arkansas, his informants must have referred to Rio Colorado, the Colorado River, which lay just beyond the Continental Divide west of South Park. This solution, as noted previously, clears up much of the "mystery" concerning Pike's continued search for a Red River which (he supposes) ran southeast into the Mississippi. Cf. Commentary to December 16th.

173. No correct delination of the Missouri had been possible until the return of Lewis and Clark in the month of September preceding.
174. Just west of the sharp elbow of the South Platte, north of Saddle Mountain.
175. South Park had long been a favorite wintering-place of the Comanches, Utes, Kiowas, etc., under the name *Bayou Salade.*
176. The fact that Pike sought to "pursue" either Spanish or Indians to get information makes ridiculous such a statement as Coues' (p. 481 n. 28) to the effect that Pike "had a chip on each shoulder for some Spaniard to please knock off; . . . and he would rather have broken some Spanish heads than have discovered the head of any river." As noted above, the party now did not have guns enough to go around. One is at a loss to explain Coues' complete change of attitude to Pike; it is as though an editor suddenly became afraid of being duped by the author being edited—fear of consequent ridicule on the part of the public. For all of Mr. Coues meticulous, if voluble, antiquarian research into the detail of Pike's voyage, it is plain he missed entirely a number of major points and spent untold wasted hours in trying to make a very imperfect map (Nau's) square with Pike's *Journal* and present-day topography (using the terminology of 1895, partially discarded today). In the present instance no one knew better than Coues that Pike's guns were dilapidated beyond description and that one man did not have a gun at all. It would not have been so bad for Coues to have repudiated Pike's purpose in now going into South Park if he had once glimpsed the real reason for his going. Missing that, it was naturally easier to ridicule than to explain.
177. The snowy mountains to the southeast formed the chain which Pike's Peak dominates. The truth here lies on the surface, and an acceptance of it simplifies every interpretation of what happens. Pike, determined to chart the upper Arkansas and Red as well, or better, than had been done by any rival on the lower rivers, was completely lost. Only a more intimate comparison of Pike's route foot by foot with his charts and diary can ever reconcile their discrepancies. As to Pike's main movements in South Park there can be little uncertainty.
178. Following the north bank of the South Platte, Pike passed the mouth of the Little South Platte (which, Coues to the contrary, he did not ascend) and the present site of Hartsell's Ranch and Hartsell postoffice. Camp was pitched on the south bank two miles above the fork. Pike's Chart (p. 150) shows islands here which do not now exist.
179. F. S. Dellenbaugh, *The Colorado River*, 118; the "large camp" noted was that of Comanches and Kiowas with whom James Purcell had been hunting— *An Account of Expeditions*, App. to Pt. III, 17.
180. *An Account of Expeditions*, 5.
181. *American State Papers*, "Indian Affairs," I, 731.
182. Camp was pitched above the confluence of Badger Creek and the Arkansas. The carrying place mentioned was in the canon below Salida.
183. Howard, Colo., in Pleasant Valley.
184. At Coaldale, Colo., above the sharp elbow of the river. On the south the

valley of Hayden Creek offered another outlet from the trap into which the party was dragging itself, the Royal Gorge.

185. Passing present-day Cotopaxi, camp was pitched near the mouth of Bernard Creek. The decreasing accuracy of Pike's Charts here is a mute witness to his tragic abstractions. The changes in a generation are illustrated by Coues' statement that Cotopaxi is the nearest the modern road approaches the Royal Gorge. One now crosses the Gorge on the "highest Suspension Bridge in the World."

186. Near the mouth of Texas Creek, at the Texas Creek station on the Denver and Rio Grande Railroad. By ascending this creek as the railway spur to Westcliffe, Colo., does, Pike might, again, have escaped the Gorge and reached Wet Mountain Valley in two days, instead of the two weeks required by the Royal Gorge track chosen, had he known it.

187. In these three days of gorge travel the elbow which the Arkansas makes at Parkdale was reached. The forlorn party was now at the entrance of the Royal Gorge. At near present Spikebuck Pike took his latitude as 38° 20′ which was only about eleven miles in error. This much greater accuracy than shown on October 24th or November 30th proves that Pike's instruments were not being damaged by the journey so much as supposed; but, rather, that unfavorable weather conditions must explain Pike's mistakes.

188. Pike reached about the site of the present-day scenic "Hanging Bridge," built over the waters of the Arkansas by the Denver and Rio Grande Railway for a right-of-way in the narrowest part of the canon, and then climbed the north wall on Robinson's track. The face of the precipice has doubtless been greatly changed by the storms and frosts of a century and a quarter; Robinson's course, therefore, cannot be picked out with great accuracy. Numerous strong words have been used by commentators in criticism of Pike's ruthlessness in remaining in this great crevass so long when good routes around it on either side were available. It has not been sufficiently emphasized, however, that, in the first place the consensus of the party's best judgment was always followed; and, in the second, the party was living, if you call it that, from hand to mouth and all but starving, and that it was in the bottom of the valley near water where game was most likely to be found. No one knew for a certainty of the safe routes around and the circumstances, perhaps, did not encourage the long delay that exploration would have required. Deep canons are rarely very long.

189. Noonan's Peak. Pike now recognized the site of encampment 29 which he had left Dec. 10th (p. 148). There can be no doubt of Pike's surprise at finding that he was actually on the Arkansas, though the suspicion of this was evident as early as Dec. 31st.

190. Yellowstone River. We have analyzed the reason which led Pike to conceive that he had become acquainted, at a distance, with the divide on which this river had its rise.

191. The blockhouse on the camp site in Canon City, see Note 166.

192. Active game hunting had evidently discovered to Pike's men what was sought for in vain on their previous visit to this camp (p. 147), namely, the "Spanish

Trace" possibly followed by the Malgares column. Amount of snowfall may have made the difference between success and failure in this instance. The pathway now followed cut in behind the ridge at the mouth of Grape Creek and followed practically the present Canon City-Webster Park road to Grape Creek crossing. Camp was pitched a mile or so beyond, where the hills enclose the stream. Despite Pike's incorrect mapping of the south bank of the Arkansas from Canon City to Grape Creek (a fact which he recognized) the main topographical features—bluffs, ridges, streams, etc.—are all easily recognizable. The twelve men who now marched from the Arkansas with "the doctor and myself" were Meek, Brown, Sparks, Jackson, Carter, Dougherty, Gorden, Miller, Menaugh, Mountjoy, Roy and Stoute.

193. The main Wet Mountain range. The party mushed on by the junction of Pine Creek with Grape Creek and camped just short of the Fremont-Custer county line.

194. Below Silver Creek. Pike's Chart here adds nothing to our actual information. The problem was, now, to keep alive—and the chance seemed slim.

195. The Sangre de Cristo Range.

196. At the confluence of Johnson's Gulch, or Silver Creek, with Grape Creek.

197. A pass through the Bull Domingo Hills.

198. The route was by the present Bull Domingo Mine and the west side of Round Mountain, shown perfectly on Pike's Chart 19; then, turning sharply southward, the track lay through modern Silver Cliff, Colo., and southwest across the valley, fording Grape Creek, to the memorable campsite on Spring, or Cottonwood, Creek at the foot of the Sangre de Cristo Range.

199. In instances like this Pike's *Journal* carries plain evidence of having been only slightly, if at all, "touched up" for publication. Otherwise, considering the party's plight, with starvation so hard on their track, the leader who had an opportunity in the rewriting might inexcusably have at least touched upon the phase of his reputed qualities as leader which, as Secretary of War Dearborn said, were "held in high estimation by President Jefferson," and were deemed by the Secretary as "enterprising, persevering and judicious— *An Account of Expeditions*, App. to Pt. III, 67.

200. The human quality of Pike maps is illustrated by a mark beside the trail on Chart No. 19 and the following words near by in Pike's own handwriting: "Here I left Dougherty & Sparks Two who were froze so bad as not to be able to March."

201. The party marched southeast, parallel with Grape Creek and along the edge of the lowest timbered slope of the Sangre de Cristo Range looking for an easy break through the icy barrier. Luckily Pike forebore to attempt a direct crossing for it would probably have led to the destruction of the party in the heart of the Crestone group containing some of the highest and most rugged mountains in the entire West. For this reason, despite the snow which covered the ground, the men must have known that they were following for the most part an aborigines' trail; progress would otherwise have been more impeded, drinking places more poorly spaced and no sure outlet at the end. Camp tonight was pitched on Colony Creek.

202. Probably on a small ridge between Crystal Falls and Grape Creek, due east of Music Pass.
203. Pike now crossed the divide between Grape Creek and the Huerfano River.
204. Camp was pitched on Muddy Creek at the confluence of North and South Muddy about two miles west of Bradford, Huerfano Co., and due east of Medano Pass.
205. Contrary to Pike's *Journal* at large this rhetorical outburst reads as though it had been written out at a later date; but it was probably based on some kind of a reprimand delivered at the time. It reads a little like propaganda for bounty for men who deserved, but never received it.
206. Again Pike's Chart No. 19 carries the quaint entry of one of the party being left behind: "Here left Menaugh who was froze & gave oute."
207. Following almost exactly the old wagon road over the Sangre de Cristo range by Medano (Sand Hill) Pass as proven by Pike's Chart and as correctly figured out by Mr. Coues from the data afforded by Pike's mileages.
208. Medano Creek, at the head of which Pike pitched camp on the night of the 27th, was, of course, not a tributary of Red River; nor was it the tributary of any other river; its waters sink beneath the sand dunes at the bottom of the western slopes of the Sangre de Cristo range. Pike was, however, in the Rio Grande drainage area, and, because west of Red River and south of the Arkansas, certainly in a region never ceded by France as "Louisiana," although the right to navigate the Rio Grande had been France's and became, automatically, a right of the United States.
209. Fifteen years later this Medanos Pass route is called by Fowler "the Spanish Road leading to Pike's gap In the Mountain"—*Journal of Jacob Fowler* (Coues ed.) 129.
   The route Pike followed to Medanos Pass was not a much used pathway. It joined at the Pass another from the Huerfano valley which was important—doubtless the main track from the upper Arkansas to Taos via the San Luis Valley. See Pike's map of San Luis Valley (p. 169).
210. The San Juan range.
211. Camp was pitched above the junction of Medano and Mosca creeks which is, approximately, on the Alamosa-Saguache county line.
212. The Rio Grande.
213. The San Luis Valley.
214. Following the route of the old road across Zapata Creek and camping either on Veracca or Zapata Creek.
215. Pike's course was practically straight for the twenty-four miles from the timber point camp to the Rio Grande River, striking the river at an island about four miles below Alamosa, Colo. This entry shows on the face of it that the record was not contemporaneously made; indeed from this date forward the diary seems to have been rewritten, at leisure, for publication. Pike's Chart (p. 169), carries the following entry opposite a mark on the north bank of the Rio Grande where Encampment 11 (from the Arkansas) was pitched: "Red River 200 yds. wide No Timber."

Pike's Traverse Table (Chart No. 16) for these days carries its own succinct account:

"30 Jany. To ye Banks of Red River [crossed out] Rio Del Nord
31 Jany. To the W. Branche of red River about [blank] M. above its confluence with the N. Br [Rio Grande]"

The entry shows that Pike did not make the correction in the name of the Rio Grande in each case. The correction is not made in the entry of the 28th when the Sangre de Cristo range was crossed. The Traverse Table for that day reads: "Across the divide to a small run [crossed out] branche of the Waters of red river." The gist of the thing is that it is preposterous to think of the man's entering "Red River" more than a dozen times on his maps and tables in order to "bluff" the Spaniards. The party, as it reached the Rio Grande, consisted of Pike, Robinson, Meek, Brown, Jackson, Carter, Gorden, Miller, Mountjoy, Roy and Stoute; eleven in all.

216. Incredulity smacking of a lack of practical plainsman has been expressed by former commentators who have explained each act of Pike's on the basis of comic-opera political designs. In the present situation such editors have deemed that he knew he was not on Red River; and, if he beguiled himself into thinking he was, he knew that, in crossing it, he placed himself on foreign soil. As though a party as desperately circumstanced as was Pike's, living in mid-winter from hand to mouth, with comrades on the trail behind them with frozen feet, would be expected to stand on ceremony before moving to the nearest wood in sight to build fires! Do such editors think he should have stood on a timberless shore and slapped his arms against his body to keep warm?

217. The Conejos River. The eighteen miles probably means the entire distance. Such a wooded place as this, like a thousand others accessible from western treeless plains, was a boon indescribable to all travellers red and white—life-saving stations in winter. As a defense from all chance comers, Pike also needed timber for shelter and protection.

218. The Pike Chart (p. 169) sets at rest any remaining doubt of the site of the Conejos stockade. Concerning it the Colorado legislature passed the following act:

AN ACT
PROVIDING FOR THE PURCHASE BY THE STATE OF 160
ACRES OF GROUND IN CONEJOS COUNTY, COLORADO,
CONTAINING SITE WHERE LIEUTENANT ZEBULON
MONTGOMERY PIKE LOCATED A FORTRESS OR STOCKADE
IN 1807, AND MAKING AN APPROPRIATION TO CARRY OUT
THE PURPOSE OF THIS ACT.
Be It Enacted by the General Assembly of the State of Colorado:
Section 1. That there is hereby appropriated out of any money in the state treasury, not otherwise appropriated, the sum of three thousand ($3,000)

dollars, or so much thereof, as may be necessary for the purchase of 120 acres of land in Conejos County, Colorado, containing the location of the fortress or stockade erected by Lieutenant Zebulon Montgomery Pike in 1807, and where on the American flag was first raised within the present boundary of the State of Colorado, the boundary of said tract to be determined by the president of the State Historical Society in conjunction with the Governor of the State of Colorado. Said tract of land when so acquired shall be and is hereby dedicated, to the use of the public as a memorial park to perpetuate the memory of Lieutenant Pike, and said park shall be under the supervision and control of the State Historical Society.

Section 2. The General Assembly hereby finds, determines and declares that this Act is necessary for the immediate preservation of the public peace, health and safety.

Section 3. In the opinion of the General Assembly an emergency exists; therefore, this Act shall take effect and be in force from and after its passage. Approved April 24, 1925.

219. Trinchera Creek and road leading, by way of Sierra Blanca Peak, through La Veta Pass to the Huerfano Valley.

220. Dr. Robinson was the bearer of papers establishing the claim of William Morrison of Kaskaskia, Ill., against one Baptiste Lalande, an absconding employee said to be living in Santa Fé. It has been asked why he should have been thus commissioned if Pike's party was not expected to go to Santa Fé. The question is a fair one. No leading question about Dr. Robinson has ever been answered. Was his going with Pike merely a sporting event? Mere adventure? We do not, and may never know. As to his bearing papers for Morrison, the answer of course is that, no regular means of communicating with Santa Fé being in existence, any party going in that direction might have been taken advantage of by Lalande's creditor on the chance that directly, or by a trading party being met up with, the papers might reach their destination and somehow be enforced. So far as strengthening the "spy" theory of Pike's expedition this Robinson episode gains little for the theory that Wilkinson used the Doctor to further his intrigue with Spain. When Robinson later returned to Mexico he fought four years with the rebels against Spain! Looking the actual facts in the face it seems most probable that Robinson now went "in" to Santa Fé to save the lives of Pike and his men. They had small chance of outlasting the winter unless rescued. Even if game could be secured with the necessary regularity, the number of men able to get it on a continually widening circumference was questionable. By the 26th about 1000 portions of deer meat (from twelve deer) must have been served in Pike's camp. Some of these deer had been brought from as far as five miles away. The frozen river could not, of course, be descended—and Pike's entry for Feb. 14th shows the Rio Grande to be frozen a little below the mouth of the Conejos. No effort had been made to cut a single piece of timber for canoe or raft, a fact that shows the brave Captain was bluffing royally to pretending that Robinson was stepping over to Santa Fé during a mere lull

in the party's activities! What a chance those "spy" advocates missed in not pointing out Pike's neglect of making any preparation to descend the "Red River"! It is not believable that many of those 600 lead bullets could still be left, though Pike does not mention this matter. It is sure no proper medical supplies could have remained to succor the injured men. The one hope of life was an appeal to the humanitarian instincts of the generous Spaniard—doing it with as gallant a gesture as possible. The pitiful condition of Pike's men is pathetically shown on the day of their "capture" by the suddenly rallying (when formalities were dispensed with) of the Spanish soldiers about them offering them blankets, etc. All this is so plain between the lines of Pike's record (but what cocky Captain would let them get into the lines!) that small doubt remains that Pike could have been court-martialled for not thus seeking succor. Is it the part of scholarship to ignore these plain facts in order to see in Pike's every action the stealthy antics of some Alexander Dumas guardsman engaged in furthering a sly international burlesque! Far more tenable would be the theory that Robinson's "mission" was to double-cross the Spaniard and aid the Mexican revolutionists! Cf. p. 60. For Lelande see Dr. L. B. Bloom, *n. Mexican Hist. Review*, II, 376.

221. It is plain that this entry was rewritten. Those who have not believed that Pike was honest in stating that he did not know he was on the Rio Grande have relied only on their suspicions. We have seen how often he had deleted "Red River" on his maps when he found out the facts. But on the mountain barrier between the Arkansas and Rio Grande basin his map carries the words "Red River"—not crossed out. On the river itself we read: "Red River," not deleted. If the Arkansas was mistaken for the Red, how much more likely the Rio Grande? But, suppose for a moment that Pike was "bluffing" the Dons and knew the truth but had purposely inscribed his map wrongly. Who was Dr. Robinson "bluffing" when, *three weeks later*, he met Pike and told him that, soon after leaving him on the Conejos, he had met some Indians who told him that the party was on the Rio Grande and not the Red, "and I was embarrassed whether I should not immediately return and apprise you of it"?—*An Account of Expeditions*, 225. Who was Pike "bluffing" when, *sixty days later*, he wrote General Wilkinson specifically as to his reason for believing that it was the Red River he fell on after crossing the Sangre de Cristo range? Who was Pike "bluffing" months later when he outlined for Secretary of War Dearborn a sketch of his journey and stated he thought the Rio Grande was the Red? And, years later, when he fashioned his diary for publication, what object was there in "bluffing" the American people into thinking he made the mistake mentioned? With his good name under a cloud because of Wilkinson's disgrace, would not common sense have dictated the wisdom of abandoning any alibi he had given the Spaniards instead of endlessly repeating a fact which showed him capable of making a serious geographical mistake? Particularly as he was desirous of securing an appointment as head of a boundary survey commission? The suspicion of his critics in this regard has no merit save one: it strengthened their pet "spy" theory; not a single fact supports it.

222. This is very evident friendly propaganda incorporated into the *Journal* when it was prepared for publication. It bore no fruit. Pike's men were never granted a bounty for what they underwent.

223. *An Account of Expeditions*, App. to Pt. III, 71.

224. *An Account of Expeditions*, App. to Pt. III, 53–55.

225. *An Account of Expeditions*, App. to Pt. III, 57–63.

226. Lalande, as Pike spells it, and Dr. Robinson's relations with him, was treated of in the previous chapter, see Index.

227. Philip Nolan in 1801 led an "expedition" into Mexican territory to "hunt wild horses," his friends claimed. The Spaniards saw the episode in another light, treated Nolan as an invader, attacked and killed him; hanging one of his men, the rest were imprisoned, including Solomon Colly. Colly therefore, probably antedated both Lalande and Purcell (Pursely) as the first "American" in Santa Fé. Cf. R. L. Duffus, *The Santa Fe Trail*, 34–36.

228. Z. M. Pike, *An Account of Expeditions*, App. to Pt III, 70.

229. *Id.* 69.

230. The *Jornada del Muerto* here mentioned (one of a dozen such in the west) was seventy-eight miles in length; the absence of water in this distance made this run the longest in the present United States which was absolutely dry. The two longest dry runs on the Forty-Niners' Overland trail were forty miles each.

231. Elliott, the Pennsylvania surveyor laid out the city of Washington; becoming U. S. Surveyor-General in 1792, he ran the boundary line between Spain and the United States, 1796–1800.

232. Z. M. Pike *An Account of Expeditions*, App. to Pt. III, 73.

233. An itemized list of Pike's papers as found by Dr. H. E. Bolton in Mexico in 1908 is published in Stephen Hart's introductory essay.

234. In passing, it is an item of interest that Captain Pike now actually arrives at the Red River for which he started eleven months and one day ago—and after perhaps writing the name a hundred times under a misapprehension as to its length and location.

235. The editor takes this, the only opportunity that offers, to express regret that the Nebraska State Historical Society contention as to the location of the Pike Republican Pawnee Village within that State was not mentioned in our Volume I. See *Neb. Hist. Mag.* X, 160–258. The Kansas argument is outlined in the *Kan. State Hist. Soc. 25th Bien. Report*, 101–129.

Index

Since the entire content of this volume is either by or about Zebulon Montgomery Pike, references to persons, places, and events have to do with his relationship to them. Brackets indicate alternative spellings or usages appearing in the text or notes. Many personal and place names have been edited in earlier editions and some appear in both Spanish and English. They are indexed here under the most common usage in this volume with the alternative in brackets as per, "Santa Fe [Santa Fé]." Endnotes are indicated by the letter *n* following the page number. The number after the *n* indicates the note number on that page.

letter from Pike to General Wilkinson, July 26, 1806, 76

letter to Pike from General Wilkinson, August 6, 1806, 91–93

letter from Pike to General Wilkinson, August 14, 1806, 86–87

Pike's address to the Osage, August 20, 1806, 97, 248n66

letter from Pike to General Wilkinson, August 28, 1806, 97–101

letter from Pike to Secretary Dearborn, October 1, 1806, 115–17

letter from Pike to General Wilkinson, October 2, 1806, 118–21

Governor Alencaster's orders regarding Pike, October 18, 1806, 97

letter from Pike to General Wilkinson, October 24, 1806, 46–47, 127–29

letter to Pike from Lt. Wilkinson, October 26, 1806, 177–79

letter from Lt. Wilkinson to General Wilkinson, October 26, 1806, 132–34

letter from Lt. Wilkinson to General Wilkinson, October 28, 1806, 19

inventory of Pike's papers in New Spain, April 8, 1807, 20–22

letter from Pike to General Wilkinson, July 5, 1807, 179–85

letter from H. L. Wilson to C. Creel, May 17, 1910, 23–24

letter from C. Creel to H. L. Wilson, July 15, 1910, 25

letter from H. L. Wilson to C. Creel, July 17, 1910, 25–26

letter from Pike to General Dearborn, undated, 27–28

letter from Pike to his father, undated, 17

Dodge City, 258n131

Dougherty, Private Thomas, 135, 165, 172, 244n38, 265n192, 265n200

Duchouquette
. *See* Larme, Baptiste [Duchouquette]

Dunbar, William, 42, 43, 47, 51, 157–58, 197
. *See also* Freeman, Thomas

Echararria, Lieutenant John, 235

Expeditions of Zebulon M. Pike (Coues), 13–14, 27, 30, 67, 70–71, 242n17, 243n22, 245n42, 246n52

fandango, 206, 215

Femme Osage River, 70

Fernandez, Lieutenant Don B., 54, 174–75, 189

Fero, David, Jr., 214, 217

Florada River, 220

Fort Aubrey, 259n135

Fort Carondolet, 89

Fort Scott, 105

Forty-Niners (Hulbert), 7

Fountain Creek, 143

Frank (Pawnee Indian), 72, 109, 111, 115

Franklin County, Missouri, 71, 245n49

Freeman, Thomas, 42, 43, 47, 51, 157–58, 197
. *See also* Dunbar, William

Fulton, Kansas, 106

Garcia, Don Francisco, 209

Gasconade River, 73–74, 76, 246n51

Gorden, Private William, 135, 244n38, 265n192, 267n215

Graham, Lieutenant Henry Richard, 183

Grand Peste, 60, 249n66

Grand River, 84, 108–9

Grape Creek, 265n201

Gravel Creek, 247n56

Great Bend, Kansas, 38, 45–46, 159
    Arkansas River at, 256n114
Greely, General A. W., 14
Gregg, Josiah, 5
Guerra, Ambrosio, 201
Guloo, Don Hymen, 220, 226
Guodiana, Lieutenant (Spanish officer),
    238

Hart, R. H., 26
Hart, Stephen Harding, 6, 9
    Overland to the Pacific, 6–9, 10n15,
    11n20, 11n21
    "Zebulon Pike: His Life and
    Papers," 13–30
Henderson, Martin, 228–29
Henry, George, 65, 67, 68, 80–81, 103,
    105, 245n45
Herrara, Don Simon de, 191, 231–35,
    237, 238
Hogles Creek, 247n57
Hoosier Pass, 151
horses, wild, 136, 190, 230–31, 236,
    270n227
Huddleston, Private Solomon, 135, 141,
    244, 244n38
Huerfano River, 260n149
Hulbert, Archer Butler, 6–9
    Forty-Niners, 7
    Overland to the Pacific, 6–7, 9,
    10n15, 11n20, 11n21
    "Purpose of Pike's Expedition,
    The," 31–56
    Zebulon Pike's Arkansaw Journal, 7
Humboldt, Alexander von, 41, 46,
    155–56, 241n3, 242n21, 243n28
Hunt, Colonel Thomas, 31, 93, 102
Hunter, George, 47, 51, 157

Jackson, Corporal Jeremiah, 135, 244n38
Jackson, Donald, 9
    Journals of Zebulon Montgomery
    Pike, 9
    . See also Account of Expeditions,
    An (Pike)

Jefferson, Thomas, 14, 42, 56
Journals of Zebulon Montgomery Pike
    (Jackson), 9
Juarez, 207

Kansas, 14–15, 32, 35, 44, 84, 254n95,
    259n136
    Bourbon County, 105–6
    prairies, 104–7
    Republic County, 9
Kansas [Kans] Indians, 14, 43, 44, 86,
    118–20
Kansas [Kans] River, 105, 110–11, 125
Kearny, Stephen Watts, 5
Kennerman, Private Henry, 54, 71, 72,
    73, 244n38
Keres [Queres] Indians, 199
Kwiktaka (White Bull), 254n97

Labardie (agent of Manuel Lisa), 99
La Belle Roche, 81
La Joya, Old, 207
Lalande, Baptiste, 53, 192, 193, 204,
    268n220, 270n226
Larme, Baptiste [Duchouquette], 95,
    96, 98
La Timpas River, 260n145
Lewis, Governor, 88
Lewis & Clark Expedition, 1–4, 14, 40,
    42–43, 46–47, 54, 120–21
    Pike and, 129, 156–58, 257n119
Library of American Biography, 13
Lisa [de Liza], Manuel, 35, 44, 66, 75,
    86–88, 91–92, 99, 245n46, 246n52
Little Monegaw Creek, 88
Little Osage River, 104
Little Osages village, 90
Little South Platte River, 151–52,
    263n178
Long, Major, 41, 243n28
    and Pike's Peak, 144
Long's Peak, 50
Louisiana Purchase, 14, 43, 55

Maguire, William M., 30
Malgares, Lieutenant Don Facundo,
15, 18, 34, 39, 41, 145m, 180, 204–21,
254n94
  Spanish Trace, 44, 46–47, 50, 52,
  261n164
Many, Captain James B., 229
Marchon, Captain Eugene, 235
Mariano River, 231
Marthasville, 71
Maugraine [Noal] (interpreter), 60, 99,
102–3
Mayner, Don Alberto, 213–14
Medano Creek, 266n208
Medanos Pass, 168, 266n209
Meek, Sergeant W. E., 135, 173, 187, 189,
265n192, 267n215
Melcher [Michon], Don, 226, 227
Menaugh, Private Hugh, 54, 135, 172,
244n38, 265n192, 266n206
Mexico, 19–22
Miller, Private Theodore, 135, 142,
148, 154, 160, 173, 244n38, 265n192,
267n215
  "Mount Miller," 9, 144
Miller's Landing, 245n49
mines, 222
Mississippi expedition, 2, 14
Missouri River, 4–5, 14, 64–71, 77, 149,
253n94
  Gen. Wilkinson's instructions and,
  57–59
  Lewis & Clark Expedition and,
  263n173
  maps and sketches, 19, 23, 155–56
  tributaries, 246n51
Montelovez, 221, 223, 225–26, 230, 233
Morrison, James, 65
Morrison, William, 268
Mountjoy, Private John, 135, 154,
244n38, 265n192, 267n215
mourning chants, Indian, 74–75

Nacogdoches
  . See Natchitoches, Louisiana
Natchez River, 237
Natchitoches, Louisiana, 16, 39, 239
National Archives, 9
Nau, Antoine, 28, 183
  maps, 28–30, 49, 67, 70, 76, 78,
  81–89, 95, 104, 142–43, 156,
  243n21, 246n51, 247n55, 247n56
Neosho [White] River, 51, 105–7, 117,
157–58, 251n73, 252n78
New Mexico [New Spain], 55, 121, 175,
178, 242n21, 253n94
  boundaries, 74, 138
  commercial opportunities, 5,
  245n46
  Gen. Wilkinson's instructions and,
  58
  Pike's intentions concerning, 32,
  34, 36, 38–42, 45, 48–49, 52,
  258n129
  population, 193, 200
  rivers, 155
  routes to, 159
  Spanish government of, 171, 209
  . See also Burr-Wilkinson
  conspiracy
Nezuma, 90
Niangua River, 82
Nolan, Philip, 195, 214, 218, 270n227
Nueces [Noissour] River, 230
Nueva Vizcaya, 5

Ojo Caliente, 53, 54, 190
Osage Bluff, 78
Osage Indians, 18–19, 32, 42, 90,
109–24, 131, 157–58, 228, 258n123
  Bel Oiseau, 88, 89
  "Big" or "Grand," 83, 95, 100–101,
  105
  Cheveux Blanche, 81, 92–94, 97,
  98, 100, 105, 250n67

San Juan Mountains, 168, 189, 272n210
San Luis Range, 16
San Luis Valley Section map, 169
Sans Oreille, 77, 83, 87, 100, 104, 106
Santa Fe [Santa Fé], 4, 16–19, 32–34,
    53–54, 171–88, 197, 254n94, 268n220,
    270n227
    "hostile advance on," 34
    route to, 121
    trade, 5, 44
Santa Fe [Santa Fé] Trail, 5, 35, 41, 44,
    46, 258n122, 258n133, 259n144
    Arkansas River and, 260n145
    caravans, 207–8
    "Cimarron Desert" route, 243n31,
        258n128
    main track, 252n81
    Malgares trace and, 262n164
    navigational confusion and,
        257n118, 258n123
    strands of, 258n125
Santa Rosalia, 220
Sibley, John, 35, 43, 47, 157–58, 184
Smith, Private Patrick, 135, 239, 244n38
Smoky Hill River, 252n82, 255n108
Soldier of Oak, 90
Solomon Fork [Solomon's Creek], 111,
    123, 252n90, 255n104
South Park, 15, 29
    map, 150
Southwestern expedition, 2, 14–17
    ammunition supplies, 258n129
    funding of, 257n119
    geographical mistakes, 153–59
    hardships, 147, 157, 166–67, 172–73
    instructions governing, 57–60
    journals, 5–6, 9, 16–26
    map, 62
    New Spain, 176
    papers, inventory of, 20–22
    party, 63–64, 135, 244n38
    purposes, 17, 25n113, 31–56, 241n3,
        246n52, 247n61, 251n68, 253n94,
        263n176

significance, 4–5
. See also specific locations and
    events; under documents and
    letters
Southwestern expedition, major
    segments
    St. Louis to Pike's Peak, 57–144
    South Park to the Rio Grande,
        145–76
    New Spain (New Mexico), 189–219
    Chihuahua to Natchitoches, 219–
        39
Spanish military detachment, 174–76
Spanish Trace, 49, 50, 148–49, 151–52,
    262n164
Spanish visitors, 171–72
Sparks, Private John, 82–83, 135, 244n38,
    265n192, 265n200
    physical condition, 125, 165
Spring [Cottonwood] Creek, 265n198
Squaw Creek, 157
St. Charles County, Missouri, 64
St. Clair County, Missouri, 86
St. Domingo, 199
Stewart, Philip B., 7
Stewart Commission of Colorado
    College, 6, 7
St. Louis, 18, 44, 64, 253n94
    Osage Indians in, 42
    trade routes and, 44
Stoute, Private Freegift, 135, 160,
    244n38, 265n192, 267n215
St. Thomas [Tomé], 206

Tancard Indians, 236
Taos, 159, 186, 243n31, 258n128,
    266n209
Tetau [Comanche] Indians, 46, 74, 92,
    254n94
    interpreter, 119–21
    Pawnees and, 111, 120–21, 140,
        253n94
    search for, 137–46
Texas Creek, 264n186